The Central Asian Arabs of Afghanistan

The Central Asian Arabs of Afghanistan

Pastoral Nomadism in Transition

by Thomas J. Barfield

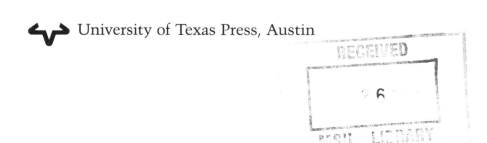 University of Texas Press, Austin

Copyright © 1981 by the University of Texas Press
All rights reserved
Printed in the United States of America

Requests for permission to reproduce material
from this work should be sent to
    Permissions
    University of Texas Press
    Box 7819
    Austin, Texas 78712.

Library of Congress Cataloging in Publication Data

Barfield, Thomas J. (Thomas Jefferson), 1950–
    The central Asian Arabs of Afghanistan.
    Originally presented as the author's thesis
(Ph.D.—Harvard, 1980)
    Bibliography: p.
    Includes index.
    1. Bedouins—Afghanistan—Economic conditions.
2. Afghanistan—Economic conditions. I. Title.
DS354.6.A7B37   1981   958'.1   81-11405
ISBN 0-292-71066-6   AACR2

Contents

Note to the Reader   ix

Acknowledgments   xi

Introduction: The Central Asian Arabs and the
Problems of Pure Nomadism   xiii

1. Central Asian Arabs: Historical and Ecological Background   3

2. Nomadic Pastoralism in Qataghan   33

3. Social Organization of the Central Asian Arabs:
The Decline of the Clan   59

4. The Role of the Arabs in the Provincial Economy   82

5. The Commercialization of Pastoralism and
Its Impact on the Arabs   110

6. The Arabs and National Institutions   138

Conclusion   165

Bibliography   171

Index   177

579421

Maps, Figures, and Tables

Maps

1. Distribution of Ethnic Groups in Afghanistan   xix
2. Regions Described in This Book   xxi

Figures

1. Arab Dwellings   48
2. Heads of Households Descended from Rahim Bai   73
3. Serai Imam Khan   87
4. Quarterly Wheat Prices in Kunduz   100
5. Afghan Wheat Prices   101
6. Afghan Mutton Prices   101

Tables

1. Population of Afghan Turkestan in 1884   16
2. Percentage of Population in Qataghan   31
3. Costs of Sheep Pasturing: Three Strategies   132

Note to the Reader

The Persian terms have been transliterated into common English following the nonstandard dialect of Persian (mixed with Uzbeki vocabulary) spoken by the Arabs in northeastern Afghanistan. I have tried to limit my use of Persian terms for the sake of the general reader and have included only those that make the analysis easier to follow or that would be useful to researchers in comparing material from elsewhere in Afghanistan or Central Asia. Variant spellings of places and tribes are commonly found in the literature, and most variations are easily recognized. In this work I use the more modern *Turkmen* in preference to *Turkoman*. Plurals of foreign words have been formed by adding *s*.

Three local measures are used throughout the work because they are found all over Afghanistan, and to translate them into exact numbers would create the illusion of false specificity:

> 1 jerib =.2 hectares
> 1 seer =7.1 kilograms
> 55 Afghanis =1 U.S. dollar during the research period, but the exchange rate varied from 94 Afs. to the dollar in 1971 to 45 Afs. to the dollar in 1977.

Acknowledgments

Social anthropology is a venture requiring the cooperation of two distinct groups of people who never meet. First are those people who introduce and explain the ways of a different culture to the anthropologist. Theirs is a time-consuming task that requires patient teaching until the anthropologist understands, and sometimes internalizes, the important information, values, and judgments that are necessary for living within the bounds of another culture.

The other group of people are members of the anthropological community with whose cooperation the unique perspective of the other culture is put into a cross-cultural and analytical framework. Theirs is a frustrating task that requires transmitting this knowledge in a form which is meaningful to others but which can never capture the true complexity of another culture.

My debts to both groups of people are large. It is they who provided the training and opportunity to make the work possible, and to them much of the credit for this book must go. All errors in fact or interpretation are, of course, my own.

This book originally took the form of a doctoral dissertation presented to Harvard University in 1978. With the exception of some revisions it remains basically the same work. At Harvard I was aided by the constructive criticism of Professor Michael Fischer, who helped draw up the research design, and by Professors Ruth Tringham and John Pelzel, who both actively supported the work. I also wish to thank Dr. Max Goldensohn for his trenchant reading of the book while it was in progress. The study was funded by a Fulbright-Hays Doctoral Dissertation Research Fellowship for Afghanistan through the Department of Health, Education and Welfare, which was most generous in accepting receipts in Persian for horses, donkeys, and silk turbans.

In Kabul, Afghanistan, I wish to thank the Cultural Section of the Ministry of Foreign Affairs for its help in arranging for the necessary visas and permissions. Other official institutions in Kabul that rendered aid were the Afghan American Educational Commission, under Larry Beck, which smoothed over many problems, and both the British Institute for Afghan Studies and the Heidelberg South Asia Institute, which provided libraries and hospitality.

During the last six months of the research I was greatly assisted by Donna Wilker, who accompanied me on the migration to Badakhshan. With her insights many aspects of Arab life were made clearer to me. In addition, in the role of a nomadic woman she was responsible for most of the work on the migration, while I in a culturally appropriate male role drank my tea and engaged in idle talk. Her ability and willingness to deal with many problems of the research made it a really cooperative study.

Finally, it is impossible to thank all the people in Imam Saheb who helped, and I promised not to use their names to protect their privacy. The names used in this work are typical of the area, but not the real names of the people discussed. I have not followed the suggestion of one friend who said I could use the stories of his adulterous affairs provided I substituted the name of his next-door neighbor in place of his own. I had hoped to be able to return to Afghanistan in the near future to thank everyone individually, but civil war and foreign invasion have now engulfed the country, making this impossible. It is indeed a tragedy, and in addition to my thanks must be added the hope that they will survive this terrible time.

Introduction
The Central Asian Arabs and
the Problems of Pure Nomadism

This study presents an ethnographic description of the Central Asian Arabs, a little-known people of northeastern Afghanistan, and an account of the changes that have taken place in their way of life over the last fifty years. The Arabs, as I will refer to them in this work, are nomadic pastoralists, seasonally moving from lowland river valleys to high mountain peaks. In many ways they seem typical of most Central Asian nomadic pastoralists, and yet when the ethnographic facts are applied to the standard categories of nomadic pastoralists, it would take an anthropological Procrustes to stretch the Arabs to fit neatly in the categories. This is because their way of life is too complex for typologies that use lack of agriculture and presence of regular movement as defining characteristics. This not only is true for the Arabs today but was so even in more traditional times. This study illustrates the wide-ranging complexity of pastoral nomadism, its integration into a regional economy, and the structural changes within the pastoral economy itself. These changes contradict the argument that nomadic pastoralism is a specialization without potential for development.

The first issue that must be raised, if only to be abandoned immediately thereafter, is what a pastoral nomad is. The study of nomads has been plagued by a fascination with typologies that borders on scholasticism. These typologies, legacies of cultural geography, have done more to obscure our understanding of nomadism than to bring about deeper insights into the nature of this way of life.

A classical and often-quoted definition of nomadism is that offered by Bacon (1954). This model divided nomads into three classes—the purely nomadic, the seminomadic, and the semi-sedentary—based on the amount of time spent in portable dwellings and the amount of agriculture done. The pure nomad lived in a tent year-round and only raised animals whereas the semisedentary lived in a house, did some farming, raised animals, and spent only part of the year in a tent.

There are immediate problems with this type of definition. Movement and lack of agriculture without a specific context tell very little. On the face of it, a pure nomad should be very different from a semisedentary one. This may not be the case when a close look is taken at why some nomads are more mobile than others. To draw an example from the Arabs in northeastern Afghanistan, there are families that by Bacon's definition are purely nomadic living next to families that are semisedentary. Both groups have similar livestock holdings, do similar amounts of agricultural work, and engage in the same migration. Does the fact that one family lives in a house part of the year and another in a yurt make enough difference to consider these people different? The obvious answer is no. There is a great deal of variation in dwellings, stock composition, or interest in agriculture even within a single extended family, let alone among large numbers of nomadic pastoralists. The amount of time spent in a tent is a function of land ownership. Those who bought property eventually built houses, and those who owned no land camped in areas open to all. All Arabs used to live in yurts, but many gave them up without changing their pastoral routine. Bacon's typology is an attempt to make sense out of nomadism in general at the expense of the variation within any nomadic community and that community's relation with the outside world. The seeming precision of categories without contexts has obscured and mystified the variety found among nomads. Movement becomes an end in itself and agriculture is regarded as somehow polluting. It would be more useful to make typologies only for a specific purpose and not define what should be empirically investigated.

An unfortunate result of such typologies has been to perpetuate the myth of the "pure nomad." The best nomads are, of course, pure nomads, who live in yurts or tents year round and never engage in agriculture. Central Asia, the southern border of which is the locale of this study, is the traditional homeland of pure nomads:

> The Central Asians scorn agriculture and engage in it only when on the borders of agricultural peoples and under severe economic pressure. Such goods as they obtain in trade are

usually luxury items; economically they are self-sufficient, able to subsist indefinitely on milk products and meat, with clothing, shelter, and equipment, derived chiefly from animal products. The symbiosis between steppe and town which is characteristic of Southwest Asia does not appear to be present in Central Asia. (Bacon 1954: 46)

In good legendary style, the pure Central Asian nomads eat only meat, marrow, and milk products (preferably fermented). They despise farmers, farming, and grain, and move great distances with their portable dwellings, wreaking havoc and destruction everywhere, but always with great élan. They are always hospitable and never pay taxes. This type of pure nomad was first described by Herodotus in the fifth century B.C., and these Scythians set the style in pure nomadism for the millennia to follow, although it must be allowed that there were farming Scythians and that even nomadic Scythians were suspiciously connected to the great grain-exporting city-states founded by the Greeks. In spite of this first example, the pure nomad has remained remarkably elusive over the centuries. The Hsiung-nu who lived on the Chinese frontier in the second century B.C. seemed to be exemplary pure nomads until it was revealed that one-fifth of the yearly Chinese imperial revenue was used to buy them off (Yü 1967: 36–64). It was not just luxury goods but staples like grain and wine that were in demand, so much so that advisors to the nomads told them to give up these goods before they became dependent on them (Watson 1961, II: 170). From that time forward nomadic tribes on the Chinese frontier had trade and extortion relations with the Chinese Empire that on a closer look produced only a few stragglers who were really pure nomads. This led Lattimore to declare that "the only pure nomad is a poor nomad" (1940: 522).

In other parts of Central Asia the Kazakh were found living in semisubterranean houses (Bacon 1954: 56–57); the Turkmen were discovered doing irrigated agriculture along with camel raising and slave trading (Irons 1974: 638). The Central Asian Arabs were completely pastoral, yet they had sheep barns and paid taxes. The list could be extended almost indefinitely. The point is that, in an attempt to describe a pure nomadism, what is most interesting in terms of political relationships, trade, and alternative subsistence strategy gets lost or becomes some kind of "acculturation" that must be explained away by recourse to processes of degeneration or contact with other groups. Uniformity in Central Asian pastoralism is an artifact of an analysis that is blind to all the evidence.

But nomads, who are not above romanticizing themselves, care nothing for purity and often act in ways which are not purely nomadic. Ethnographic and historical material must be reexamined without definitional blinders in order to come to an understanding of what the actual relationship of nomads was to their environment, other nomads, and sedentary people. This will not be a uniform pattern, for the immensity of Central and Inner Asia argues against any single adaptation that can be labeled "pure nomadic pastoralism."

For these reasons I feel it is fruitless to join the debate about what nomadism is. Most definitions seem to be drawn loosely enough so as to include the anthropologist's own group, but strictly enough to exclude as many other groups as possible. Second, some of the romantic nature of the enterprise is lost by entitling an ethnography *Semisedentaries of Central Asia.* The description of the Central Asian Arabs reveals a people who live from pastoralism and do migrate. But there is nothing to be gained by worrying about exactly where they should be placed in some classification. I hope the details of the many links the Arabs have to the wider world will show that traditional classifications tend to bind the world of the nomad too tightly. In this way further comparison with other nomadic pastoralists, or farmers, can be encouraged rather than foreclosed.

The Problem

In the anthropological literature the work of Fredrik Barth has been used as a theoretical basis for much of the current writing about nomadic pastoralists. One of the important models he employed in *Nomads of South Persia* (1961) explained how nomads maintained an economic, social, and demographic balance by losing both rich and poor nomads to the sedentary society. He posited that as nomads became wealthy, they invested in land. As their land holdings grew, they began to devote more time and interest to them, eventually dropping out of pastoralism by abandoning sheep raising for the role of sedentary landlords. At the opposite end of the economic spectrum, poor nomads got themselves into debt and sold animals to make payments. Eventually their declining number of sheep were not enough to support the family, so the nomads were forced to settle and became landless peasants. Barth claimed that shepherding jobs were few, so there was little a poor nomad could do to stave off sedentarization resulting from poverty. In this way the society kept its numbers in balance by losing members to the surrounding population, and it remained egalitarian because only middle-range pastoralists who shared common goals remained in pastoralism. On a national scale pastoral nomads represented a middle ground between the landed elite and the peasant masses.

This model received overwhelming acceptance from most anthropologists, but Jacob Black (1972) strongly attacked it, using data from the Lurs, a tribal group who lived near the Basseri studied by Barth. Among the Lurs this model had not worked. Instead, the wealthy nomads formed "agro-pastoral combines" and mixed land holding with sheep raising. Poor nomads were hired by rich nomads to take care of sheep on contract. Far from leaving pastoralism, the wealthy strata came to own the vast majority of all sheep, and the poorer Lurs were forced into exploitative shepherd contracts because they lacked alternative opportunities. Black argued that the Luri data demonstrated that Barth's model was not universal but stemmed from an over-emphasis on the supposed egalitarian nature of tribal societies—which, in his view, was illusory.

The wide acceptance of Barth's model, combined with the counter hypothesis proposed by Black, made the issue of economic organization among nomadic pastoralists very significant. The two appeared to be totally at odds, so I decided to take up this issue as the focus for a study of a pastoral nomadic group in northeastern Afghanistan. Afghanistan is home to many nomads, who have been estimated at 10–15 percent of the total population and who play an important part in the economy there. The research design was aimed at coming to an understanding of the pastoral economy and its relationship to nomadic social structure. In the field it soon became apparent that the research would have to be expanded to consider the nomads as part of a regional system and to include their connections with urban markets, farming villages, and governmental structures. A too narrow concentration on a single nomadic camp group would have exaggerated the Arabs' isolation. As the following pages will show, the debate between Black and Barth was central to understanding the changing nature of pastoralism among the Arabs in Qataghan. A big trade in sheep had resulted in a situation like that described by Black when the Arabs changed from a subsistence-oriented economy to a cash economy. Barth's model would have worked in a subsistence economy where sheep provided low cash returns and made them an unattractive investment compared to land, but when the price of sheep rose in cash value, these same sheep became lucrative investments for both rich nomads and merchants who had money to invest. The structure of pastoral nomadism changed to reflect this new orientation. This shift would have been easier to see among farmers, where changing from a subsistence crop like wheat to a cash crop like cotton required a different type of agriculture. But among the nomads the sheep remained the same; it was changes in the regional economy that transformed the sheep from a "subsistence crop" to a "cash crop" without any conscious decision by the nomads themselves.

The Research

With this anthropological problem in mind I arrived in Afghanistan in January 1975. I had made two exploratory trips in the summers of 1973 and 1974. Although they provided no ethnographic data, they enabled me to make contacts that later proved very helpful. With the help of an Afghan friend I had picked the area of Imam Saheb in the province of Kunduz as the most promising place to work. It was the winter home of thousands of nomads who migrated eastward to Badakhshan. They were reputedly the wealthiest nomads in the country. After obtaining permission from the government to work, I had the problem of choosing among the many different tribes of nomads, almost all of which had permanent winter villages in the area. Pashtuns, with their black tents, were the most numerous pastoral nomads, but in Imam Saheb there were also Uzbeks, Turkmen, Arabs, and Farsiwans (Persian-speaking nomads lumped together under a generic term), who were pastoral or who had pastoral components. The Arabs attracted my interest because they were traditionally yurt dwellers and engaged in long-distance migration, and (I must admit) because I had never heard of any Arabs in Central Asia. Furthermore, they spoke Persian, which was far easier to learn than Pashtu. An Afghan friend congratulated me: "If you had gone with the Pashtuns I would have felt obligated to give you a rifle, but with these Arabs your knife should be sufficient!" With these words of encouragement I absorbed my first lesson on the relative status of the two groups (Barfield 1978).

I was introduced to an Arab leader the next day. He arrived on a motorcycle, an indication that things were not quite as I had imagined them. I lived at this man's shepherd camp during the

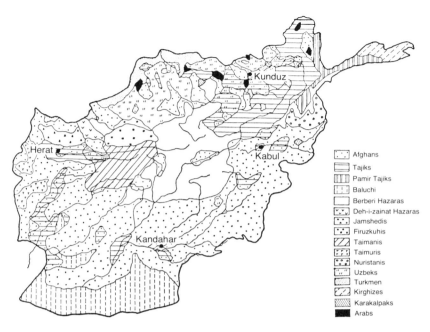

	Afghans
	Tajiks
	Pamir Tajiks
	Baluchi
	Berberi Hazaras
	Deh-i-zainat Hazaras
	Jamshedis
	Firuzkuhis
	Taimanis
	Taimuris
	Nuristanis
	Uzbeks
	Turkmen
	Kirghizes
	Karakalpaks
	Arabs

Map 1. Distribution of ethnic groups in Afghanistan. Adapted from *The Emergence of Modern Afghanistan*, by Vartan Gregorian (Stanford: Stanford University Press, 1969).

spring of 1975. I was disappointed at not being with a family group, but later I discovered that shepherd camps were the wave of the future and that there were fewer family groups involved in pastoralism than in the past. I learned a lot about sheep, and with a motorcycle at our disposal we often went visiting. I found my Persian improving rapidly since I was working alone. The Arabs enjoyed conversation, and I was told in no uncertain terms that part of my value was to talk. My first night in the camp a voice had bellowed:

> Arab Bai: "Make conversation!"
> Me: "I don't speak good Persian."
> Arab Bai: "I don't care, you must talk."
> Me: "I don't have anything to talk about."
> Arab Bai: "That's a lie. Either you make conversation or you go to your tent and sleep. You can't sit here and just listen."
> Me: "Do you know in my country we have roads eight

lanes wide with so many cars on them you can't go anywhere?"
Arab Bai: "Now that's interesting conversation!"

Of course no one could believe such statements, but the nomads loved good stories, and I could always be counted on to say something unusual. At first I felt put upon, but I soon discovered that anyone else who failed to take part in conversations was likewise berated. In many cases we exchanged customs and beliefs because when asked to describe something most of the nomads would say very little, but when comparing themselves with their neighbors or the foreign ways I described, the conversations always blossomed into long and detailed stories that exemplified their way of life, which they loved telling about.

During the spring and summer I gathered data on commercial pastoralism because access to a traditional family group was not immediately possible. I rode into the mountains of Badakhshan until my horse ate some poisonous plants and died. Afterward, everybody told me about the danger of poisonous plants. The rest of the trip was on foot, following a salt caravan to the highest mountain pastures. There just below the snow line I spent the summer. I left with some shepherds, and we walked for seven days to the nearest road.

The focus of the research changed from sheep to people in the winter camp, a nucleated settlement in the valley of Imam Saheb itself. I stayed in the guest houses of various Arabs and had the use of a house in the town of Imam Saheb. This turned out to be a good arrangement since within Imam Saheb I gained information about the town which helped me understand the integration of the town with the countryside. In this I was greatly aided by an Afghan friend who spoke English and was unstinting in his help, not only with practical problems but also in providing me with a great many insights as to exactly what I was observing. Without his aid the study would not have been possible.

As spring came I wanted to study the more traditional family groups. Since the Arabs objected to taking along a single male, I was joined by Donna Wilker. With her help I was able to gather data on women that I had been unable to acquire before and to make the traditional three-week migration to the mountains, 300 kilometers from Imam Saheb. This was perhaps the most interesting part of the research, since, although the migration is not the core of Arab life by any means, it was an unparalleled opportunity to observe the Arabs dealing with a wide range of

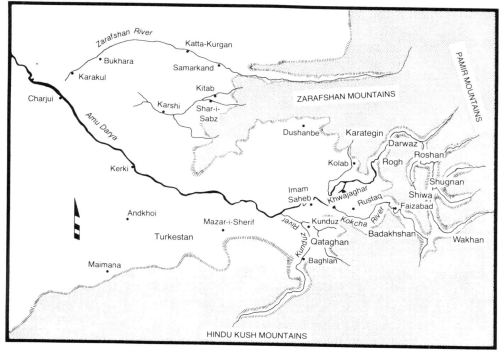

Map 2. Regions described in this book. Dotted area is 1,500 m and above in altitude. The area shown is partly in Afghanistan and partly in the USSR.

problems. It was also a contest in that the Arabs constantly played games—for example, seeing if they could catch one sleeping and thus late for predawn moves, or making one admit to being tired first. My coming up for the second time also surprised many people who had seen me the summer before, and their reception was far friendlier. Some traders who had cheated me in a business deal even apologized, though they didn't repay me.

During the research I was fortunate enough to be able to look at pastoralism from many perspectives. The Arabs and many other Afghans in Qataghan were extremely helpful in teaching me about pastoralism, from the politics of acquiring commodities from the cotton monopoly to judging the virtues of sheep and donkeys. The green fields of Imam Saheb and the vast reed swamps, the spring pasture covered with flowers, and the snowy peaks of Badakhshan, where out of nowhere a hundred horsemen showed up and played the polo-like game of *buzkashi* for three days, are all scenes that remain vital memories. An ethnography cannot easily capture the liveliness and beauty of the experience nor the happiness or frustrations involved in the research. In a sense it is merely an introduction to a land and people who gave me an opportunity to share their lives and to whom I will forever be grateful. In the chapters that follow, the complexity of nomadic pastoralism will become clear. There will be no pure nomads, but I hope that a picture of the problems nomadic pastoralists face in the modern world will emerge.

Statements in present tense throughout the book describe the situation as it was at the time of my research. I do not have sufficient information to determine how the Arabs may have been affected by more recent developments in Afghanistan.

The Central Asian Arabs of Afghanistan

1. Central Asian Arabs: Historical and Ecological Background

For millennia Central Asia was one of the world's great crossroads. At one time or another, nomadic tribes, invading armies, and representatives of many civilizations have occupied it. One legacy of Central Asia's long and complex history is the presence of ethnic minorities whose numbers, though small, are a constant reminder that some of the invaders never left. The Central Asian Arabs are one such minority.

This study focuses on the Central Asian Arabs in northeastern Afghanistan. They are pastoral nomads, taking their sheep seasonally from the lowlands in the Amu River Valley to the high mountains in Badakhshan. It is a story of their adaptations to continually changing circumstances. For more than one hundred years politics has played an equal role with the natural ecosystem in creating the effective environment in which the Arabs have made their choices. For example, lines drawn on maps in London and St. Petersburg explain better than any naturalistic phenomena the present distribution of Arab mountain pasture, though the Arabs themselves were in complete ignorance of these decisions. For this reason an examination of the place of the Arabs in Bukharan and Afghan history is a necessary prelude to understanding their role as nomadic pastoralists in the last quarter of the twentieth century.

Who Are the Central Asian Arabs?

The Central Asian Arabs traditionally occupied territory within the old khanate of Bukhara and the northern plains of Afghan Turkestan. As far as their origin is concerned, there are two traditions about the Arabs in Central Asia: "One that they are descendents of the Arabs who introduced Mohammedanism into

3

the country, which they themselves believe, and another that they were settled by Timour after he had conquered the western powers" (Schuyler 1876, I: 110).

It is possible that both these traditions contain some truth. After the Arab conquest of Central Asia in the eighth century a number of nomadic Arab tribes moved into the region around Bukhara (Barthold 1929: 81, 94–95, 101, 106, 182–195, 276). In 1401, after sacking the city, Tamerlane deported a large number of Arabs from Damascus to his capital at Samarkand, where they were observed by a Spanish envoy (Clavijo 1928: 287–288). These new arrivals could have augmented the numbers of any Arabs left from the original Islamic conquest. In any event, about a century later Babur, founder of the Mogul dynasty in India, wrote that the Arabs were one of the three main tribes north of Kabul, i.e., north of the Hindu Kush (Beveridge 1921: 207). Since the time of Tamerlane there has been no immediate connection between the Arabs in Central Asia and those in the Near East.

The absence of links with the Near East is most striking in language. Few Arabs in Central Asia speak Arabic today. The Soviet census of 1926 reported only 2,170 native speakers of Arabic in a population of 29,000 Arabs in Soviet Central Asia (Vinnikov 1940: 10–11). Today there are only a few villages where Arabic is spoken. Two dialects have been identified, but even these have been greatly influenced by the Tajiki and Uzbeki languages spoken in the region. All the Arabic speakers are at least bilingual, and many are trilingual (Tsereteli 1970: 167–170). In Afghanistan a few Arabic-speaking villages have been reported near Balkh (Farhadi 1969: 413). None of the Arabs I met in northeastern Afghanistan spoke Arabic, nor did they know any Arabs who did. They declared that Persian (Tajiki, Dari, or Farsi) had been their native tongue for as long as anyone could remember, although many were bilingual, also speaking Uzbeki.

This is not a new situation. Even in the nineteenth century the Arabic language was rapidly disappearing in Central Asia among the Arabs. N. Khanykov, a Russian who visited Bukhara in 1841 and made a thorough study of the khanate, said of the Arabs, "They speak Arabic among themselves but it is no longer the pure language of the peninsula" (1845: 72). Later an American diplomat, Eugene Schuyler, went to Bukhara in 1873, soon after it had become a Russian dependency, and found that Arabic had disappeared in many areas. Of the Arabs in the khanate, he noted: "Those near Katta Kurgan speak Tajik and Turki, the rest speak a debased and corrupted Arabic" (1876, I: 109). In northern Afghanistan the situation was similar. Around Balkh there were "many Arabs, who though they now speak Persian are still distinguished from the Taujiks. A few Arabs, however, retain their language" (Elphinstone 1815: 473).

While language is not a necessary criterion for defining ethnic groups, the close association of Arabs with the Arabic language elsewhere in the world creates some confusion about any group of people who call themselves Arabs but who no longer speak Arabic. This confusion has been compounded by the racial and political character given to the term *Arab* in the twentieth century in response to Western imperialism (Lewis 1966: 16). In earlier times *Arab* referred to tribal people, the nomadic Bedouins in particular: "The association with nomadism is borne out by the fact that the Arabs themselves have used the word at an early date to distinguish Bedouin from the Arabic speaking town and village dwellers and indeed continue to do so to the present day" (Lewis 1966: 10–11). The Central Asian Arabs are Arabs in the original sense of the word—nomadic tribes originally from Arabia. Soviet physical anthropology supports their claim of Semitic origin (Oshanin 1964: 45–47), but in language and culture they bear no resemblance to Arabian Arabs today. This matters very little in an area which has culturally assimilated many groups of people who nevertheless have maintained some degree of social distinction. Following Barth's definition, the Arabs in Central Asia identify themselves as such and are so identified by other ethnic groups in the region, thus constituting a recognizable ethnic group (1969: 11). In the local context, *Arab* is a social label, not a linguistic one. Whether there is an actual relationship between the Arabs in Central Asia today and the Islamic armies of the eighth century is socially irrelevant. It is rarely asked why the Utarbuloqi, Sinjani, or Larkhabi (all neighbors of the Arabs with rather obscure origins) have their particular names, but Persian- or Uzbeki-speaking Arabs violate too many of our preconceived notions about what *Arab* means to go without comment and debate.

Another confusion about the Central Asian Arabs is the idea that they are *sayyids* (Schurmann 1962: 102). The *sayyids* are an endogamous group of people who claim direct patrilineal descent from the prophet Mohammed through his daughter. The Central Asian Arabs claim no such descent, nor descent from any religious leader. Their tradition holds that their ancestors were the tribal nomads who made up much of the early Islamic army. Unlike the *sayyids*, they are not rigorously endogamous but have marriage links with many other ethnic groups. The confusion arises in large part because, although *sayyids* logically have an Arab as an ultimate ancestor, in Afghanistan they do not consider themselves to be Arabs socially, particularly if they live near Central Asian Arabs. Indeed, given the vast range of physical types and different native languages (none Arabic) found among *sayyids* in Afghanistan, one is on safer ground considering them to be socially and politically, perhaps genetically, subgroups of larger ethnic groups. *Sayyids* in Imam Saheb denied any connection with the local Arab nomads, but did not deny that the nomads were Arabs. Many groups, including the *sayyids*, claim Arab ancestry, but only the Central Asian Arabs actually state that they are still Arabs today.

At present the number of Arabs in the Soviet Union is quite small, with most of them located in Uzbekistan. In 1926 there were 29,000 Arabs, but by 1959 their numbers had declined officially to 6,400. Interestingly, the number who claimed Arabic as their native language remained about the same: 2,170 in 1926 and 2,007 in 1959 (Vinnikov 1940: 10–11; Karmysheva 1964: 271). The decline in the Arab population is the result of two factors. First, a large number of Arabs came to Afghanistan during the Stalinist collectivization period in the 1930s. Second, it has been to the Arabs' advantage to officially register as Uzbeks in Uzbekistan, resulting in a large undercount, even though in daily life they continue to refer to themselves as Arabs. In Afghanistan no proper census has ever been taken, so it is quite difficult even to estimate the number of Arabs there, but they could have a population as high as 100,000. Surveys have shown that most of the Arabs in Afghanistan live in the north in an arc extending from Maimana to Kunduz, where they are nomadic pastoralists who seasonally move from the plains into the surrounding mountains and foothills (Schurmann 1962: 104). There is a second, unrelated group of Arabs who live in Jalalabad. These Arabs originally came to Afghanistan as soldiers from the Iranian Khorasan region. In the early nineteenth century they garrisoned Bala Hissar in Kabul while the rest engaged in farming near Jalalabad. They spoke Persian and numbered about 2,000 families (Elphinstone 1815: 322). Today these Arabs are more nomadic. They have adopted the Pashtun style of black goat-hair tents and migrate seasonally to the Paghman Mountains near Kabul

(Ferdinand 1969: 130; Jenkyns 1879: 5). The Arabs in the northeast had heard of the Jalalabad Arabs but said they were not related, which is not surprising in view of their different histories.

The Arabs in Nineteenth-Century Bukhara

As the nineteenth century opened, Bukhara was but a shadow of its former self, its fame and beauty better preserved in poetry than in fact. Bukhara's decline in fortune began with the collapse of the old overland caravan trade that had encompassed all Eurasia, in which Bukhara was a major hub. The caravan trade was unable to meet the competition of the new Western trading companies and their sailing ships. In a prime location for the overland trade, Bukhara was reduced to the status of a remote oasis by the new sea routes. By the middle of the sixteenth century an English trader found the merchants of Bukhara to be "beggerly and poore," forced to wait two or three years for enough business to enable them to sell all their goods and with "no hope of any good trade to be had worth the following" (Jenkinson 1886: 87). Still, if no longer a great city, Bukhara remained important regionally by exporting such goods as cotton and silk to its neighbors, including Russia, and by acting as a major market for slaves. Economic decline also engendered political fragmentation; formerly the center of Timurid and Uzbek power, Bukhara became just one of the many small khanates ruled by petty despots who were constantly at war with their neighbors.

During this same period of decline in Central Asia, Russia was advancing steadily eastward by incorporating large tracts of steppe and thereby moving ever closer to the borders of Transoxiana. The khanates of the region viewed this expansion with apprehension but felt somewhat insulated by the mountains, deserts, and steppe that still surrounded them. One result of Russian expansion was more trade with Bukhara and an increasing number of outside observers who wrote descriptions of the khanate. It is from these accounts that we first get a clear picture of the Arabs in Central Asia and the role they played in the regional economy. It is also the first information that can reliably be linked to the Arabs living in the region today.

The Arabs were an important part of the Bukharan khanate. Meyendorf visited Bukhara in 1820 and estimated the Arab population at 50,000 people. They were nomadic and lived in the northern and southern parts of the khanate. Those in the south engaged in the profitable sale of the famous *qarakul* lambskins (so-called Persian lamb, or astrakhan) (Meyendorf 1826: 187). Twenty years later Khanykov came to Bukhara as a Russian envoy and left a remarkably detailed description of the khanate and its people:

> *The Arabs*—Their number is somewhat greater than that of the Tajiks, but they are far from constituting a numerous tribe. They are chiefly dispersed over the northern parts of the Khanate, having their headquarters in the vicinity of Vardanzi and Samarkand. They have not relinquished the habits of their ancestors and continue to lead a wandering life, with this difference, that the severity of climate has induced them to exchange their tents for the *kibitka* [yurt]. Such only as are compelled by the nature of their occupations live in fixed habitations. Their features betray their origin; their large eyes are black, as well as their hair; and their skin, which is susceptible to the effects of the sun's rays often becomes nearly black from exposure. . . . Their chief occupation consists of breeding their flocks, and it is they who provide the bazaars with the brown and black *pustins*, or sheep skins. We spent too short a time among them to enable us to form any positive conclusion respecting their character; they seem however to stand higher than the Tajiks, with respect to their moral qualities; for during our whole stay in Bokhara we heard no evil reports against them. The Bokharians, it is true, reproach them with the uncouthness of their manners and their ignorance of decorum; though as far as I can judge, these defects consist in their not smothering you with flattery, as do the Tajiks. (1845: 72–73)

These descriptions of the Arabs' important place in the khanate of Bukhara raise some questions. If the Arabs were the major sheep raisers for the khanate, why have they remained so little known in comparison to those nomads—Turkmen, Kazakh, or Kirghiz—who lived on the periphery of the khanate? Second, why was there no mention of the Arabs in the political history of the region during this period? The answer to both these questions lies in the relationship that the Arabs established with the Bukharan state. A short explanation of the different positions held by ethnic groups in the khanate in the early nineteenth century will make it clear that the Arabs were quite unlike the other nomads in their dealings with Bukhara.

Bukhara was a multiethnic state. The two major groups in the khanate were the Uzbeks, the last Turkic conquerors of Transoxiana, and the Tajiks, the old Persian-speaking inhabitants of the region. Both these groups were concentrated in the major river valleys. The Uzbeks also controlled the uplands surrounding the valleys, while the Tajiks dominated the more mountainous parts of the khanate. In addition, the Arabs were also found in the Zarafshan region in the north and the Karakul Basin in the south. The Turkmen inhabited the desert to the west of Bukhara, including the oasis of Merv and parts of the lower Amu River Valley. To the north on the steppe were the Kazakh, and to the east in the mountains were the Kirghiz (Trotter 1873).

The distribution of these ethnic groups was not random; each exploited a particular niche that integrated a mode of subsistence with political realities. While it is customary to divide the inhabitants of Central Asia into two classes—nomadic and sedentary— and discuss their traditional conflicts, this division is in fact too gross. It obscures important differences within each class and hides a more interesting dynamic that explains why the Arabs were overlooked in the region's history.

Bukhara had three major types of agricultural production: intensive irrigated agriculture in the major river valleys and oases, dry farming of wheat and barley in the loessial uplands, and alpine farming in the high mountain villages (Krader 1963: 10–21).

The most important of these was the intensive irrigated agriculture that used dams and a complex system of canals to create large green strips of productivity in the major valleys and oases. The Zarafshan River Valley was the most important area for this kind of production in the khanate. It was also the home of the Sarts, who were the agricultural peasantry made up of detribalized Uzbeks and Tajiks lumped together into a single category by occupation. The common use of the term *Sart* illustrated that, although two different ethnic groups inhabited the valleys, they were all but indistinguishable in economy and lifestyle. These highly productive areas also supported the khanate's major urban centers, Bukhara and Samarkand. These cities were the seats of government, centers of international trade, and locations where the most diversity in craft specialization and education could be found.

The loessial uplands lacked the advantages of irrigation in most places but were extensively cultivated, depending on seasonal rainfall to water the crop. In most years this area produced substantial surpluses which were exported to the large cities. These cities depended on the upland production because the irrigated valleys devoted much of their land to cash crops like cotton. A crop failure in the uplands created problems for the whole region. In addition to grain farming, the people of the uplands also raised some livestock which they were able to graze locally or take on short migrations to seasonal pastures. Ethnically this was an Uzbek area, and, unlike those in the lowlands, these Uzbeks retained some degree of tribal cohesion. Villages were much further apart than in the lowlands. Some irrigated areas could be found in this region wherever the valleys that cut into the foothills made it possible. This kind of irrigation was neither as complex nor as profitable as that found in the major river valleys and oases, but it did provide the base for towns like Kolab which were of regional importance. These towns were markets for the local area, provided necessary manufactured goods, and linked the region to the outside world.

In the high mountains of the khanate, alpine agriculture supported many villages. These villages grew wheat or barley on the mountainsides and raised cows and goats using alpine pastures. The economies of these villages were subsistence-oriented and basically self-sufficient. Their surpluses were mostly milk products and live animals for sale, but their pastoral economy was severely limited by the necessity to make hay and stall-feed their livestock during the winter, which reduced the number they could raise. There were no urban centers here; the mountain villagers depended on the bazaars of the uplands to supply them with manufactured goods and commodities such as salt which they could not produce themselves. The mountainous area of Karategin was linked to Kolab in this way even when the Bukharan state had no control over that rugged region.

Pastoral nomadism was the other great tradition of Central Asia. However, the relationship of the nomads to Bukhara varied considerably, so it cannot be considered as a single uniform pattern. Many nomadic groups combined pastoralism with other activities such as raiding, trading, or agriculture to increase their standard of living. It was often these secondary activities that determined just what sort of relationship they did establish with the Bukharan state.

The Kazakh and the Kirghiz had the least contact with Bukhara. The Kazakh bordered the khanate on the north, where they made long-range migrations over the steppe in order to graze their large herds of sheep and horses. Only in the southernmost part of their traditional range did they fall within Bukhara's sphere of influence. Except in terms of providing camels and some of the work force for the caravans to Russia, the Kazakh had little business with Bukhara, and what needs they did have were fulfilled by towns on the edge of the steppe like Chimkent and Tashkent. The Kirghiz lived in the high mountains that bordered the khanate on the east. They also raised sheep and horses but migrated vertically from lower mountain valleys in the winter to high mountain pastures in the summer. Like the Kazakh, the Kirghiz had few direct relations with Bukhara, in part because they were far closer to the cities in Sinkiang or to the khanate of Kokand in the north (Krader 1955; Radloff 1893).

The Turkmen bordered Bukhara on the edge of its western desert. These Turkmen included groups that were both fully nomadic and those that were engaged in irrigated agriculture in Merv or along the Amu River. Movement from agriculture to nomadism was quite common among the Turkmen. Because of their desert environment the Turkmen were great camel breeders, but they were also famous for their *qarakul* sheep and their splendid horses. Unlike the Kazakh or Kirghiz, the Turkmen had close ties to Bukhara, where they sold carpets and slaves. Their economy owed its prosperity to slave raiding. They had become "commercial raiders" who took advantage of their central position in the desert between two enemy states. The Turkmen needed both a place to raid and a place to sell the loot because their own economy had only a limited use for slaves. Iranian Khorasan and the Uzbek states of northwestern Afghanistan were continually raided for slaves, which were then sold in Bukhara or to the west in neighboring Khiva. The Bukharan state could not control the Turkmen themselves but was content to welcome their visits to the Bukharan markets (Napier 1876; Irons 1974).

The Arabs were the other major nomadic pastoral group, but they lived within the limits of the agricultural valleys in the winter and then abandoned them for the steppe in the spring and the mountains in the summer:

> Among the settled inhabitants, many of those of Turki descent as well as the Arabs still inhabit by preference the felt tent of the nomad, and in country districts cattle are often housed in the farm buildings while the owner is encamped in the courtyard which they surround. In those parts where cultivated land borders on the steppe the inhabitants who possess large herds of cattle, sheep, and horses, spend winter only in the villages camping in the steppe in other seasons in search of pasture. (Trotter 1873: 7)

Living on the fringes of the valleys within the khanate, the Arabs were, unlike other pastoralists, in close and constant contact with sedentary farmers and urban centers. The dependability of their pasture and its richness allowed them to keep within fixed areas. The sheep they raised were sold in urban bazaars:

> The breed of sheep is chiefly attended to by the Arabs, the race is the same as the Kirghiz sheep [fat-tailed] but rather fatter; and the great care which is taken of them must be attributed to the profits this branch of trade affords. There is nothing in the sheep which is not turned to account by its owner. The mutton is sold, the wool and skin are used for clothing and felt, etc. The fleece of the lamb skins fetches a higher price the younger they are, and are made into the pustins which form a considerable article of export trade with Russia, but more especially, with Persia. (Khanykov 1845: 203–204)

It was the location of the Arabs in relation to the other nomads and, ironically, their extremely close connections with the Bukharan market that made the Arabs the invisible nomads. As subjects of the amir of Bukhara and living entirely within his borders, the Arabs exchanged the opportunity for political independence in wastelands along the khanate's edge for access to the best pasture in the region and trade with urban markets. It was the Arabs, and not the more famous nomads, who supplied Bukhara with pastoral products and who raised the largest sheep in the whole region.

The other nomads maintained their independence by avoiding the khanate's political control but were forced to stay in the less productive border areas. Khanykov described how the region's geography made this possible:

> Rivers are therefore the natural boundaries of the cultivated portions of the Khanate, while the rest offers asylum to wandering tribes, who barely escape starvation by continually changing their places of encampment. Such as approach the limits of the cultivated land, pay a certain tribute, and are in consequence held to be under the immediate control of the Khans; others enjoy their freedom and are only nominal subjects to the Amir of Bokhara. (1845: 6)

As a pastoral nomadic tribe that fell completely under the control of the Bukharan khanate, the Arabs were viewed as an anomaly. In their survey of Bukhara the British classified the Arabs as a "settled tribe" because "though they lead a pastoral life, [they] cannot be fairly called nomads, inhabiting as they do certain defined districts" (Trotter 1873: 6). The implicit assumption here was that nomadism required variable movements and the political independence with which to make them. The Arabs showed that they could be more successful pastoralists by giving up some political independence in exchange for pastures so dependable that they could migrate within fixed districts.

The political aspects of nomadism are best understood by returning to the structure of the Bukharan khanate. The main river valleys and oases with their complex irrigation systems were the heart of the Bukharan state and most subject to the government's control. Leaving these central places east to the mountains, west and south to the deserts, or north to the steppe, one entered districts of secondary importance to the Bukharan state. Here lived people with mixed economies: some, like the Arabs were pastoral; some, like the wheat farmers of Kolab were agricultural; and many villages were a mixture of both. These groups produced important surpluses and were near enough to the centers of power for that surplus to be extracted profitably. Towns in these regions were secondary centers of trade and government, and a vital part of the khanate.

The periphery of the khanate was an area under nominal rule of the amirs. All of the regions in the periphery were difficult to exploit and sparsely inhabited. Sandy wastes, high mountains, or broad steppes were not only difficult to conquer, but also could not be easily or profitably integrated into the realm. As a result, submission was not commonly obtained from the nomads who inhabited these areas, nor even from the mountainous kingdoms like Darwaz, Roshan, and Shughnan. It was not nomadism per se that allowed this independence, but the location and relation of the nomads—and alpine farmers—to the central authorities. Wasteland was the natural home for the nomads because they could live there while farmers could not. A nomad's ability to move went far beyond economic necessity because movement was a political weapon used to preserve independence. To see that nomadic pastoralism was no automatic means to political independence we need only look to the Arabs, who were under control of the government. Even the Turkmen, who were famous raiders, were powerful only when they could escape retaliation. Those Turkmen in Iranian Khorasan who lived near the Persians were noticeably better behaved than their cousins who lived further away (Irons 1974). Nomads could benefit greatly by exploiting the resources of better-watered regions, but there was a political price to pay. They were integrated into the agricultural state as pastoral specialists. It was not the Arabs who led opposition to the amir's control; they were too subject to retaliation. It was the nomads on the periphery, with their political independence, who were able to benefit from raiding and unrest. The Arabs, going about their profitable business, seem never to have been caught up in political conflicts and hardly rated as active participants in the regional history.

It is now possible to answer the two questions raised earlier about the importance of the Arabs in Bukhara. The Arabs were less well known than other nomads because they were peacefully integrated into the khanate's economy as pastoralists who supplied meat for the urban markets and skins for the international trade. The nomads on the periphery stood out as independent political actors, watched by both the Central Asian khanates and the Russians because they were potential threats. The Arabs were such a part of the local scene that early nineteenth-century descriptions of them had little more to say than that they were an important part of the population. Similarly, the Arabs did not appear in the political history of the region because they were encapsulated by the Bukharan state and did not take part in the petty wars that were so common at the time. It was the other nomads who bordered the khanate, and who could leave it when necessary, who made raids and took part in political intrigues. The Arabs chose a policy of accommodation and avoided trouble, thereby losing their place in the region's history because they were never prominent either as winners or as losers in Central Asian politics and warfare. Finally, as will be seen, a large number of Arabs left the Bukharan khanate soon after the Russian conquest. Therefore, in the late nineteenth century the Arabs no longer constituted an important part of the khanate's population, so that few writers bothered to look closely at their earlier role in Bukhara and to see that it had changed.

The Arab Emigration to Northern Afghanistan

By the mid-nineteenth century Russia had advanced its control of the steppe to the borders of the old Central Asian khanates. In two military campaigns between 1865 and 1868 Bukhara was captured and forced to pay an indemnity and cede Samarkand to direct Russian rule. Although it maintained its legal sovereignty, Bukhara became a Russian dependency in which the amirs continued to rule but were under Russian control. This state of affairs continued until after the Russian revolution when in 1920 the khanate was formally abolished. Russian rule also brought rail transport and American varieties of cotton, which made Central Asia the prime producer of cotton for Russian industry (Becker 1968).

The conquest of Bukhara had a profound effect on the Central Asian Arabs. There was apparently a wholesale migration by the nomadic Arabs to northern Afghanistan in the 1870s. Almost all of the Arabs in Qataghan province are descendents of the immigrants. According to their oral history, the Arabs refused to submit to the rule of the infidels and moved to Afghanistan, introducing their large fat-tailed sheep to Qataghan. No records directly mention such emigration, but comparison of a number of sources supports this oral history. Economic rather than religious reasons may have been the motivating factor. The sequence of events probably ran as follows:

1. The Russian conquest of Bukhara left the khanate with a government that was semiautonomous. It lacked independence but had a fairly free hand in domestic affairs. The one exception to this was the annexation of the Zarafshan district, including Samarkand, in 1868. This was the area that preconquest reporters gave as the homeland of the Arabs, and the facts support the claims of the Arabs' oral history that they fell under the direct rule of "infidels."

2. In 1871 there was a famine in Bukhara because of drought, and this, combined with a Russian administrative fiasco the next year, seems to have been the most likely cause of the emigration. In 1872 the Russians changed the taxes from in-kind payment to cash payment based on local prices. 1872 was a bad year for the harvest, and with the tax change it was disastrous:

> When it was determined to commute the payment in kind to cash, and the produce was therefore appraised at the current market rate, it became apparent that in reality taxation amounted to one-third of the gross produce. This was owing to the people, on the approach of the date for the payment of taxes, taking at once the government share of the produce to the bazaars which naturally glutted the markets and compelled them to sell nearly twice as much grain to realize a given sum of money than would have ordinarily been the case.
>
> These circumstances produced a serious derangement, economical and agricultural, in the position of the natives of the Zarafshan circle, which quickly showed itself in arrears, complaints, deputations to the Governor-General and ended

in crimes of property and in emigration. The people began to move en masse into the neighboring territories, and indeed two Kishlaks (villages) migrated bodily across the frontier. (Terentiev 1876, 2: 216–217)

As pastoral nomads, the Arabs were in a position to use their mobility to emigrate and take their sheep elsewhere. This they did.

3. Visitors to Bukhara after 1873 give a very different picture of the Arabs. Whereas both Meyendorf and Khanykov indicated that the Arabs were an important group in the khanate, later visitors listed them only as a curiosity and recorded them as being sedentary. Olufsen, at the turn of the century, gave an extensive account of all aspects of the khanate, in which he said of the Arabs, "Formerly they lived in tents in the old Arab way, but now they live in houses like the other natives, especially engaged in carpet weaving and horse dealing. They still speak a sort of Arabic and are easily recognized owing to their pitch black faces, large black eyes and black hair" (1911: 246). There is no mention of their former occupation as the khanate's major sheep raisers. It is most likely that the pastoral Arabs left behind the more sedentarized Arabs who had property and who were consequently less mobile. The Russian censuses of the period make only one mention of Arabs until the Soviet census of 1926, which included Bukhara for the first time (Krader 1956: 268). Had there been large numbers of Arabs in the Zarafshan region during the Russian occupation it is unlikely they would have been missed.

Table 1. Population of Afghan Turkestan in 1884

Ethnic Group	Number of Families
Uzbeks	30,080
Arabs	16,070
Hazaras	11,490
Tajiks	10,740
Turkmens	8,505
Baluch and Firozkuhi	3,730
Afghans	3,420
Sayyids and Khwajas	1,610
Kipchaks	1,460
Total	87,105

Source: G.A.T. 1979:14.

4. Finally, a British census of northern Afghanistan showed a remarkable and almost unheralded increase in the number of Arabs in the region. Whereas the reports of the 1830s and 1840s had indicated only pockets of Arabs, a census in the 1880s made them the second most populous group on the Turkestan plain (see Table 1). While it is not possible to determine how many of these Arabs could have come from Bukhara, the high figures for Afghan Turkestan and the absence of Arabs in Russian censuses seems best explained by an emigration of nomadic Arabs to Afghanistan.

The Arabs in Northern Afghanistan

The Arabs' move from the Zarafshan region into northern Afghanistan was not a radical change for them. It was a culturally familiar environment with Uzbeks in the plains and Tajiks in the mountains. It was also the southern range of the nomadic Arabs who had been reported throughout northern Afghanistan in the early nineteenth century in Maimana, Andkhoi, Balkh, Tashqurghan, and Baghlan (Burnes et al. 1839: 43, 108; Elphinstone 1815: 473; Wood 1872: 206). It was close enough to Bukhara for them to continue to market sheep there, and pasture was readily available in this depopulated region. The Arabs leaving Bukhara had a choice of two distinct environments. The first was the plains of Turkestan which stretched from Maimana to Tashqurghan. This was the home of most of the Arabs already living in Afghanistan but was still open as the result of wars, raids by the Turkmen, famines, and epidemics that had left this rich land free for the taking. The second environment was in the swampy valleys of Qataghan with access to the mountains of Badakhshan or part of the Hindu Kush range. This area was also underpopulated because the malarial valleys discouraged settlers.

Northern Afghanistan had consisted of many petty states whose number and size varied constantly. These states, at times independent and at times subject to Kabul or Bukhara, were constantly at war with each other or in rebellion against their overlords:

> The amount of rivalry and intrigue that exists among the petty Khans of Turkestan is perfectly incredible to anyone who has not been in the country; and instead of trying to decrease or modify either, they exert their intelligence to the utmost to complicate and carry out their paltry schemes. The certain consequence is a permanent state of warfare in

which it is impossible for the people to attempt the development of the resources of the country, or to undertake any enterprises with the view to its future improvement. (Ferrier 1976 [1857]: 204)

Irrigation agriculture was particularly vulnerable to political unrest. The number and size of the petty Uzbek states guaranteed that they would never lack for opponents. More important, however, their weakness made them vulnerable to raiding. It was this endemic raiding that turned northern Afghanistan into a political desert. These plundering raids had economic goals—the extraction of goods—rather than political aims—the conquest or submission of an opponent. The raids of the Turkmen were most infamous. Their goal was slaves, and much of Khorasan and northwestern Afghanistan was depopulated as a result. The villages in the area had "gradually succumbed to the attacks of the Turkomans one after another, in many cases being absolutely destroyed, the people—men, women, and children—all being carried off into slavery, and the result is that no one has dared to go out to those places ever since. Not only has the population of these outer districts been carried off bodily, but even that in the more settled districts along the high road has suffered in proportion" (Yate 1888: 134–135). Vambery also reported the wholesale abandonment of much of northwestern Afghanistan (1864: 237, 254, 255). As noted above, this raiding was dependent on weak neighbors and markets in Bukhara. But a more insidious form of raiding was that organized by one state to loot another. The Uzbek khanate of Kunduz, or Qataghan, was supported in large part by revenue derived from raids conducted by the mir and his subjects:

> The Meer is also entitled to the entire of whatever plunder may be taken when he himself is in the field as well as one-fifth of whatever plunder may be taken by his subjects acting under his permission but without his presence. I have no means of estimating this source of revenue, yet it cannot fail to be considerable. He seldom allows three months to pass without a regular organized foray which he directs in person: as for his subjects, they are always plundering. (Burnes et al. 1839: 112–113)

Murad Beg, the mir of Kunduz in the 1830s, was greatly feared, as the following account makes clear:

> When I was in Kunduz I saw 10,000 sheep driven from Muzar [Mazar-i-Sharif]—the product of one foray. I cannot give a

more correct idea of the extent of Murad Beg's power or the dread his name inspires, than by mentioning the simple fact, that two months after the date of this outrage, I saw the flock of 5,000 sheep belonging to Murad Beg passing *without an escort* through Muzar on their way to be sold in Bukhara. (Burnes et al. 1839: 106)

Like the Turkmen, the raiding state of Kunduz was dependent for its raids on the existence of weak states and the incapacity of larger states like Kabul and Bukhara to defend their peripheral provinces. As a state, however, Kunduz at least had the potential to annex and rule the territories it raided. Its failure to do this was evidence of its own weakness. Kunduz failed to become a new power center, and its predatory pattern of foreign relations could be maintained only in the absence of a strong opponent.

The state of anarchy in Turkestan and Qataghan that encouraged petty wars and raids began to end with the Afghan conquest of the region. Dost Muhammad of Kabul brought all the small Uzbek states in Turkestan under his rule in a series of military campaigns from 1850 to 1855. Kunduz was annexed in 1859 (G.A.T. 1979: 23). The Russian advances into Central Asia also solidified the region by forcing Bukhara to renounce its old claims to Afghan Turkestan when in 1873 both the Russians and the British agreed to accept the Amu River and the khanate of Khiva as the official border of Afghanistan (Becker 1968: 58–63). The Russian conquest of Khiva in the same year closed down the last major market for slaves and marked the beginning of a drive against the Turkmen. From their new base in Khiva the Russians reduced a series of Turkmen strongholds until the major center at Merv fell in 1884 (Becker 1968: 99–102). Since the Turkmen had been responsible for the devastation of much of northern Afghanistan, their pacification was a boon to the region. Also at this time Amir Abdur Rahman (1880–1900) attempted to settle Turkestan with Pashtuns from south of the Hindu Kush to tie the region more closely to Kabul (Tapper 1973; Kakar 1979: 131–135).

The only detailed description of the Arabs in Afghan territory at this time comes from the secret reports made by the British survey teams of the Afghan Boundary Commission. They provide considerably more material about the Arabs than is available in more modern sources. As noted in Table 1, in 1884 they found the Arabs to be the second most populous group on the Turkestan plain, and this excluded those Arabs who had settled in Qataghan. While most of these Arabs were long-time residents of this region, they had avoided becoming part of the political struggles in the region and, like their cousins in Bukhara, received little historical attention. They too suffered from the Turkmen's raids, but as nomads they were better able to avoid attack than were sedentary villagers. At the time the Arabs were leaving Bukhara the Turkestan plain was even more open than usual. A famine in 1872 was followed by a cholera epidemic which completely depopulated many districts. Afghan rule was also not too harsh, judging from this statement of J. P. Maitland in 1886: "We observed no signs of oppression or markedly unjust dealing on the part of the Afghan rulers toward the subject races. The administration was decidedly good for an Asiatic state . . . In Turkistan both Uzbaks and Turkomans allowed they had no serious cause of complaint, though they naturally feel their inferior position. This feeling is shared by the majority of the Persian speaking population" (G.A.T. 1979: 12).

Maitland estimated that there were 16,070 Arab families in Afghan Turkestan, most of which were nomadic or seminomadic, and distributed them as follows (G.A.T. 1979: 74):

Aibek with Khuram	300
Tashqurghan	1,000
Balkh-Ab	5,000
Rud-i-Band-i-Amir districts	7,000
The Hazhda-Nahr	1,500
Sangcharak	60
Sar-i-Pul	150
Shibarghan	600
Andkhoi and Daulatabad	390
Maimana	70

Maitland also noted that the Arabs, since 1850, had moved east away from Maimana where they were once strongly represented because of Turkmen raids and the settlement of Turkmen tribes in Panjdeh to the north. The Arabs in Afghan Turkestan all spoke Persian and lived in yurts similar to those of the Turkmen. They were divided into clans, each under the rule of a Mir Hazar, with the whole tribe of an area under the command of an Ilbegi. In Balkh-Ab there were ten clans: Chilkapa, Jamali, Ao Karosh, Mullai, Khanzada, Rashadi, Iskandari, and three others whose names were unknown. In Rud-i-Band-i-Amir there were eighteen clans organized like those in Balkh-Ab: Rashadi, Bausari, Kharbuza Khori, Sazi, Hazhda-Diwana, Haft Posti, Abdui Karimi, Keitukra, Alanchari, Kashkari, and eight others whose names were unknown (G.A.T. 1979: 74–75).

The Arabs in Qataghan

Qataghan as a natural area embraced the Kunduz and Khanabad rivers, together with part of the Amu River before it entered the desert. As these rivers left their mountain sources and entered the plains, they flooded the wide valleys cut into the loess. This created vast reed swamps with endemic malaria that were infamous throughout Afghanistan. "If you want to die, go to Kunduz," was a widespread proverb. Wood, visiting Kunduz in 1838, found it "a place only fit to be the residence of aquatic birds" (Wood 1872: 163). As a result, the entire region was sparsely populated.

Badakhshan was a mountainous region not afflicted with the diseases of the plains. But in the 1830s it suffered from the depredation of Mir Murad Beg of Kunduz. Not content with raiding the territories to the west, he personally depopulated Badakhshan in an attempt to people Qataghan with Tajiks from the mountains. After he had subdued Badakhshan, he put down a number of rebellions and in 1829 began to systematically move the Tajiks to the plains (Wood 1872: 162). Another source reported that "His most deadly revenge was taken by driving before him 20,000 families whom he transplanted from the beautiful hills of Badakhshan to the fens of Kundooz and Hazrut Imam, in which they have from year to year pined and languished, so that of all that great number between four and five thousand could now with difficulty be collected" (Burnes et al. 1839: 102).

On almost the very spot where the Arabs of today have their *qishloqs* (winter camps), P. B. Lord, who surveyed the area, observed:

> In riding through the fens below Huzrut Imam, a short way from the banks of the Oxus, I noticed a village of considerable size, was but of very recent construction as its half finished huts, the scarcely made paths between them, and the small portion of land around as yet brought under tillage abundantly evinced. At its termination I was astonished to see a graveyard, in which I counted no less than 300 graves, and probably half as many more remained. These too were quite recent, in so much that on few of them had the grass begun to grow. "Tell me," said I to an old man who was lingering near the spot, "what people are you and what misfortune has fallen on you?" "We are Tajiks," replied he, "from Mominabad, last month was a twelvemonth since Mahomed Beg brought 1500 families of us here, and I take an oath that not 800 *individuals* are now remaining. This graveyard,"

added he, "is only half. There is another equally large at that end of the village." (Burnes et al. 1839: 111)

Lord goes on to discuss the reason for this deadly settlement policy:

> Because the former rulers of the Kataghans lived in Kundooz [Murad Beg] thinks it right that he should live there too, and he points with great justice to the advantages of its central situation when troops are to be collected. But he goes on to argue that because he lives there, he sees no reason why the people of the hills should not live there also. I ventured to suggest that a reason might be that they invariably died. (Burnes et al. 1839: 121)

With this reputation it is no wonder the Afghan government had difficulty finding settlers willing to go to Qataghan. Amir Abdur Rahman was unsuccessful in convincing Pashtuns from the south to move there. Indeed, with an oppressive taxation policy he managed to drive many farmers out of the province into Bukharan territory. So Qataghan was used by the amir as a penal colony for his enemies (Kakar 1979: 39, 87). Qataghan would seem a most unlikely spot to settle, but the Arabs discovered that their style of nomadism was perfectly adapted to the region. The Arabs were able to take advantage of the wealth of Qataghan by moving out of the valleys in the spring and summer to avoid the malaria and returning each winter for the pasture in the lowlands. Certainly the area was perfect for a nomadic pastoralism which required rich and dependable pastures. Wood described the steppe as follows:

> Throughout this excursion I was struck with the admirable adaptation of this country to the wants of a pastoral people. West of Khulm, the valley of the Oxus, except on the immediate banks of the stream, appears to be a desert, but in the opposite direction eastward to the rocky barriers of Darwaz, all the high-lying portion of the valley is at this season [spring] a wild prairie of sweets, a verdant carpet enamelled with flowers. Were I asked to state in what respects Kabul and Kunduz most differ from each other, I should say in mountain scenery. Throughout Kabul the hills are bold and repulsive, naked and bleak, while the low swelling outlines of Kunduz are as soft to the eye as the verdant sod which carpets them is to the foot. (Wood 1872: 268)

As nomads who traditionally engaged in long-range migrations, the Arabs slipped easily into Qataghan. The seminomadic Uzbek pastoralists of the major river valleys engaged only in short-range migrations. The Tajiks of Badakhshan could exploit only a fraction of the mountain summer pasture because they had to stall-feed their animals in winter, and were consequently limited by their inability to collect sufficient fodder. The Arabs, using each pasture area at its peak, were easily able to become the dominant nomads of the region. Using the sheltered swamps in the winter, the steppe in the spring, and the mountains in the summer, they found long-distance migrations both ecologically adaptive and profitable.

Land in the swamps was readily available for winter villages. Even in the 1830s Qataghan had welcomed settlers: "Land is offered to whoever will take it on easy terms of paying, if agriculturalists one-tenth to one-eighth of the produce; if sheep farmers, one-fiftieth of their stock annually" (Burnes et al. 1839: 111). When the Arabs arrived in Qataghan in the 1870s, winter pasture in the lowland valleys was thus easy to claim. The steppe above the valley floors was equally unsettled. The Arabs said that they found it virtually unoccupied. Finally, mountain pasture was available due to the disastrous depopulation policies of Murad Beg, and later the control of Badakhshan by the Afghans, which gave the Arabs access to the highland areas. As in Bukhara, the Arabs allied themselves with the Uzbeks and came under the control of the state, in this case the Afghan state, in return for use of the best pastures in the region. Until the reign of Amanullah (1919–1929), Qataghan was ruled in a tribal fashion. Abdur Rahman in his first attempt to take the throne had recognized the importance of the old Uzbek leadership, and stated to the leader of the Qataghan Uzbeks: "When my father gave the country of Kataghan to your father, he retained for himself the Tajik, the Arab, and the old Afghan, and Hazara tribes, leaving only the Kataghan [Uzbeks] to you. I will do the same" (Sultan Mahomed Khan 1900: 69). Although the Uzbeks lost much of their power after supporting an unsuccessful revolt against Abdur Rahman in 1888, which led to the division of northern Afghanistan into smaller provinces (Kakar 1971: 139–157), it was not until 1921 that Qataghan was reorganized along more bureaucratic lines by War Minister Nadir Khan, who later became king.

Though the type of nomadism adopted by the Arabs in Qataghan was very similar to what they had practiced in Bukhara, there were some significant differences. In Qataghan the

Arabs became far more nomadic than they had been in the Zarafshan Valley, where they were a "settled tribe" of pastoral nomads with fixed *qishloqs* and even farm buildings. In Qataghan they became completely nomadic, spending one winter in Taloqan and the next in Kunduz or Imam Saheb, moving as it pleased them. For almost fifty years, until granted title to land in 1921, they were without a fixed base. For many years after that they used the land only for camping. Only in the past thirty years have their villages again begun to resemble the pastoral *qishloqs* they had left in Bukhara.

In addition to establishing a more nomadic existence, the Arabs found themselves more cut off from trade. Having controlled the profitable urban sheep market in Bukhara, they now found themselves in an economic backwater. Qataghan was productive, but it choked on its surpluses, which could not be easily exported. Internally Qataghan had no real markets of importance. Even in the 1920s Kunduz lay in ruins, Khanabad was a small administrative center, and Imam Saheb was a town of two hundred households and one hundred shops (Kushkaki 1923: 81). Not surprisingly the Arabs continued to market their sheep in Bukhara, despite the distance, until well into the Soviet period when the border was closed to trade.

Let us turn from the Arab emigration to Qataghan to the ecology of the region they now inhabited. The focus will be on north Qataghan, the Amu River Valley region where a large number of Arabs settled. Until 1935 the region remained as it had been one hundred years earlier. But in the past fifty years such vast changes have taken place that the swamps and river valleys have been transformed. Because the impact of these changes is critical to understanding the Arabs today, we must first look in detail at the regional ecology, both to understand how the Arabs made use of seasonal pastures and to gauge the effect of changes in the ecology on the regional economy.

Ecology in Northeastern Afghanistan

Rivers have traditionally represented the centers of kingdoms, not their boundaries. In mountain areas, to cross from one watershed into another is to move from one district to the next. A map of river drainage is thus far more useful in understanding a natural region than are the modern provincial units, which change regularly. Fortunately, the traditional names Qataghan and

Badakhshan are analytically useful in both geographical and political senses.

As the Sorkh Ab River leaves the mountains for the plains, it becomes the Kunduz River. It joins with the Khanabad River to debouch into the Amu River. These three rivers, as they cut into the loessial plains, define the territory of Qataghan. To the east in the mountains lies Badakhshan. Badakhshan proper consists of the watershed of the Kokcha River and its tributaries together with the lower reaches of the Darya Panj and its left-bank tributaries before they enter the plains. The Darya Panj, sometimes called the Upper Oxus, also drains the high Pamirs and the formerly independent states of Roshan, Darwaz, and Shughnan. These mountain districts are now split between Afghanistan and the Soviet Union because a nineteenth-century treaty used the river as an international boundary. The Kokcha joins the Panj near Khwajaghar on the plains of Qataghan. From this point onward the river is often called the Amu.

The Arabs move seasonally from one natural region to another. In addition to their three pasture areas they migrate three hundred kilometers through a number of ecologically and ethnically distinct zones. By using Arabs of Imam Saheb as an example we can come to an understanding of the major land uses in Qataghan as a whole.

Imam Saheb lies in the Amu River Valley between its junction with the Kokcha River to the east and its junction with the Kunduz River to the west. The western boundary is defined by the end of the loessial plains and the beginning of a great sand desert which dogs the course of the Amu from this point on. Its southern border is the loessial plain out of which the river has carved its valley. This area of steppe separates Imam Saheb from the Kunduz valley. To the north the river has cut sharp cliffs from the loessial plain. The northern bank, now in the Soviet Union, is continually cut by the river and the alluvial soil deposited on the southern bank. As a result, the Afghan side consists of a wide alluvial valley ranging from five to fifteen kilometers from the loessial steppe. Conversely the steppe reaches to the very edge of the river on the Soviet side so that the flood plain there is extremely narrow. Water for irrigating Imam Saheb is drawn from the Amu via the Shahrawan Canal, which diverts the water about fifteen kilometers below the Kokcha junction.

The Amu River is quite shallow at Imam Saheb. Before the border was closed, the river was forded here. The channels of the river change frequently, and from above, the whole valley reflects braided knots of its alluvial past. Above the immediate river banks is a large swamp of reeds. It is the home of boars, ducks, and pheasants, and is one of the most famous hunting spots in Afghanistan. The nomads graze their sheep in this area in the winter and cut reeds for building material. It is the *jangal*—a wild overgrown place—a peculiar sight in an arid country.

This immediate flood plain varies slightly in elevation, and these slight changes mean the difference between grassy meadow and wet reed swamp. The low points, usually former river channels, enclose what could be called swamp islands. Only one meter higher than the swamp, these islands are grass-covered plains in the midst of the reeds. One of these plains, perhaps fifteen square kilometers, is occupied by some Arab nomads whose sheep graze on the steppe grasses. Their *qishloq* in the center is not subject to flooding.

The alluvial terrace of the valley is marked by sharp cliffs ten to fifteen meters high that separate the floor of the valley from the immediate flood plain. The alluvial terrace is the agricultural heart of the valley. The vast majority of the population and the town of Imam Saheb are centered here. The agricultural land is irrigated by the Shahrawan Canal, which hugs the edge of the valley below the loessial cliffs. In this way the water is distributed by taking advantage of the gentle slope toward the river. The canal flows from east to west, and water is diverted from southeast to northwest by subsidiary canals. Excess water falls from the terrace into the swamp, which in part is now planted in wet rice. The main crops of the valley are cotton, wheat, and melons. Much of this rich agricultural land was swamp as late as thirty years ago. Now only reeds growing along irrigation channels and decaying causeways give testimony to its former state.

The settlement pattern of the valley reflects this history. The original Uzbek settlements were along the main canal. The land grants to the nomads were at the fringes of the system. Thus the more pastoral Turkmen and Arab villages are found at the extreme end of the canal system. In the last fifty years the valley's population has expanded from this original area to include the whole alluvial terrace above the flood plain.

The loessial plain rises above the alluvial terrace and forms the border of the agricultural settlement. In the spring these dry plains offer luxuriant pasture to the nomads of the region, but there is no regular source of water on this plain. These waterless grasslands are referred to as *chul* (in Uzbeki) or *dasht* (in Persian), though *dasht* is also used for any uncultivated plain, even well-watered ones in the mountains. Much humor is derived from the fact that *chul* also means "penis." The steppe is sharply limited on the west by sandy desert (*reg*), which is of little use to the Arabs. The major grazing lands are Dasht-i-Shirmahi, Dasht-i-Abdali, and Dasht-i-Archi, together with a host of other named pastures within this area.

The Migration Route

To get to their summer pastures the Arabs leave the river valleys for the mountains. Their migration takes them through a number of different ecological zones where they have developed symbiotic relationships with the inhabitants.

The plains of Qataghan are left behind as the nomads pour over a bridge on the Kokcha River near Khwajaghar. They border a range of deeply eroded loessial hills that tower over the flat river plain. The hills range from 1,000 to 1,500 meters in altitude. On the tops of the hills are Uzbek villages. They have no irrigated fields but rely completely on rainfall for a successful wheat crop. This type of unirrigated agriculture (*lalmi*) is typical of all the highland areas. Whole hillsides are plowed, some on what seem impossibly steep slopes. Land is no longer measured in jeribs (one jerib equals .2 hectares) but in hillsides or amount of seed sown. Saline streams flow through the area, so farmers hollow out large cisterns (*yekhdons*) to store the snow through the winter; it melts slowly through the rest of the year, providing fresh water.

On the other side of this range is the Rustaq Valley. Rustaq, with an altitude of 1,000 meters, is a major trading center for mountainous Badakhshan. It is one of those anomalous districts that create ideal links between regions. The valley is not part of the Qataghan plain, but neither is it part of the mountains. "The town of Rustak is pleasantly situated and has much garden land around it. In every part of the country fruit is plentiful, apples and pears thrive in the higher valleys, and below towards the Oxus watermelons and the production of hot climates flourish. The crops are likewise both of cold and warm climate" (G.A.B. 1972 [1914]: 143).

The mix of highlands and lowland also shows up ethnically, with Uzbeks giving way to Tajiks as one moves into the mountains.

Rustaq was traditionally Badakhshan's major commercial center (G.A.B. 1972: 143). Though almost unknown today, its bazaar is still considerably larger and more lively than that in Faizabad, the provincial capital of Badakhshan. Rustaq's trade advantage is derived from its central location in relation to its mountainous hinterland and easy access to the plains. Traditionally roads led from it to Khanabad and Tashqurghan, as well as to Imam Saheb and the ferries across the Amu. There was considerable trade with Bukhara. Today it is oriented toward Kunduz, but retains a competitive advantage over Faizabad because trucks can serve it more easily. There are no roads into the mountains suitable for motor vehicles, so access to a market is important to the Tajiks in Shahr-i-bozorg and Rogh. Even today, markets are scarce in Badakhshan. A trip to a market is required to obtain goods such as salt, tea, sugar, manufactured goods, or rice. At one time, the Arabs used pasture in this area, but they no longer do so. They still use the Rustaq bazaar before going into the mountains. They have close ties with the Uzbeks there, who also take their sheep to pastures near the Arab holdings. These ties are reinforced by a number of marriage connections.

The passes east and north of Rustaq lie at an altitude of about 2,500 meters. Crossing them, one enters Shahr-i-bozorg, a district of Badakhshan. Despite its name ("big city"), Shahr-i-bozorg (1,500 meters) lacks bazaars and consists of scattered villages surrounded by *lalmi* wheat fields. Streams have deeply eroded the land, so that the settlement pattern is one of nucleated villages sitting atop loess-covered peaks. Pistachio trees dot the area. Springs are plentiful, and therefore there are no *yechdons*. The population is exclusively Tajik.

Higher up in the mountains one finds true alpine villages and summer pasture for the nomads' sheep. The first of these districts is Rogh. Here the settlement pattern changes from that found in Shahr-i-bozorg. This high-mountain pattern takes two forms. Where the valleys are narrow and deep, settlements cluster along the river banks—or just above them if the river runs through a gorge. These valleys are far warmer and more protected than upland areas. The pattern at higher elevations is a cluster of houses along mountain streams that are the tributaries to the deep-cut rivers. These small valleys, surrounded by snow-covered mountains, are some of the most beautiful in Badakhshan. Although dependent on *lalmi* agriculture, mountain villagers often divert small streams to water mulberry or walnut groves and small gardens. In Rogh and other mountain communities mulberries are a staple food. At higher altitudes villages lack orchards; the best that can be managed is a few poplars to provide building material. The highest villages are located at about 2,500 meters. At this altitude villages in Darwaz can grow only barley, for which the nomads have a great contempt; they claim it is food fit only for animals and that barley bread causes farts.

Above 3,000 meters the agriculture zone comes to an end. Alpine pasture is available up to about 4,000 meters, where ice fields and bare rock begin. This area is the summer pasture for both nomads and villagers. The villagers generally have only one *ailoq* (summer village or camp). This is often directly above their *qishloq* (winter village). Today most of the pasture is controlled by the nomads, although the ruins of stone houses show that at one time the Tajiks controlled more.

These mountain pastures in Badakhshan are perhaps the finest in all of Afghanistan. There are two major pasture districts, Dasht-i-Ish in southern Darwaz north of Rogh, and Dasht-i-Shiwa between Faizabad and Shughnan. Both of these areas are large mountain plateaus. The mountain slopes above the plateaus are also valuable pasture land, as well as a source of asafoetida, which is an export of Badakhshan. Nomads from north Qataghan use Dasht-i-Ish; those from Kunduz and Baghlan use Dasht-i-Shiwa. Pasture becomes available in June and is used by most nomads until mid-August. Others risk snow by staying until late September.

Development in Qataghan

Until the mid-1930s the ecology of the lowland valleys remained exactly as described by British reports of the 1830s—it was an area of malarial swamps. But in the last fifty years it has become one of the most productive agricultural areas in Afghanistan. These changes have had a direct impact on the Arabs which will be discussed in detail in later chapters. Here the basic course of development which resulted in this radical change in the ecology will be outlined.

Although Nadir Khan reorganized the administration of Qataghan and Badakhshan in 1921, the area remained sparsely populated. Then in 1935 it began to stir. Impressed by the potential richness of Qataghan, especially for commercial cotton growth, a number of Afghan capitalists combined with the new governor, Shir Khan, to develop the province. Using corvée labor to drain the swamps, Shir Khan began to reclaim land in Khanabad, which became a major rice-producing area, and in Kunduz, which became the cotton-growing center in Afghanistan. In the forties this development was extended to Baghlan, Pul-i-Khumri, and Archi. Investment in a sugar beet factory, cotton gins, and cotton mills made Qataghan the center of Afghanistan's first private industries, with great profit to the investors in the monopoly cotton company—Spinzar or "white gold" (Jarring 1937; Etienne 1972).

A motorable road through the Hindu Kush via the Shibar Pass gave Qataghan an economic link to Kabul for the first time. More important, cotton was exported to the Soviet Union at the Amu River port of Qizil Qala, later renamed Shir Khan Bander after the governor. This link gave Qataghan a great competitive advantage because even the poor roads of the region were adequate for getting cotton to the border.

Attracted by cheap land and the decreased danger of malaria as the swamp draining proceeded, immigrants began to pour into Qataghan, swelling its population and changing the ethnic character of the region. Most of the new settlers were Pashtuns from the south and Turkic refugees from the Soviet Union. A dramatic turn for the better came in the early 1950s when the local administration, with the help of the United Nations, eradicated malaria in Qataghan altogether (Franck 1955: 28–29). By 1965 the population had tripled the 1921 figures. In the mountainous hinterland, however, the population remained static, and its ethnic composition did not change (Grötzbach 1972: 74–84).

As striking as the ecological transformation was the great increase in Pashtun settlements in what had traditionally been an Uzbek territory. Pashtun settlement was encouraged by the central government in order to tie the border regions more closely to Kabul. By the mid-1960s the Kunduz-Khanabad basin had the ethnic composition shown in Table 2. The most striking pattern in the table is that the percentage of Pashtuns is highest in those areas where development occurred the latest and was most extensive. Thus, Taloqan, which was not part of the reclamation project, kept its Uzbek majority. Kunduz and Khanabad, developed in the 1930s, have a large Pashtun population but not a majority, reflecting the freer policy of land sales and distribution that marked the initial development of the region. Those investors who financed the original development seem not to have been interested in playing ethnic politics so much as making money. In the 1940s, when the proven profitability of Qataghan was known, the government showed more interest in seeing that Pashtuns got preferential treatment. Baghlan and Pul-i-Khumri

Table 2. Percentage of Population in Qataghan

	Pashtuns	Tajiks	Uzbeks	Turkmen	Hazaras
Baghlan area	56	30	10	2	—
Pul-i-Khumri area	61	14	14	5	6
Kunduz area	41	43	13	2	1
Khanabad area	45	36	6	3	10
Taloqan area	10	10	60	1	10

Source: Etienne 1972: 83.

have Pashtun majorities as a result of this favoritism. Pul-i-Khumri is an especially good example, since it was created as a new town in a sparsely populated area.

Because the frontier was expanding and land was plentiful, conflict between Uzbeks and Pashtuns was muted. Nevertheless, the government was forced to come to the defense of the settlement policy, which was not popular with the native inhabitants (Akhramovich 1962: 40). By the early 1950s the frontier was closing, and rising land prices reflected the end of unlimited land, though prices remained comparatively cheap compared with those in the overpopulated mountain valleys (Grötzbach 1972: 267–278).

The Arabs in northern Qataghan got caught up by this development only in the late 1940s. Until then the Amu River region was left untouched. In 1947, however, the government began creating irrigated farm land on the Dasht-i-Archi. By diverting water from the Kokcha River, an area equal in size to the Imam Saheb Valley was created. It was settled exclusively by Pashtuns. Many were deported there for their part in the 1949 Safi rebellion in Jalalabad. Because of their numbers they became an important force in the Amu Valley. Many of the Pashtuns who came to Archi were nomads—so many in fact that they soon became the majority of nomads of the region. They adopted many features of Arab nomadism and today coexist with the Arabs—but as the dominant ethnic group (Barfield 1978).

This initial development of Qataghan was a spectacular success. The valley system was so much changed that the Arabs found themselves adapting to new conditions as the area was transformed. The very swamps in which they camped became valuable cotton land, malaria was a problem of the past, and Pashtun nomads had come to dominate the region. Although this development was accomplished by the Afghans themselves, using traditional technology, its effect showed that an environment could be radically restructured. In spite of the many new features in the valley, the Arabs were able to adapt their nomadic pastoralism to these changing conditions. Far from being a "timeless people," the Central Asian Arabs have continually responded to political and ecological changes throughout their history.

2. Nomadic Pastoralism in Qataghan

The Arabs are nomadic pastoralists. In large part it is this mode of production which structures daily life and sets the pace and rhythm of the year. However, the Arabs in Qataghan, like most nomads, are neither politically nor economically independent of the sedentary agriculturalists or urban artisans. They are in reality specialists who raise sheep for sale to the bazaar in order to buy the basic necessities of life. They are totally dependent on the agricultural producers for grain, which makes up the bulk of even a nomadic pastoralist's diet, and must also obtain various manufactured goods in urban markets. In later chapters these links will be explored in more detail, but first it is necessary to understand the basics of the pastoral economy on which Arab life is based. To be a successful pastoralist one must possess animals, pasture, and labor. These are the very basis of nomadic pastoralism in northeastern Afghanistan.

Animals

Productive Animals

The Arabs raise the largest fat-tailed sheep in Afghanistan, and these sheep are the productive core of their economy. This breed of sheep is locally known as Turki. The animals weigh up to eighty-five kilograms and are most famous for their distinctive fat tails, which alone can weigh as much as fifteen kilograms. They are raised for the meat market, the sheep fat being a delicacy much in demand, especially for cooking oil. The wool is of a very poor quality and is shed by the sheep in the spring.

Qarakuli sheep are also kept in the herds of wealthier Arabs. Qarakuli sheep are much smaller than Turki sheep, rarely half their size, but produce excellent carpet wool and the lambskins which are a major export of Afghanistan. These skins are obtained by slaughtering newborn lambs within a few hours of birth in order to obtain the tight curl characteristic of these lambskins. Qarakuli sheep are mainly in the hands of the Turkmen herders; the Arabs have started to acquire them only within the past thirty years.

Sheep are divided into classes by age and sex. A herd owner knows not only the number of animals in the herd but the composition of the herd as well. This classification applies to both Turki and Qarakuli sheep, but is mainly of significance for Turki, since they vary significantly in size from one age group to another.

A *bara* is a lamb under six months of age. At about four months the male lambs are castrated. This is done at the mountain pastures. These castrated sheep are meat producers that the Arabs sell in the bazaar. Castrated sheep are classed as *tokhali* (six months to two years), *shishak* (two to three years) and *chari* (three to four years). Castrated male lambs become *tokhalis* on their return from the *ailoq*. The other classes advance each spring at lambing time. The fall herd contains no *baras*, because though it is technically possible to lamb twice a year, the Arabs control breeding so that lambing occurs only in the spring. The Arabs explain that lambs born in the winter have a low rate of survival, and that they lack the resources to keep the ewes in good enough condition for two lambings a year, which would require stabling and stall-feeding ewes and lambs throughout the winter. The castrated sheep grow to enormous size, reaching the maximum as *charis*. *Charis* are twice the size of *tokhalis*. Naturally there is a substantial price differential between the two.

If castrated sheep are the pastoralists' major source of income, the ewes or *mish* are their capital. The number of ewes in the herd determines its productivity. The Arabs first breed their ewes at six to eight months of age. This is possible because the sheep quickly grow to a large size thanks to the lush spring and summer pasture. Breeding takes place in October, lambing in March and April. Ewes produce one lamb each spring, and twinning is rare. Ewes are able to reproduce for ten years on the average. During the winter old ewes (*pir mish*) are culled from the herd. This is not a matter of absolute age, but of teeth condition. When the teeth start to rot the Arabs say that a ewe's reproductive life is at an end. This may occur as early as six years or as late as twelve. Because of excellent pasture and selective culling, the infertility rate is quite low. Throughout the spring and summer the ewes produce milk, which is an important part of the traditional diet. On the average, ewes produce one kilogram of milk per day, but informants said that on poor pasture half that amount was more likely and that on good pasture double that amount was possible. For economic reasons that will be examined later, milking sheep in many herds is now minimal. Ewes are milked after the birth of the lamb for especially creamy milk, and they produce milk until late July or August, when they go dry.

Rams, or *kutch*, are impressive animals. They are five times as valuable as *charis*, often selling for as much as 15,000 Afghanis (Afs.) if they can be bought, and are highly prized by their owners. Owners are extremely particular about their breeding stock. Out of a whole spring lamb crop none may be thought good enough. Those rams that do become adults grow into aggressive horned animals that are difficult to control. They can easily injure an unwary shepherd. The rams are run with the herd from October, when they tup the ewes, until after lambing, when they are separated from the ewes to prevent lambing out of season. The rams from about a dozen Arab herds will be kept together in the *ailoq*. The ratio of rams to ewes is low. The Arabs calculate they need one ram to service between 50 and 70 ewes on the average. They point out, perhaps bragging, that their exceptional rams, if Turki, can tup 150 ewes; if Qarakuli, 100.

The composition of a herd tells as much as its size about the economic status of an Arab pastoralist. Poor pastoralists have to sell their *tokhalis* immediately upon their return from the *ailoq* in order to buy provisions for the winter. Pastoralists who have more security can afford to wait the extra time, and take the calculated risks, until their sheep become *charis* and can bring the maximum profit. A *tokhali* during my stay sold in the fall for around 1,500 Afs., in the spring for 2,000 Afs. A *chari* sold in the winter for 3,000 Afs., exceptional ones for 3,500 Afs. The rule of thumb was that the sooner one sold, the less one made—with the exception of *charis* that have reached their maximum. *Charis* in a herd reflect an owner of means.

Given these alternate strategies of selling sheep, the distribution of sheep classes can be used as an analytical tool. For example, the composition of the herd of one wealthy Arab just before migration was as follows (excluding rams):

Charis	48
Shishaks	73
Tokhalis	74
Mish without lambs	21 (This does not represent infertility, but mostly lamb mortality.)
Mish with lambs	233
Baras	234 (Includes one set of twins.)

Those doing the counting noted that the *charis* were far fewer than expected. This could have been due to either the legacy of an earlier pastoral disaster or, in this case, the sudden need for cash a few years earlier. The ability to predict the number that should have been *charis* indicates that the Arabs have their own model of herd composition. A mature herd like the one above approximates an ideal proportion of one-third castrates, one-third ewes, and one-third lambs in the spring. A poorer herd owner has no castrates, one-half ewes, and one-half lambs in the spring. The percentage of ewes to the total number of sheep is a measure of how well the herd is doing. Large herds, reflecting wealth, naturally tend toward the 1 : 3 pattern. Small herd owners are unable to hold on to their castrates and thus have herds of the 1 : 2 type. This ratio is a useful tool in determining whether a flock is being pushed to the maximum or whether it is upwardly mobile. The presence or absence of *charis* indicates whether one pastoralist is in reality wealthier than another, though both have the same number of animals.

These two basic patterns of sheep holding have demographic ramifications. In a mature herd the growth rate expressed as a percentage is lower than that found in a herd composed solely of ewes. Probability dictates that half the lambs will be females. Thus a mature herd in spring increases by around 50 percent, an immature herd by about 100 percent. But this is deceptive, for in the fall all the male lambs in an immature herd will be sold off, reducing the herd size by one-fourth. In a mature herd only the *charis* are sold (leaving aside culled ewes), just one-ninth or less of the total herd. These percentages are based on an ideal in which a high percentage of lambs survive. In fact, the mature herd has another significant advantage based on the differential mortality of lambs versus mature sheep. Even in a good year an Arab pastoralist expects a 10–15 percent mortality rate. Mortality is highest among newborn lambs. Thus a mature herd is less at risk than a herd in which half the herd is newborn lambs.

The total number of sheep, herd ratio, and growth rate can therefore be used in combination to spot pastoralists who are in the process of rising, those who are stable, and those who may be under strain. A large herd with a deviant ratio may indicate a herd owner forced to dip into his reserves for some reason. Conversely, a small herd owned by an urban investor often shows a mature pattern even though it numbers only one hundred. The Arabs use these two models implicitly in judging their own herds and those of others.

Pastoralism is renowned for its high growth rate in comparison with agriculture. Its geometric growth rate is seen to be its great virtue as a means of getting wealthy. The potential gains are easy to calculate, but they must be offset by the risk of loss. Losses cannot be judged on the basis of "average years." In fact no year is ever quite average for everyone. It is the extreme year, the freak loss, or "unseasonable conditions" that are the greatest concern. A bad year can destroy a pastoralist. These losses must be considered along with the growth rate, though they are not as predictable.

Despite this, it must be admitted that pastoralists in Qataghan and Badakhshan are situated in a region that is ideal for pastoralism. Nomadic pastoralism is common in harsh, marginal regions, but this lack of resources is reflected in the small size of the sheep or goats raised there. The sheep in Qataghan are the largest in Afghanistan because resources are dependable. During the drought years of the early 1970s, the pastoralists of Qataghan suffered from poor pasture, but their sheep did not die of thirst as they did in Maimana. The region has permanent rivers and springs which are insurance against drought. Pastoralists in Qataghan worry far more about weight loss in their marketable sheep than about the remote possibility of the sheep dying of starvation or thirst.

The Arabs in Qataghan have a better chance to realize the potential growth rate in their herds than do other pastoralists in Afghanistan. But even here there are many pitfalls. The worst disaster that can strike a pastoralist is a spring blizzard that coats the steppe with ice. Such a freeze does an incredible amount of damage. The ewes give birth, but the lambs cannot survive. If the cold keeps up, even the grown sheep, unable to graze, weaken from hunger and cold, and die. Such a storm, the greatest fear of pastoralists, may occur only once in a generation, but its aftermath is felt for decades. In the early 1950s many Arabs were destroyed by such a storm. Flocks of three thousand were reduced to three hundred. Some Arabs left pastoralism completely; others, even after a generation, have only begun to catch up. This was an atypical event, but it is the atypical events which have been the most disastrous.

Disease is another killer. Sheep diseases can decimate a flock in a few days. There has been some attempt to combat sheep diseases by the national government, but no drugs or remedies can be found in major towns. The Arabs would be quite willing to purchase them if they were available. Because herds are scattered, an epidemic that destroys one flock may not touch another. While a spring blizzard brings disaster to all, diseases may be capricious.

The losses most frequently encountered are the result of a high mortality rate in the newborn lambs. Even in a favorable year many of the lambs will not survive—they are most subject to disease, they are attacked by flies that lay eggs in cuts, and they may become bloated from drinking too much milk on a hot day—all of which can have fatal results. Lambs are also the favorite target of thieves, who find them easy to carry, or they may simply be lost by a careless shepherd. Losses among the lambs are avoided by careful shepherding, but with the total lack of veterinary service, the Arabs resign themselves to losses.

The migration itself does not present a great danger to the flocks. On the whole, herds make the trip with very few losses, even among the lambs that have grown quickly on the spring pasture. But on occasion disaster will strike. On a high plain in the mountains I saw sixty sheep carcasses strewn about. Three days previously a freezing wind had swept out of the north and had frozen the sheep, just sheared before the start of the migration. The sheep that preceded them and those that followed had no difficulties. Arabs passing the spot sought out information as to whose sheep had died, for their sheep had preceded them, and each feared from a distance that the dead ones might be his own. Such instances abound: sheep falling off cliffs, getting swept away by a stream, attacked by predators—all of which the Arabs attribute to fate, or *kismet*. Fate or not, nomadic pastoralists are aware at all times how vulnerable their sheep are to conditions beyond their control. Even a good year may be rewarded by lower prices reflecting the increased supply. There are no price supports in Afghanistan, but when the concept was explained to a group of nomads, one laughed and said, "Here when the price falls too low, we eat the sheep!"

As an aid to herding, the Arabs keep two or three large goats. These goats, *shah buz*, lead the herd in migration, sheep being docile followers if they have a goat to follow.

Transport Animals

Although sheep are the productive units in a pastoral economy, other animals are also required for nomadic movements.

The bulk of a nomadic household is moved by camels. Until the advent of motorized transport, camels also moved most of the trade in the area. Arab families who migrate use two or three camels. On migration the camels and their loads are often decorated with fancy carpets, beads, and tassels. Camel wool is highly valued.

Donkeys are the major form of transport in the towns and mountains. They cannot carry enough to be good long-range transport, but in the mountains the sure-footed donkey is at home whereas the camel is not. Donkeys are indefatigable travelers, require little care, and are comparatively cheap. The donkeys of Qataghan are highly admired in Badakhshan for their size and endurance. An Arab family will own at least two or three donkeys.

Qataghan has traditionally been famous for its horses. Wealthy Arabs vie for expensive horses used to play *buzkashi*, but the average household owns horses that can double as baggage animals. A family usually owns a stallion and a mare so it can replace the stock without having to enter the marketplace.

Riding has its etiquette. The symbolic value of each animal is represented by what is, and is not, proper to ride. A fully equipped Arab family going on migration would be mounted as follows. The male head of household should be riding a stallion. This is more than just symbolic of strength. Since horses are never gelded in Afghanistan, it takes a strong man to make his horse obey. His wife, with the small children, should be on a mare. Men are ridiculed for riding mares, though some put discretion before valor when riding on narrow mountain trails where a stallion's misbehavior could result in a fatal fall. Unmarried daughters ride on the top of the loaded camels. To mount, they vault to the camel's neck and jump up. This keeps them out of the way and has the secondary purpose of advertising a daughter's availability to other families interested in negotiating a marriage. Boys and sometimes their younger sisters will ride on donkeys. A man also has the choice of walking, whereas a woman is not permitted to walk unless the terrain makes riding difficult.

Protective Animals

The final animal found in a camp is the dog. These are vicious mastiffs, with their ears and tails docked. They provide protection by attacking all who approach the camp. For this reason no one walks around without a stick to beat off the dogs. They are not voice-trained; if a dog attacks, a member of the family must go out and drive it off. The dogs are quite territorial. On the migration trail they are peaceful, but as soon as the tent goes up, the dog stakes out a territory and starts to attack people. Dogs provide a large measure of privacy to a nomad family.

Pasture

Pasture is the second requirement of a pastoralist. Pasture is available in abundance but on a seasonal basis. Thus the Arabs are nomadic, moving seasonally from drying pastures to fresh ones. The Arabs regard it as having two springs—one on the plains and one in the mountains.

The Arabs in north Qataghan have three pasture areas: the winter camp in the valley of the Amu River, the spring pastures on the nearby loessial steppes, and the summer pastures in the mountains of Badakhshan. The Arabs spend three months on the steppe, four months in the mountains, and five months in the river valley. The pasturage in between their seasonal camps is only of minor importance. The migration from spring to summer camp takes three weeks and is devoted solely to travel—a distance of about three hundred kilometers.

The nomads in Qataghan are very different from most nomads in Afghanistan in that they own their spring and summer pastures. Pasture is owned by an individual family and is neither common nor tribal property. The nomads do not actually own the land per se; they own the exclusive right to use the pasture of a particular area. As confirmation of this right they have a deed, or firman, issued by the government naming the pasture to which they have rights. These firmans have been handed down through the generations. The pasture rights (and, as one nomad told me, since snow covers it in the winter, pasture is the only thing worth having rights to) can be bought and sold, rented, or inherited. A nomad's rights are not dependent on tribal affiliation but on property rights, ultimately guaranteed by the state.

Let us go back for a moment to explain how it was that in Badakhshan pasture came to be individually owned.

When the Arabs arrived from Bukhara there was little competition. Pasture was available for the taking. Some of the Arab clans used the upper Zerendaw Valley in Rogh for their summer pasture. The sheep were grazed on the sides of the mountain there. The pasture was good, but the area was limited. This valley at its headwaters was also an international boundary between Afghanistan and the autonomous kingdom of Darwaz. The other mountain kingdoms of the Upper Oxus were in the hands of the Afghans. Pasture north of Zerendaw, in Darwaz, was thus not available for political reasons. The Tajiks of Darwaz, transhumant themselves, were not about to give up their own pasture. Then in 1895 some gentlemen in London and St. Petersburg, concerned that undefined frontiers might create trouble between their respective empires, signed a treaty. This treaty defined the boundaries of the Pamir region and the Upper Oxus between British India and Russian Turkestan. Both parties had been unsatisfied on previous occasions when they tried to use mountains as boundaries. Maps being what they were in the nineteenth century, valleys would later appear where the mountain was supposed to be, or the mountain named would share that designation with three others. This kind of thing led to trouble. So it was determined that the Darya Panj—the Upper Oxus River—would be the official boundary. This cut all the mountain kingdoms in half. Afghanistan received left bank Darwaz and ceded right bank Roshan and Shughnan to Bukhara. The amir of Afghanistan complained he was getting the worse end of the deal. Left bank Darwaz was poor and mountainous— traditionally a grain-deficit area (G.A.B. 1972: 58). Right bank Shughnan and Roshan were far more valuable. Nevertheless, the treaty was signed and implemented. The Afghans moved into Darwaz to govern it, though collection of taxes seemed to be the impelling motive:

> An unforeseen consequence of the 1895 settlement was a sizable emigration from Afghanistan. In 1897 the Beg of Darvaz [Darwaz] reported that over 700 families had left their homes in left bank Darvaz after vainly resisting the Afghan takeover there; 100 of these families settled in Bukharan Darvaz, the rest in Kulab and Karategin. In July 1898 Ignatiev reported to Tashkent that the total number of refugees from southern Darwaz had reached 1,164 families. (Becker 1968: 158)

For Darwaz this was a massive exodus. For the Arabs it was an opportunity. With Darwaz now under Afghan rule, its villages deserted, and the Arabs living next door, it was only logical that some of the larger herd owners would explore the now empty pasture areas. The best pasture area, Dasht-i-Ish, a mountain plateau, was taken by the Afghan government for the government horse herds. But the more mountainous area was open to all, and for the next twenty years or so Arabs staked out claims there. Because the mountain pastures of Darwaz were at a higher elevation than the Zerendaw pasture, the wealthier Arabs had two camps—one in Zerendaw for the women and children, and one high in Darwaz, two days away, for the men and most of the sheep. Only the larger herd owners took pasture in Darwaz because it was they who were beginning to become cramped for pasture. Though the Arabs have never heard of the 1895 treaty, they were the beneficiaries of global geopolitics.

Privately owned pastures came into being when Nadir Khan reorganized Qataghan and Badakhshan in 1921. Nomads who were using a particular pasture at that time had their rights confirmed in a government title that could be used as evidence if a dispute arose. While nomads received individual titles to pasture use, mountain villages received collective title to their traditional summer pasture. This was probably done for administrative ease: mountain villages could easily be associated with one or two pasture areas, but the nomads were scattered all over the mountains and steppe. Granting title to nomads for pasture was not new: Amir Abdur Rahman had given similar rights to Pashtuns in the Hazarajat (Ferdinand 1962: 128–130). These rights were interpreted quite differently in the northeast than in central Afghanistan. In the Hazarajat the pasture was considered to be the common property of all the descendants of the original owner and was both indivisible and inalienable. In the northeast the Arabs saw titles as personal property that could be divided by inheritance and sold or rented by the present owner.

This interpretation of pasture rights had many ramifications. First, because the pastures were dependable, they were valuable resources. Second, although tribal groups often occupied whole pasture areas, an individual's rights were separate from that of the group and not dependent on tribal membership. The nomadic pastoralists in Qataghan and Badakhshan had rights to their pasture based upon their relation to the state, not to a tribal organization. This combination of rights and dependability of pasture made the dynamics of nomadic pastoralism very different from those found in other parts of the country. It also laid the basis for pastoralism's later transformation into commercial ranching.

Just how different Qataghan-Badakhshan was from the rest of the country was illustrated by the impact of Pashtuns who settled in north Qataghan after World War II. Until then Pashtun nomads had been confined to the Kunduz and Baghlan areas, from which they moved seasonally to the Khawak Pass in the Hindu Kush or Dasht-i-Shiwa in Badakhshan.

As part of a large development project begun in 1947, Pashtuns poured into the Amu River Valley for the first time in large numbers. Many of them immediately took up long-range nomadism. Had all the pasture in the area been owned by the Arabs, conflict with the new Pashtun immigrants would have been inevitable. But as a legacy of the Treaty of 1895, which gave Darwaz to Afghanistan, the government had reserved the best pasture in the area, Dasht-i-Ish, for its own use in maintaining government animals. As state pasture (*sarkari*) it was prohibited to the Arabs. The pastures granted to the Arabs by Nadir Khan were on the mountainsides above and below the Ish plateau. The government eventually stopped keeping animals, most of which had disappeared during the Saqaoist uprising in 1929, and when the Pashtuns arrived in Archi, they were granted title to the pasture in Dasht-i-Ish.

Arabs and Pashtuns today both hold their own areas with the same type of firman. Each nomad family that had acquired property rights found it advantageous to uphold the status quo. Tribal solidarity was weakened, as established Pashtuns felt under no obligation to share their own pasture with newly arrived Pashtuns, nor was there any incentive in helping new Pashtuns wrest pasture from the Arabs. The principle of private ownership was new to the Pashtuns, but once it was accepted they became staunch supporters of the rights of pasture holders.

With no new *ailoq* territory available, there is now considerable competition for pastureland in Badakhshan. This competition is regulated by the state and occurs at the family level, so that it rarely threatens the system as a whole. At present there are three ways for a nomad who lacks summer pasture to acquire it—purchase, theft, or rental.

Pastoralism is a risky business. Because of various disasters, nomads face the possibility of losing all of their sheep. A nomad in such a situation who owns a good *ailoq* in a secure area may be able to sell it to another nomad and salvage something from the disaster. Sales of *ailoqs* occur mostly in Darwaz. This is because *ailoqs* in Darwaz are usually quite large, capable of supporting a thousand sheep or more for the summer, and because it is an area firmly controlled by the Arabs, so that squatters are prevented from moving in on it. There is a strong demand for such *ailoqs* from Pashtuns who own poorer pasture and would like to trade up. The expense involved in buying an *ailoq* requires that the buyer be fairly wealthy. In the mid-1950s the Arabs suffered from a number of pastoral disasters, and some of them lost all their sheep. An *ailoq* in Darwaz sold to a Pashtun at this time brought the former owner 80,000 Afs. for a pasture that could support one thousand sheep. In one case a Pashtun who used the pasture was troubled by his Arab neighbors stealing his sheep. Ten years after he purchased the *ailoq*, he began paying a bribe to the former owner of 4,000 Afs. a year in order to stop the thefts. The sheep thieves were relatives of the old owner and agreed to stop their unneighborly behavior. The price of sheep at this time was high enough to justify the "insurance premium." It has become common practice for Arabs who have sold their pasture to receive continuing payments.

An owner of good pasture in Darwaz holds not merely a pastoral asset but also an investment that provides protection against complete disaster. Selling these pasture rights, however, makes it unlikely that the nomad will be able to reenter the pastoral economy.

For the poor nomad, theft of an *ailoq* is a way of becoming established. A Pashtun cannot force an Arab out, but Arabs in a marginal area who are unable to use their pasture will soon find it occupied by Pashtuns. Marginal areas are those in which the pasture is comparatively poor and the ethnic composition mixed. The pastures in the highlands of Rogh are far more at risk than those in Darwaz because the *ailoqs* in Rogh are smaller and the nomads poorer. Arabs who lose their sheep here are unlikely to receive compensation for their pastures.

The Zerendaw Valley in upper Rogh is an area into which Pashtuns have been moving. Up until World War II this valley was used exclusively by the Arabs. Then wealthy families began abandoning their low *ailoqs* in Zerendaw and moving their families to the high Darwaz *ailoqs*. It may be that the increased number of Pashtuns encouraged some Arabs to give up their less productive *ailoqs*, or it may simply have been a desire to ease the work by keeping only one *ailoq*. In any event, in the past twenty-five years the number of Arab tents in Zerendaw has dropped from sixty or seventy to only twenty-five. The abandoned *ailoqs* fell into the hands of the Pashtuns who migrate through Zerendaw to reach the pastures in Dasht-i-Ish. In this situation Arabs who lost pasture received no compensation. Nomads who move into abandoned *ailoqs* can claim them as their own, for right to pasture is confirmed by use. A squatter can even get legal title by claiming that no one was using the pasture. Since this interaction takes place between poor Pashtuns and poor Arabs and does not involve the displacement of active pastoralists, the conflict is of little interest to better-established nomads of either ethnic group. The existence of private property transfers the burden of direct competition to the more marginal members of each group. The holdings of large pastoralists or of the ethnic group as a whole are rarely at issue.

By far the most common means of acquiring access to mountain pasture today is by renting it. Because of private ownership a pastoralist can graze sheep only in a designated area. Though the size of an *ailoq* does not vary, the number of sheep an individual owns does. Therefore, there are many people who may own more pasture than they can use. They are often willing to rent part of an *ailoq*, or even a whole one, to another pastoralist who has no pasture rights. These cash rentals are not automatically renewable and must be renegotiated annually. Charges range from 3,000 to 5,000 Afs. a season in upper Rogh and from 4,000 to 15,000 Afs. for grazing in Darwaz. The price differential reflects the larger size and higher quality of *ailoqs* in Darwaz. The cheaper rents are obtained by sharing part of an *ailoq* with the owner. The highest rents are for whole *ailoqs*. Price-gouging is not unknown. An Arab who rented a Pashtun an *ailoq* for 15,000 Afs. admitted that the price was excessive, but explained, "What can he do? He is *majbur* [compelled], he has no *ailoq*."

In terms of rationalizing pasture use, the system works quite well to conserve the resource by preventing overgrazing, while providing the necessary flexibility to handle fluctuations in individual sheep holdings. Each *ailoq* is described in terms of the number of herds of sheep (*ramas*) it can support. A *rama* traditionally was a unit of 1,000 sheep, so the capacity of each pasture is well known. A rental allows use up to the *ailoq*'s limit, but the owner has a vested interest in making sure the resource is not abused by overgrazing. The owner, or relatives, can inspect that pasture during the summer to make sure the contracted number of sheep is not exceeded. An Arab who owns a 3,000-sheep *ailoq* but now owns only 300 sheep makes a good deal of money by renting the excess pasture. Should the owner's herds recover, less pasture will be rented out to others. The renting of pasture reduces conflict by making mountain pasture available to those outside the system for a price while reinforcing the concept of private ownership. The stability of the system is backed by the government. Until recently it posted troops in Dasht-i-Ish and Dasht-i-Shiwa to keep the peace. In an area far from any government centers, peace has been maintained at a minimum of cost because of the flexibility of the system and the common vested interest of all pasture owners in maintaining the status quo.

Winter Pasture

Until the 1920s the Arabs had no permanent *qishloqs*. At that time they were granted permanent winter villages in Imam Saheb as part of King Amanullah's settlement program in Qataghan. The land the Arabs received was swamp, but it sufficed for their pastoral needs. They saw the land not for its agricultural potential but as a permanent camp that could be seasonally abandoned. The government encouraged the settlement of nomads because nomads with at least one fixed abode were far easier to govern. Unlike the present Afghan government policy, settlement of nomads did not imply that they would give up pastoralism, only that their nomadic pastoralism would become more regular.

When the Arabs acquired *qishloqs* in Imam Saheb, they gained permanent access to the vast swampy areas in the flood plain of the Amu River. This *jangal* provided both ample water and grazing. The valley itself provided considerable protection from the winter winds and storms. Today grazing has been extended to the agricultural plain, where harvested cotton fields are grazed by the sheep. Grazing in the valley lasts from late September or October to February.

By law and custom in Afghanistan the jungle along the banks of the Amu Darya is a wasteland and is open to all for free grazing. But these pastures are, in fact, rented pastures because a hefty bribe is required to use them. To understand why, one must turn to a combination of international and local politics.

Like most settled areas Imam Saheb has both a local police force and a civil government. In addition, however, it has another set of officials, who monitor the border. The Amu Darya is the boundary between Afghanistan and the Soviet Union. As part of the border agreement both the Afghans and the Soviets agreed to appoint respective commissars for each border segment in order to resolve local problems when they arise. Imam Saheb is the headquarters of the Afghan side between Shir Khan Bander and Yangi Qala. The commissar has jurisdiction over the border area—mostly swampy lowlands—to the exclusion of other authorities. Even Afghan nationals need his permission to visit the area, when going hunting, for example.

The sheep of the area traditionally graze in the swamp under the commissar's jurisdiction. But the commissar can at any time close part of the border to grazing for "political" reasons. In the winter of 1975 he collected for each herd grazed 2,000 Afs. and one *chari* sheep. A refusal to pay would have resulted in the expulsion of the nomad's herd from this prime grazing area. Because of this, relatives with separate *ailoqs* often combine their animals for winter grazing to lower the cost of this "herd tax."

The commissar also used Russian complaints to mulct the border villages. In 1974 some Russians reported a cow missing and claimed that it had wandered or been taken to the Afghan side. They demanded its return. The commissar had the men of the border villages look for it—but no cow or sign of a cow was seen. The commissar pronounced the border villages collectively guilty and fined them each 10,000 Afs.—the price of two Afghan cows. Since about ten villages were included, he profited mightily after compensating the Russian owners. "We can't afford any more Russian cows," complained a village leader.

When the Arabs took land in Imam Saheb for their *qishloqs*, they did so as clan groups, although title remained in the hands of individuals. Originally they erected their yurts here. They were of two types: one with a wooden frame covered with felt, like those of the Turkmen and common to Central Asia, and the other a dome-shaped reed structure that used no wood or felt (Figure 1). Today these clusters of yurts have been replaced by flat-roofed mudbrick houses surrounded by walled compounds. The yurt-like reed huts can still be found in the middle of the swamp inhabited by one Arab clan that lacks formal ownership of the land it camps on. A more portable tent of bent poles covered with felt is still used in the spring and summer.

The development of permanent winter villages in Imam Saheb has given the Arabs a rather sophisticated view of land. As a pastoral people their first concern in obtaining land was to have a place of their own where they had rights to the surrounding winter pasture. Nomads in Afghanistan are particularly sensitive about having secure access to pasture. Owning nearby land is a certain way of establishing those rights. The Arabs spend five months in the Imam Saheb Valley during the scarcity of the

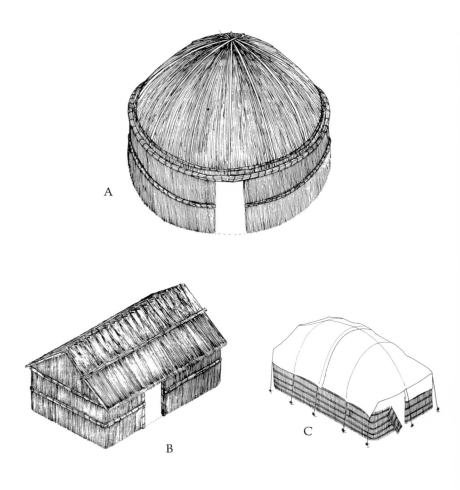

Figure 1. Arab dwellings. (A) *Kapachamshi*. This dome-shaped structure is made entirely of reeds to provide year-round shelter. Because it cannot be moved, nomadic families who migrate simply abandon it during the spring and summer. More affluent Arabs who have built mudbrick houses now use this structure as a cookhouse. (B) *Chubdara*. This building is also of reeds but has wooden beams to support it. It is a permanent structure used year round for storage and abandoned seasonally if the family who owns it migrates. (C) Summer tent. This is a portable dwelling that uses a number of saplings that are bent over to create the frame. A felt cover is thrown over the supports for the roof, and reed fencing is used for the sides. Drawings by Albert Szabo.

winter. Owning land there provides them with a secure base and the right to exploit the nearby swamp.

Viewing land in terms of its pastoral value is still prevalent today. Only a few families have acquired agricultural land beyond the original land grant. I once asked about land owning and was told that very few people owned land. When I objected that the *qishloq* consisted of three hundred walled compounds, my informant chided me, "A man who owns less than five jeribs [one hectare] is not a land owner, just a householder." Although one U.N. report indicates that three jeribs of irrigated land could support a family (U.N. 1973), the Arabs see land owning as an investment which is different from having land around one's house even if a crop is planted there. Many "householding" pastoralists are better off than sharecropping farmers.

Arabs admire the productivity of irrigated agricultural land. "It cannot die, it cannot be stolen, and it always produces a crop," they say. They are openly contemptuous of Tajik hill farming, not because it represents agriculture, but because of the low yield and high risks. Ownership of agricultural land is highly valued, but as will be seen, there is a reluctance by many to get into an area about which they know little.

Spring Pasture

Spring pasture is found on the steppe above the river valley. It is quite extensive, but seasonal. Depending on the weather, grass begins to appear in mid-February or early March. Spring begins officially on March 21, the Persian New Year. Though many nomads start moving their sheep onto the steppe in early March, they prefer to wait until the New Year, when it is warm, to bring their families out.

The grass, watered by the melted snow and spring rains, grows in abundance. The richest pasture is reserved for horses and cattle, while some lush sections are left almost ungrazed to be hayed for winter fodder. Like the *ailoqs*, spring pasture is privately owned. This results in tents scattered equidistantly over the plain. Private ownership encourages not only reserving pasture for haying, but capital investment as well. The most common investment is a *yekhdon*, or cistern, to store the winter's snow for drinking water throughout the spring. The plain itself is waterless. Large stock may be occasionally driven to a few wells or riverbanks to drink, but sheep on green pasture do not need watering at all. For three months they subsist on dew and grass. Only when the grass grows dry in mid-May are the sheep taken to drink. Taking the sheep to water marks the end of the spring camp, and the animals are immediately driven off to the mountains.

The pasture between the spring and summer camps is only of marginal importance. The sheep are pushed through as fast as possible in order to reach the *ailoq*. Most of the area is used in growing wheat. The return from the *ailoq* is equally swift, but the sheep can now graze on harvested wheat fields over the entire migration route.

Salt

In addition to pasture, sheep require salt. Salt is a basic dietary requirement for human beings and livestock, but because of the number of sheep their total requirement becomes quite significant and puts a burden on the sheep owner. An adequate supply of salt increases the ability of sheep to gain weight (Stoddard and Smith 1943: 298).

In the winter when the sheep are kept in the Amu River Valley the sheep get salt naturally by grazing in the salt marshes or drinking from saline streams. Only in a few scattered areas must salt be fed to the sheep. Salt must be transported to the spring camps, but because of the short distance from the town to the steppe, transport is only a minor problem, and the salt is inexpensive, costing 12 Afs. per seer (1 seer = 7.1 kilograms).

It is in the summer camps that salt takes on critical importance. High in the mountains, the *ailoqs* are far from any markets and salt is expensive. It may take six days' round trip from the pastures in Dasht-i-Ish to Faizabad, where salt costs 40–50 Afs. a seer. Not only is this four times the salt's cost in the lowlands; it must also be transported by horse or donkey over mountain trails.

The amount of salt required is calculated on the basis of ten seers to every one hundred animals. It may require two or three trips for a large herd owner to transport this much salt. The salt trade is the major force in the economy of Badakhshan because it is bought not only by nomads but also by Tajik hill farmers. In order to buy salt they must make long trips to the bazaar, where they purchase other goods as well. With more than a million head of livestock in Badakhshan during the summer, the trade is quite brisk. The salt itself has a distinctive red color and is brought in large blocks from mines near Taloqan, which have traditionally supplied a large part of Afghanistan with salt. Today it is often forgotten how, in a province like Badakhshan, a critical commodity like salt can still be the major impetus to trade.

Labor

Traditional subsistence-oriented pastoralism among the Arabs is centered around the nuclear family, or in some cases an extended family, rather than on camp groups or larger units. The reasons for this are based on the private property aspects of pasture rights in the area. Private ownership and inheritance practices play a large role in determining the social organization of labor needed to make the pastoral enterprise viable.

Private ownership of pasture means that most families are self-sufficient in pasture. Cooperation in herding with others requires sharing a valuable privately owned resource. The advantage of maintaining exclusive rights to a pasture may often outweigh the benefits of cooperative herding, especially among large herd owners. Cooperative herding is usually based on a common inherited pasture. Inherited pasture is divisible, and an Arab who shares an inheritance can demand that it be split evenly. This occurs with large *ailoqs*. But if the pasture is small, the descendants continue to use it in common because it is not practical to split it. In addition, the owners of smaller *ailoqs* can take advantage of sharing labor. Camps in Darwaz that have been split remain the property of nuclear families. Those in upper Rogh are more often used in common, where they average four tents per *ailoq*. The smaller herd owners in upper Rogh are most likely to include a nonrelative, though usually an Arab of the same clan, because the outsider's labor value outweighs the marginal utility of the pasture.

Some Arab camps are made up of extended families. Unlike many pastoral people, an Arab son inherits only at the death of his father. While a new tent hold is created at marriage, this nuclear family does not become truly independent until it inherits pasture and animals. Sons may have acquired some stock of their own through trade and labor, but the family estate remains intact. A father not only owns the animals but has a significant pool of labor available to herd them. Should the father become mentally incompetent, the oldest son manages the estate in practice but is not the legal owner. These extended families rarely survive the patriarch's death, although the divided stock may still be run in common, since they may inherit only a single pasture. Economically independent families are often established rather late in life as a result of this inheritance pattern. Problems of declining shares of pasture have not yet come to pass, since the pasture was claimed only sixty years ago. In the future the difficulty of having enough pasture through inheritance may become a problem.

Another reason for the focus on the nuclear family is that all decisions about migration are made independently. There is neither a tribal nor a governmental official who supervises the migrations. Each family decides when to initiate migration and where to stop along the way. The basic reason for this is that the sheep are being driven to a particular pasture, and there is no attempt to exploit pasture along the way except to maintain the sheep's health. In fact, Arab families traditionally send the sheep to the mountains a week before the families leave, so that herds and people meet only at the *ailoq*. The family not only provides the basic labor of sheep raising, but is responsible for all decision making.

Pastoral labor is of two types—the maintenance of sheep and procurement of raw materials on the one hand and processing activities on the other. The first are male roles intimately connected with herding and marketing. The second are female roles that are equally vital not only for maintaining the family but for providing critical equipment used in production. There is an attempt in subsistence pastoralism to integrate the family's labor so that the maximum yield can be obtained from the herd. As we shall see later, there is a difference between the maximum yield in terms of subsistence products and the maximum profit in terms of cash. In a subsistence strategy men's and women's work are only analytically separate—in reality the maintenance of the family depends on both cooperating. The major distinction between subsistence pastoralism and commercial pastoralism is that in a commercial regime the two spheres actually do become separable.

Herding sheep is the major responsibility of adult males. For the Arabs, the upper limit on a single flock lies between 800 and 1,000 sheep. However, a flock of this size is almost always split into two unequal herds for daily grazing. In the spring a milking herd is separated from the rest, in the summer there is a separate lamb flock, and in the winter *tokhalis* may be grazed separately. A single shepherd can care for all the sheep in a pinch, however. The reason for this is that once the permanent camp is reached a shepherd makes a circuit only within his pasture. The chances of sheep straying are small, and if they do they are still to be found nearby. Dogs do not assist in shepherding.

A flock of 800–1,000 sheep is unusual today. The average combined flock of subsistence pastoralists is about 250. A small herd owner running between 50 and 100 sheep usually combines them with relatives' herds—sharing the same pasture—to reach 250 because both in driving the sheep on migration and in taking them out to graze, the difference between 100 and 300 sheep is almost nothing in terms of labor. Cooperation is especially · important to those who own under 100 sheep because it allows them to engage in alternate money-making activities. The minimum number of animals needed to support a family is irrelevant to the Arabs because they engage in outside work, but it takes at least 100 animals to be a full-time pastoralist without other means of income.

A wealthy household is most often short of labor to handle herding. Even though the camps and pastures are together, a large herd owner requires a shepherd's help if there are no adult sons in the family. In the past there were a number of Arabs with over 1,000 sheep, and these owners required many shepherds.

The traditional means of hiring shepherds was through payments in kind. Today cash payments have been substituted for sheep. Just how profound a change this was can only be understood in light of the dynamics of the traditional system.

Arab herding contracts do not involve a transfer of risk. The shepherd is hired to do his job in return for an agreed-upon payment. He does not profit from the herd's increase, nor is he responsible financially for its loss.

There are three kinds of shepherding positions. The most important is that of *chopan*, the shepherd. It is a very respectable position, since sound knowledge of sheep and their handling is the key to a successful herding venture. In general, the *chopan* is an established middle-aged man who is poor in animals. The *chopan* is assisted by a *chakar*, or shepherd's assistant. He is usually a young man working to earn money for bride price. Muscle is preferred to brains, as *chakars* are considered too immature to make important decisions. They are often called upon to play buffoon roles in joking relations with the owner, whereas the owner never shows any disrespect to the *chopan*. The third kind of position is that of a *muzdur*, traditionally a wage laborer and therefore not paid in sheep. He was hired to do work on the fringes of the pastoral sphere. Today, with cash payments for everything, the distinction between *muzdur* and *chakar* has been blurred.

Arab shepherds are hired for six-month contracts. These contracts coincide with the winter residence and summer residence. A change of personnel takes place in the spring and fall. Before the introduction of cash wages, the six-month contract paid on average five or six ewes to the *chopan*, three or four to the *chakar*. The Arabs were quite specific that only ewes could be used as payment. The rate was calculated on the basis on one ewe for every one hundred sheep herded for the *chopan*. The *chakar* received proportionately less. The average number obtained through discussion with *chopans* indicated that they were running herds smaller than I observed during my stay. In addition to the ewes, the owner provided the shepherd with food, a felt cape (*kaybanak*) to sleep in, and shepherd boots (*chambuz*).

The payment in the form of ewes was a very high price to a large herd owner because these wages were taken from the owner's productive capital—ewes. This put a brake on a large herd's rate of reproduction. When the herd grew to the point where hired labor was required, then the more labor hired, the greater the capital drain. From the shepherd's point of view the system was quite lucrative, since he acquired the capital to build his own herd while working. After a number of years he could have the nucleus of an independent herd.

This system of payment provided considerable stabilization with Arab pastoralism. The more sheep the wealthy acquired, the greater their capital drain. This drain supported poorer Arabs who were able to rebuild their herds. Given the potential of great gain or loss, payments in ewes provided a homeostatic device that kept pastoralism among the Arabs in rough equilibrium. In addition, even wealthy Arabs remained directly involved in pastoralism because the labor supplied by the family could be replaced only in an unacceptable price in ewes. While shepherding was important, it was an expensive adjunct to the family's labor.

Pastoral labor is also called for in shearing. The shearer (*kalgar*) takes a percentage of the wool in payment. A *kalgar* can shear about thirty Qarakuli sheep a day and considerably more Turki. He takes one-eleventh of the Turki wool (which is of such poor quality that many owners don't bother with it) and one-fifteenth of the Qarakuli wool. The Qarakuli wool is taken from adult sheep. It is coarse but lustrous, and highly valued for making carpet wool. A shearer cuts off a wool pelt, which weighs

3.5 kilograms, uncleaned. In 1975 the market price for the wool ranged from 300 to 350 Afs. per seer. Qarakuli lambswool is sheared in the mountains three months later. It is highly prized for felt, and the white wool in 1975 brought 500 Afs. per seer; the black, 350 Afs. per seer. In a clipping I measured, eighty lambs had produced three seers. A shepherd is responsible for this Qarakuli lamb shearing. In celebration of the shearing the owner slaughters a lamb for a meal called a *tuimaida*. In addition, most shepherds pocket some wool to bring back to their wives. "Women complain if you don't bring them something," explained one shepherd. Shearing is most important among wealthy pastoralists, since only they have Qarakuli sheep. An Arab with Turki sheep can do the shearing himself.

Women do not have responsibility for herding, but they are completely in charge of setting up the camp, providing necessary equipment that can be produced at home, processing milk, and feeding the family. Their work not only maintains the family but also allows the greatest benefits to be derived from the herd.

Women are responsible for making and breaking camp. While men may assist, most of the work is in the hands of the women. Nowhere is this more observable than at the end of a day's migration. The men immediately sit and wait for their tea, which is the first responsibility of the women. As the men drink tea, the women erect a shelter, begin making bread, get water, and so forth. The man can nap at this time, but a woman should always look busy, even if it is through a make-work project. It is no wonder that at the end of the three weeks' migration the women are quite irritable—the major burdens of traveling fall on them.

Much of the equipment that the Arabs use is obtained by purchase in the bazaar, but certain items are made by the women. Felt is perhaps the most important product. Wool from sheared sheep is cleaned, beaten, and rolled to create the type of felt needed. Felt is used in lining robes, as saddle blankets, and as flooring. Other wool is spun into yarn out of which a heavy wool cloth is made. The women also make a heavy wool rope. In addition to these products, the women make a light reed fencing, *buria*, held together with wool thread. This fencing is used for wind screens and the sides of summer tents. While Arab women do not make knotted carpets, they do make a deep-pile rug resembling a Scandinavian rya rug.

Milking is in the hands of the women. The ewes are rounded up by the men and held in place or, in more organized camps, tied together while the women milk them. The milk is strained through a cotton cloth to remove sticks, rocks, or sheep dung, and then boiled. Uncooked milk is never drunk because it is believed to cause stomachaches. The boiled milk is skimmed for clotted cream, *qaimaq*, which is quite a delicacy. That milk which is not used for cooking is turned into yoghurt, *kattugh*, which is consumed fresh or allowed to dry to a solid residue called *qrut* which can be stored indefinitely. *Qrut* making is a major summer activity. The Arabs produce neither cheese nor butter. They do make a sour milk, *doq* or *chelao*, which is quite refreshing but is reputed to make one drowsy. Milking runs from lambing season in March until early August when the ewes have gone dry. The exploitation of the milk products provided by the flock is the hallmark of subsistence pastoralism. As this falls within the women's sphere, it is they who are responsible for reducing the surplus milk to *qrut*. In shepherd camps, without women, the men may milk some sheep to make *kattugh*, but they never get involved in turning surplus milk into *qrut*.

The women's major responsibility is preparing food for their families. The basic Arab diet is bread and tea. Bread is made from wheat flour in the form of large unleavened flat cakes weighing about a kilogram. These are baked on a flat hot rock. Baking bread is a never-ending process. Cold bread is looked upon with disfavor, and a proper wife is expected to have fresh bread or at least reheated bread to serve. Guests at any time of day should be served fresh bread. Since Qataghan is a rice-producing area, the Arabs have far more rice in their diet than other people in Afghanistan because it is relatively cheap. Rice is served in the evening, baked in sheep fat if possible. In the spring and summer rice is cooked in sheep's milk. While the Arabs do not slaughter many healthy sheep to eat, enough dying sheep are slaughtered to produce a more regular supply of meat than is seen in agricultural villages. In shepherd camps cooking is done by men, but the food suffers. One shepherd boiled water, oil, and salt for two hours and announced he had made soup, after which he was verbally abused by his hungry compatriots. Bread made by women is immediately distinguishable from that made by men by its superior quality. In subsistence pastoralism women's labor in cooking could not be replaced except at a very high cost. Even a large herd owner would not be willing to replace his wife's labor with that of a shepherd who had to be paid in ewes—especially if he had to eat the shepherd's cooking.

Ownership and Herd Management

Knowledge of sheep and their needs is critical not only for the shepherd herding them, but even for a herd owner not actively involved in the day-to-day work. Important decisions must be constantly made in light of one's herd, market conditions, and alternative possibilities, all of which demand that pastoralists constantly review their position.

Ownership of sheep is marked by special cuts on the ears. Each owner has a particular mark. This facilitates separating sheep when herds mix and is important in proving ownership in cases of theft. While Arabs do have a detailed knowledge of their sheep, marking is critical when dealing with large numbers of sheep. Soon after a lamb is born its ears are marked. This is done by the owner personally or by a shepherd under the owner's immediate supervision. A shepherd may point out lambs that have been missed, but he will never do any cutting without express permission. Ear cutting is a ritual act by which owners mark the lambs as their own. Pragmatically the owners also want to make sure that the lambs are not switched by their shepherds. Marks of herd owners are well known.

An especially important aspect of herd management is determining when a sheep is about to die. Arabs dislike slaughtering sheep for their own consumption, but dying animals provide a varying supply of meat. But the meat can be eaten only if the sheep was slaughtered by having its throat slit while alive, according to Islamic law. If the sheep is killed in this manner, the meat is *halal*, or clean, and is permissible to eat. Should the sheep die before being slaughtered in this manner, the meat is *haram*, or forbidden, and cannot be eaten regardless of the cause of death. In this case, the animal is skinned, and the hide and intestines (exported for sausage casings) are sold in the bazaar. The meat is given to the dogs. Arabs respect this prohibition even when hungry for meat, though optimistic decisions are often rendered in questionable cases. It is always "other people," like Tajiks or Pashtuns, who are accused of not being too particular.

Even when convinced of the ultimate fate of a sheep, the Arabs wait until the last possible moment to slit its throat. This often leads to mistakes, and should the sheep die *haram* a general argument breaks out over who is responsible. Herd owners naturally want to wait until the last moment because they hate to lose a valuable animal. Shepherds wait until the last possible moment so they will not be accused of slaughtering healthy sheep for dinner. If present, the herd owner gives the command; in the owner's absence it is the *chopan's* responsibility. It is a common belief among herd owners that shepherds will steal or eat their sheep if given a chance. They demand to see the skin of each sheep that dies or is slaughtered to assure themselves that their livestock is not being sold. In fact, most shepherds show remarkable restraint in killing animals, but since they will often *hope* a sheep will die, their interest and that of the herd owners is in conflict. I was once in a shepherd camp on a mountainside that was suddenly overrun by sheep. The shepherds beat the sheep back with their sticks. One shepherd stunned a sheep with a blow to the head. The other shepherd told him to watch what he was doing. Instead, he cried out, "Die, you sheep, so that we will have something to eat!" The sheep ran off unharmed, but this sort of attitude creates suspicion between owners and shepherds.

I was often struck by the Arabs' detailed knowledge of their own herds. In addition to the precise counts of the type and class of sheep they owned, they knew the qualities of many individual sheep. Their largest sheep wore charms to protect them. But the defects and merits of more average sheep were also recognized. This was brought home to me forcefully when I went to visit a rich Arab who was believed to be dying, although he later recovered. He was in great pain when his *chopan* arrived. He told the people there that he intended to give away ten sheep as a religious offering before he went to the hospital. Five sheep had already been disposed of, and he had called his *chopan* to give instructions on the selection of the other five. He then described the five particular sheep he intended to give, out of a herd of seven hundred. He specified three *pir mish* (old ewes) that would have to be culled anyway, an undersized *chari* which would not bring as much as his other *charis*, and a *shishak* that was as big as a *chari*, since he had far more *shishaks* than *charis*. Even though everyone believed that he would not recover, the herd owner used his detailed knowledge of the herd to make sure his gift would have as little impact on his herd as possible.

3. Social Organization of the Central Asian Arabs: The Decline of the Clan

At the grossest level of identification the Central Asian Arabs in Qataghan consider themselves all to be *qaum-i-Arab*—of the Arab tribe or people. For outsiders this label usually suffices, but among themselves and to other people with whom they have close relations, the relevant term of reference is the *taifa*, or clan. In Imam Saheb the Arabs are divided into thirteen clans:

1. Kal dolati	5. Aw foroush	10. Qurdon
2. Hajda dewana	6. Kur Ashi	11. Tubatai
3. Shal bofeo	7. Kata poi	12. Ali Momati
4. Kuta qara	8. Turk	13. Shahri
	9. Bongseri	

These *taifa* are no longer organized as political units. In the nineteenth century Maitland noted that each clan had a leader such that all were under a tribal chieftain (G.A.T. 1979: 74–75), but such organization seems to have disappeared about fifty years ago after the Arabs acquired land in Imam Saheb.

Although a founding ancestor can be named for each *taifa*, I discovered that many Arabs were ignorant of the links between the founder and themselves, or even of the name of the local founder. In no case were links between one part of a single clan and other parts known even within the same village. After receiving a detailed list from one informant, I asked why it excluded most of the households in the *qishloq*. He assured me that they too were clan members, having the same ancestor five generations back, but how they were linked he did not know. He suggested I ask them if I was really interested.

Indeed, I discovered that the Arabs were profoundly bored with genealogies. It irritated them when I asked so many questions that they felt were irrelevant. On one notable occasion, as I tried to separate out a large set of brothers, half of whom had two names, Nik Momat impatiently interrupted me and asked, "You know these men are dead?" When I admitted I did, he replied, "Then why talk of these? They are dead. Ask about the living."

I was witnessing not the death of traditional culture but a process that has occurred among different nomadic peoples of Central Asia for some time—the change from a genealogical clan to a patronymic one. Whereas knowledge of genealogical links is necessary to validate one's position vis-à-vis others in a genealogical clan, in a patronymic clan the links are irrelevant: one is an Aw foroush because one's father was an Aw foroush. What is most striking about the Arab clans is that they are still in the process of changing from one system to another, a process that has been historically documented among other Central Asian nomads.

From historical records Krader has shown not only that the change from a clan system based on detailed genealogical knowledge to a clan system in which affiliation is based on the inheritance of the same clan name was widespread among the historically known steppe nomads, but that the nature of the change and the reasons for it were similar despite differences in location and historical period. Comparing the Mongols, Buryats, Kalmuks, Kazakhs, and Mongours, he came to this conclusion:

> Measured against the criteria of the corporative kin group of the former genealogical clan-lineage formation, the present-day groups whose membership and marriage relations are based only on a common patronymic are weak exemplifications of that structure. During the course of the retreat of the genealogical principle before the patronymic principle, the political rule has been taken over by outside forces. Even if the personnel is indigenous the new political organization is not. With the new rule many functions of the society have fallen away, among them the pasturage distribution, the administration of native justice, the clan leadership, and the genealogical process of reckoning degrees of agnatic relationship in the society. In the social structure based upon genealogies, the counting of generations is a crucial act; past time is thus inherent in the social system. In societies based upon the patronymic principle the past itself loses—or changes— its relevance. Time is not counted, the patronymic principle is synchronic, it is cyclically recreated with every generation; its ties to the past are not detailed and tend to be vague. The patronymic sib is a weak corporate body, whether as kin group or as a political group; it is the expression of an era in

which the sinews of steppe society are those of a political system that lies outside the steppe. (1963: 332–33)

The clans of the Central Asian Arabs do differ significantly in some ways from those among the steppe tribes. Perhaps most important, Arab clans are not exogamous. There is a preference for marriages within the clan, although not necessarily with patrilineal first cousins. Second, the Arab clans seem never to have been divided hierarchically between noble and common clans. In spite of this the Arab clan is far more understandable as a variant of the clans of Turkic-Mongol pastoral nomads than of any type found among Arab tribes in the Middle East. Certainly the process of transformation from the genealogical clan to the patronymic clan accurately describes many of the present problems of Arab social organization. It is also quite probable that the Arab clan was never independent of state authority and that its structure reflected from the beginning a weakened form of genealogical clan.

While Krader presents a model posing two ideal types, one degenerating into the other, I would suggest that for many nomadic pastoralists an intermediate position of a weakened, but firmly genealogical clan is more probable. This has to do with the nature of state control. Take away the clan's basic raison d'être and it withers, living on in name but impotent in action. The Central Asian Arabs were, more than other pastoralists, under the control of the state and thus never had untrammeled rights to pasture, administration of justice, or independent clan leadership. But the nature of state control in nineteenth-century Bukhara was qualitatively different from that found in Afghanistan in the last quarter of the twentieth century.

Until comparatively recently, administration of nomadic peoples, where they could be administered, was indirect. Although the clan was not independent, the concept of the clan as a unit and the clan leader as a representative was critical in maintaining order in areas where direct rule was impractical or expensive. This gave the clan political significance within the state structure as well as an illusion of solidarity. In fact, the clan was maintained as a device used by the sedentary state to control people whose mode of life could not be handled in the same fashion as that of dependent sedentary villagers.

Even in the 1830s Lord found that the Uzbek clan had become an administrative convenience in the hands of a strong ruler:

In affairs of internal policy Murad Beg seems to attend to two objects, first that as many of the sirdars [leaders] as possible should be relatives or creatures of his own, and in this he is not a little assisted by the singular fact that the Ooroughs or clans of the Uzbeks though so carefully distinguished have nothing like hereditary chiefs. "Who is the head of your clan?" said I to Mingh Kul, the present governor in the great Oorough of Munas: "I am now," replied he, "but you may be tomorrow if the Meer wishes" . . . The other object of his internal policy is that an order sent by him should be implicitly obeyed throughout his dominions. (Burnes et al. 1839: 120–121)

Attaching a tribal organization as a form of administration to a sedentary state allowed for the administration of people mapped through social space rather than physical space. A nomad was always a member of a particular clan and could be dealt with through that clan, though the nomad might move through a number of different sedentary administrative districts during the year. The drawback of the system was that the state was forced to deal with problems through the clan and clan leader. Though the clan leader might be a creature of the government, the clan acted as a buffer to direct rule. Until recently a sedentary state demanded only submission to its authority and payment of taxes from tribal people. But with modern weapons in the hands of the state, government became more and more centralized. Disputes and transgressions that had been left to the will of customary law now found their way into government hands. The tribal groups that had been so useful as a means of indirect rule were now obstacles to the implementation of direct rule. The Afghan policy toward settlement of nomads had little to do in reality with improving the nomads' lot, but everything to do with breaking down political structures incompatible with direct state control. The modern state became unwilling to strike deals with the semiautonomous groups that preserved order in the nineteenth century. Giving them land was, as we will see, not only an excellent way of breaking down social solidarity; it was private ownership of resources rather than state control per se that accelerated the decline of the genealogical clan.

The *Bai* and Dispute Resolution

A wealthy Arab pastoralist is referred to as a *bai* or *boi*. This title refers quite specifically to animal wealth and is attached to the end of a name. Informally the term is often applied quite freely as a mark of respect even to very poor nomads. But this informal use is not reflected in a more public arena for fear of the ridicule which would follow a poor man who would claim a status far above his means. Even a wealthy Arab may come in for criticism should his values be perceived as misplaced. In a teahouse two poor Arabs were discussing the affairs of a rich Arab, when one of them declared, "He is no *bai*; he puts his land first!" A *bai* is a man of considerable animal wealth and one who views his sheep holdings as his primary resource, no matter what other investments he may have.

The *bai* is more than wealthy; he is the closest thing the Arabs have to a leader. He is much like a Kazakh *bii* (Krader 1963: 209–213). The Arabs, who recognize no formal lines of authority among themselves, turn to the *bais* for help in resolving disputes. A *bai* has a social status rather than an institutional position. Wealth is only one criterion—the man must also be respected for his judgment and honesty, for the political power of a *bai* rests on the willingness of people to defer to him.

In the past it appears that *bais* often had their own power because they were recognized by the state as important people to whom local disputes could be legally delegated. Thus a description of Imam Saheb made as a result of Nadir Khan's reorganization trip to Qataghan lists sixteen notables and their tribes, of which three were Arab (Kushkeki 1923: 87). These locally important men were recognized as such by the government. Today with political authority in the hands of the Afghan state there are two distinct positions, that of the *bai*, who is unofficial but handles many of the problems within and between *qishloqs*, and that of the *arbob*, who is the legal link between the *qishloq* and the local administration. (The position of the *arbob* will be examined in detail in Chapter 5.) There are significant differences between a *bai* and an *arbob*. The greatest difference is that the *bai* mediates disputes within the clan, or between clans and ethnic groups if they are willing, while an *arbob* is charged with handling affairs between the government and the residents of the *qishloq*. Instead of a *primus inter pares* like the *bai*, the *arbob* is a man who links two alien systems. The *arbob*'s power flows from the state; the *bai*'s is derived from the consent of his clan. As an individual acting on his own, the *arbob* often has little or no influence. A *bai* and an *arbob* are sometimes the same person, but the mode of operation characteristic of each is so different that there is no confusion about which role is being filled in any given situation.

Although a *bai* has no legal power to resolve disputes, he still plays a powerful part at the local level. He often switches from the role of mediator, trying to bring about an agreeable settlement between two parties, to that of arbitrator, one who decides a case at the behest of the disputing parties. In any event he is a well-known insider who is far more trusted than the local government administration. His justice may be personal, but he has the background and knowledge to come up with a solution that will meet with community approval.

In spite of the local government's claim to jurisdiction in all disputes, most people seek informal arbitration of their complaints whenever possible. The fear of being caught up in a process handled by provincial administrators—resulting in demands for bribes and bringing government scrutiny on individuals who would prefer to remain anonymous—is enough to give these negotiators power to resolve most disputes. Either party can ignore the judgment and go to the government for adjudication, but the difficulties involved in such a course are usually enough to convince the loser of the battle that there is nothing to be gained by appealing to the government—and often a lot to lose.

Let us examine two cases typical of those that are resolved by appeal to a *bai*. They represent the historical way in which most disputes were settled in the absence of strong authorities, and they are important in maintaining the cohesion of the Arabs as a tribal group organized on different principles from those of the governmental bureaucratic administration. These resolutions of disputes keep the Arabs insulated from the government and make the *qishloq* opaque to government scrutiny, as very little of what goes on there comes to the attention of the "authorities."

The first dispute concerned an Arab's accusation of sheep stealing by a Pashtun. It marks the kind of low-level problem which, at least in the initial stages, is easiest to handle informally. In fact, as in many disputes, the very informality allows the disputants to gauge the reaction to their cases before committing themselves to a specific course of action. Discussion among friends and relatives is not good enough for this purpose because they generally claim to agree with whichever party they happen to be talking to at the time.

During the spring an Arab accused a Pashtun of stealing six sheep. This occurred on the plains above Imam Saheb. The Arab, having visited the Pashtun camp, where the theft was denied, contacted an Arab *bai* and asked for a hearing. This particular *bai*, Juma Khan, had his own spring pasture near the camp of the accused Pashtun, and thus as a neighbor of the Pashtun and fellow clansman of the Arab arranged for a meeting at his tent. He invited two neutral parties, a Tajik and a Pashtun, to listen to the case. These two old men arrived first and engaged in drinking tea and idle talk. About an hour later the Pashtun arrived, closely followed by the Arab. Juma Khan welcomed each in a friendly manner. Though he had arranged the meeting, he acted only as host and did not take part in the discussion, which became heated, among the two disputants and the old men.

The Arab proceeded to tell his story. He said he had seen two men off in the distance near where his sheep had been grazing. Later he discovered six sheep missing from that flock. At this point the Pashtun interrupted and objected, "Whenever you Arabs find something missing you say we Kandaharis [Pashtuns] did it!" "That's because you do!" responded the Arab. Immediately the Pashtun and the Arab began leveling charges at each other, quite loudly magnified since I sat between them. The two old men told both of them to quiet down, and the Arab continued his story. The Arab said he had gone to the Pashtun camp and, though failing to find his sheep, had recognized the meat he saw in the camp as that from his stolen animals. A number of people laughed at this claim, but others said that it was possible to recognize meat. The Pashtun denied any responsibility for the theft or knowledge about it.

The two old men, *mui safid* ("white-haired"), began to examine both men about the facts of the case, especially about the circumstances surrounding the loss. This they did in a very impartial manner. The Arab was forced to admit that his evidence was circumstantial, that he had not recognized the men he saw because he was too far away, and that he had not discovered the theft until later. The Pashtun proclaimed his innocence and called upon Juma Khan to vouch that over the years he had been a good neighbor. After about an hour of reviewing the facts, which were few, and the various possibilities, which were many, the Pashtun rose to leave. Laughing, he stroked the Arab's beard on the way out and asked God to witness that this dispute was over. This the Arab hotly denied, but the Pashtun left, accompanied past the dogs by Juma Khan.

The old Pashtun, who had been neutral, now began to take on the absent Pashtun's case. But nothing was really accomplished other than repeating the case again. After more tea the two old men left, again accompanied by Juma Khan, who thanked them for making the trip out to his camp. No decision was given even at this time, and the case was just left to hang.

Juma Khan had taken no part in the dispute. He feigned boredom and left the tent once or twice. Having arranged the meeting and acting as a neutral party, he was overtly friendly to everyone. But when the others had left, he turned to the Arab and berated him openly for bringing such flimsy evidence on which to base such a serious accusation. While no one had delivered a judgment, it was obvious to all that the case was too weak to take further. This accounted for the light-hearted manner in which the Pashtun laughed off the charges. The Arab dropped the case.

This informal resolution of conflict allows even very weak cases to be heard with no liability. The loss of six sheep was serious, but by the end of the discussion even the Arab realized he had no case. But since no decision was publicly made, he was not forced to admit he might be wrong. The *bai*, as a powerful Arab, was able to provide a neutral meeting place, could call upon impartial people to hear the dispute, and had contacts outside of the Arab community that facilitated getting cooperation from the Pashtuns. Since this was all unofficial and voluntary, the success of the gathering was dependent on the high status and good reputation of the *bai*. As a fellow Arab, he saved his harsh words until everyone else had gone. The *bai*'s ability to arrange such a meeting shows that in many instances the tribal system provides far more flexibility and impartiality than does the bureaucratic administration of the town.

The second case illustrates the role of the *bai* as an arbitrator. This role is particularly common in the disputes of Arabs among themselves. This dispute involved repayment of a debt between two Arabs of the Kata poi clan. The Kata poi have neither a *bai* nor an *arbob* because they are a poor clan and their *qishloq* is not registered. As a result, the Kata poi have no one among themselves who is of sufficient stature to handle dispute settlements, especially the minor ones that generate much heat. On social occasions such as weddings, when prominent Arabs visit the Kata poi *qishloq*, the Kata poi combine the festive event with often rancorous disputes, using the prominent Arabs from other clans as judges. Jamil, an *arbob* of the Aw foroush but acting in the role of a *bai*, spoke for them.

This particular dispute took place during a wedding feast in the Kata poi *qishloq*. The guests were all inside the reed-yurt mosque. Outside waited an old woman named Gul-i-sib ("Apple Blossom"). Between one of the many courses of food, she entered, salaamed, and, squatting in the middle of the yurt, began her story. She complained in a very loud voice how she had lent 125 Afs. ($2.50) and some small items to a man named Rustam and had never gotten any of it back. Rustam, sitting in the circle of men, became agitated and began to curse at Gul-i-sib, denying everything she said. They both became very angry and suddenly jumped at each other, but were caught by the bystanders before any blows could land. Rustam was told to sit down and shut up. At this point more food arrived, and the judges used the opportunity to halt the proceedings while things cooled down. They whispered back and forth over what should be done. Jamil then announced that of Gul-i-sib's many claims, Rustam was immediately liable for 125 Afs., which he was ordered to pay on the spot. Rustam pulled out a plastic wrapper that contained his money. He had exactly 120 Afs., which he claimed was the only money he had. Gul-i-sib was about to object when everyone said in unison, "He can owe you the 5 Afs." Gul-i-sib was then picked up bodily and carried over to Rustam, who was pushed toward Gul-i-sib, so that they could shake hands while holding the money between them as everyone prayed—a standard way of finalizing any important financial arrangement. As they shook hands, looking like two cats with their fur up, everyone declared that they must now consider the dispute settled. Gul-i-sib left the yurt and stood outside declaring loudly what a rotten person Rustam was. Inside, Rustam mumbled to his friends about how much he had given that ungrateful woman in the past. Jamil called Gul-i-sib back into the yurt and warned her not to go to the government with this dispute because that would just mean more trouble for everyone. Gul-i-sib replied, "You are my government," and left.

This dispute showed a *bai* in a more traditional role as arbitrator. As the last statement indicated, the *bai* had no legal authority to settle anything, but nevertheless his word was accepted. Because of his position he was able to make a decision which stuck because of the support of the community, not because of any coercive power. The Kata poi wanted a settlement, and therefore public opinion backed the *bai*'s judgment. Jamil did not give Gul-i-sib everything she wanted but satisfied her basic demand. This was not unexpected, even by Rustam, who "by chance" had only slightly less than the exact amount he was liable for. The warning about "not going to the government" is a theme that runs through most disputes, and it may be said to give the arbitrator his real power. In this sense most disputes are seen as family matters that should not involve outsiders. The *bai* is the only figure with enough authority among the Arabs to fill the role of judge, which generations ago was legally his.

While a *bai* arbitrates disputes, he does not have the power of command. Internally the *qishloq* is highly egalitarian, almost anarchic. Wealth and status differences are recognized, but the power of command does not come with wealth. Each family acts independently.

Nowhere is this more true than in labor relations. An Arab shepherd sells his labor, not his fealty. Shepherds rarely work for the same sheep owner more than three contract periods in a row. As will be shown, rich sheep owners have come to dominate the scene, and yet there is no patron-client relationship among shepherds and owners. One reason for this is that patrons would have little use for clients in the money economy. They are interested in labor, not particular people. An Arab with clients would have no political arena to use them in—so support as a patron, rather than as just an employer, would yield little. When poor Arabs object to agricultural work it is not the work they object to as much as the lack of independence to sell one's labor as one pleases. In this sense, the traditional values of freedom of action associated with nomads remain strong among the Arabs.

The Clan Village

When the Arabs left Bukhara in the 1870s their clan structure seems to have received a vital stimulus. Because they became completely nomadic for fifty years, social identification became more important in determining rights to resources and cooperation. Therefore when land was granted to the Arabs in the 1920s for permanent *qishloqs*, the Afghan government dealt with the clans as corporate groups. As a result, the Arab *qishloqs* in Imam Saheb today are clan villages. But though the *qishloqs* may have been granted to each clan as a corporate group, the land was considered the private property of each householder. The kinship ties, or personal differences, that determined where families first settled have been perpetuated through time. The Arab clan structure circa 1920 has been preserved on the ground by the land holdings and essentially represents the corporate nature of the clan at the time—a corporate nature that has ceased to exist except in social terms. Over time, through the inheritance process, spatial proximity has coincided with patrilineal relationship—adjacent houses were those of brothers; nearby houses, those of cousins.

While granting land to the clan preserved its unity spatially, the clan declined in importance politically and economically. With privately owned pasture and permanent land holdings in Imam Saheb, the importance of maintaining kinship ties was reduced. Private ownership of land now guaranteed one's place and the place of one's descendants in the *qishloq*. In the fifty years before the land grant, an annually changing *qishloq* necessitated close cooperation among members of a clan. Here knowledge of genealogical links was important for political and economic support, but with private property clan affiliation was only socially important. With the clan transferred to this more marginal place in Arab life, the patronymic principle sufficed to bring order in the social world. No particular benefits now accrued from clan membership. Critical resources were now private property, and preservation of private property was in the hands of the Afghan state, not a local kin group. Over time, with each family secure in its resources and with no political responsibilities to kin, the Arab clan as a corporate group with political or economic significance became moribund. Collective interests had become irrelevant in the face of private property. Individuals now were in a position to push their own interests without having to consult with or gain the backing of their kin. Krader (1963) attributes the decline of the clan in part to nomads picking up agriculture. Yet it is not agriculture per se but the aspect of private landholdings that attacked the very basis of politics for a nomadic people—a corporate pastoral resource that necessitated collective action and consultation.

There is one exception to this general rule: the Kata poi clan did not get title to land. They show a much higher degree of clan unity than do other Arab clans. Unfortunately, they also provide evidence that abandoning the clan as a political and economic group was highly adaptive to the changing conditions of Qataghan in the last fifty years. The Kata poi are the most traditional of all Arab nomads; they are also the poorest and most endangered. A comparison between them and the Aw foroush, their nearest neighbors and the richest Arab clan, is revealing.

The Kata poi and the Aw foroush have been in the Imam Saheb area for about the same length of time. The Aw foroush live on the edge of the agricultural plain above the swamps. The Kata poi live in the midst of the swamp on a grassy plain that can be reached only by a narrow causeway. The Aw foroush say that the Kata poi failed to get title to their *qishloq*, and camp on it collectively by right of prior possession. It appears that, since they were living in the midst of the swamp, title to the land, which was otherwise unusable, was thought to be unimportant.

The Kata poi *qishloq* consists of sixty households divided into approximately twenty compounds. The compounds are created by combining high reed fencing with reed huts, which look like reed castles with walls and bastions. The compounds contain from one to six households. In the center of their camp is a reed mosque. The Kata poi are a poor clan, and their reed huts, their conservatism, and their location in the swamp are derided by the Aw foroush, who call them the *bay akal mardum*, "the witless people."

In the Aw foroush *qishloq*, I never heard clan or tribal affiliation used to support arguments or create solidarity. Any sense of clan or Arab identity the Aw foroush have comes out most often in opposition—when they compare themselves with Tajiks or Pashtuns. The Kata poi, by contrast, cannot assemble without the constant refrain "We are all of the same *quam*" to bring the group together or cool down arguments. While the Kata poi stress tribal solidarity, the Aw foroush studiously ignore it. Indeed the Aw foroush spend more time in slanderous gossip about near relations and other members of the clan than in efforts at camaraderie. But the Kata poi *qishloq* is based on kin affiliation, and though they may have as many nasty things to say about their kin as do the Aw foroush, they are obligated in everyone's self-interest to keep the collectivity intact. The right to camp on Kata poi land is based on descent within the clan, not property rights. At the moment, however, they face a collective threat to their land. While the Aw foroush basically lost their clan but gained individual rights to land, the Kata poi have their clan but are now threatened with the loss of their land because they do not "own" it. This corporate threat strengthens the clan, but the Kata poi have no clan leaders and are dependent on the advice of influential Arabs from other clans. We will return to their story in Chapter 6, which will show that at the present time the clan is a unit incapable of dealing with the Afghan state as it did in the 1920s, leaving the Kata poi vulnerable to the loss of their land. The present troubles of the Kata poi are evidence that abandonment of the genealogical clan for a different kind of relationship to the state is not only due to internal dissolution of kin ties, but is the most adaptive way to deal with a state that has been able to impose direct rule on the inhabitants of Qataghan. In times of rapid change conservatism may be as dangerous as taking on new risks.

Lineage Development and Private Property

The effect of freezing the social structure of the 1920s can best be observed by looking in more detail at the Aw foroush *qishloq*. In this *qishloq* of 240 households the clan is not the major social group; the lineage has replaced it. The Arabs have no particular term for lineage, nor are these de facto lineages named. But since the members of a lineage share a common known patrilineal ancestor, live adjacent to each other, and tend to know how they are linked genealogically to one another, it is a definable social unit.

The Aw foroush *qishloq* has over the years been transformed from scattered groupings of yurts into clusters of walled compounds. Geographically the *qishloq* was originally divided into upper, middle, and lower sections separated by swamp that is now agricultural land. Families that originally settled together in each of these areas have therefore remained neighbors (or descendants of neighbors). Within these three major sections lineages have developed. Their existence is reflected in the six different mosque congregations in the *qishloq*, each averaging about forty families. There are three in the lower *qishloq*, one in the middle, and two in the upper. Member households are descended from the founder of the mosque and are responsible for its upkeep and the support of a local *akhund* or mullah. Most of these *akhunds* are Arabs, and each mosque has its own. The mosque is a common meeting ground for prayer and is the only corporate property of the lineage. (The only clan property is a clan cemetery.)

Households are more likely to think of themselves as *khish* (relatives) who have a common mosque rather than a particular social group. They support a single *akhund* by providing food in rotation, gifts, shelter, and a salary of 15,000 Afs. a year. The *akhund* conducts prayers, does Koranic recitations, and presides over ritual occasions. In addition, he runs a *maktab*, a school for young children where they learn to recite prayers, read the Koran during the winter, and learn the basics of Sunni Islam.

The most intense social relations take place within the mosque congregations of the *qishloq*. Social engagements bring large numbers of people together and stress the solidarity of the *qishloq*. Visiting patterns at the lineage level reveal that there are, however, deep divisions not only within the mosque congregation but within smaller descent groups. A person who attends a wedding or circumcision may not in the ordinary course of events have anything to do with the family giving the feast. These divisions go beyond the factors responsible for the demise of the clan; they reflect underlying differences in strategies that various families have chosen to deal with the changing conditions of the past fifty years. The success of these different strategies is measured by wealth, and the major difference has come over the desirability of purchasing agricultural land.

After settling down in Imam Saheb a number of Arab *bais* invested money in land. Most of the purchases were in the vicinity of the *qishloq* and were made only after World War II. The land in the neighborhood of the *qishloq* is of average quality for the valley and is supplied with adequate water from the local irrigation system. The question of diversification by acquiring land was and still is a hot issue in the *qishloq*. Many Arabs felt it was a bad idea to sell off sheep to buy agricultural land. Profits in sheep raising were larger, they said, and land buying required not just the investment of profits, but usually selling off many more sheep than usual to make the purchase because land was not easily acquired piecemeal. Given the organization of Arab herding, a pastoralist might have a substantial surplus invested in the herd to produce *charis*, the most valuable size of castrated sheep. To buy land meant not only selling off the annual *chari* crop, but dipping into future profits by selling almost all of the castrates. This meant a large sacrifice most pastoralists were unwilling or unable to make. Other than having their own land to live on, which was often a fair-sized piece in local terms, the majority of nomadic Arabs were not interested in acquiring agricultural land. Despite the fact that land values have been appreciating considerably over the years at a rate greater than that of inflation, at any time during the recent past the major objection to buying land has been that it was "too expensive" when it came down to putting up cash. In retrospect many people admit land was very cheap, but it was the economically more aggressive Arabs who recognized this at the time and diversified their holdings. Although sheep herding has had greater profitability than agriculture in the last decade, the families that combined sheep owning with other investments are now the wealthiest people in the village, though they had the same resource base as their relatives.

A split in strategy is illustrated by a case which concerns a group of brothers and their descendants (Figure 2). Malang

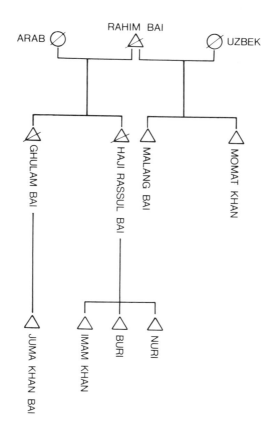

Figure 2. Heads of households descended from Rahim Bai.

("Crazy") Bai decided to purchase land in 1963. In order to raise the cash, he was prepared to sell off a substantial portion of his flock. Momat Khan, his brother, came to visit him and told him he would truly be crazy if he sold sheep to buy land. He, for one, would stick to sheep. Malang Bai bought forty jeribs from a Turkmen friend at a cost of 1,100 Afs. per jerib. Today the land is worth approximately 10,000 Afs. per jerib. In 1974 he purchased another ten jeribs at the now much higher price. Says Malang Bai, "Momat Khan has 300 sheep, and I also have 300 sheep now—plus fifty jeribs of land," and he pointed to the fact that he had gotten 350 seers of cotton from his new ten-jerib purchase that

73

brought 35,000 Afs. Then he asked, "Who is the *malang* now?" and laughed, "If you buy land you can always rebuild your herd, but if you have only your own sheep and lose them, then you will go hungry."

Malang Bai was not the first in the family to acquire land. His half-brother, Ghulam Bai, had purchased eighty jeribs twenty-five years before. In addition, Ghulam Bai purchased urban property—a large caravanserai which not only provided a good return for the money but also allowed the family to engage in profitable trade in the town. The caravanserai was used by other Arabs on bazaar days and became an important link between the Arabs and the town. When Ghulam Bai died, his widow ran the estate for many years, controlling land, urban investments, and sheep with great skill until her son came of age. Juma Khan, the son, now manages the enterprise, and his mother, though retired, is famous in the town as an example of a widow who actively managed and preserved the family estate.

The present generation is now split because of their alternative strategies. Malang Bai and his nephew Juma Khan are wealthy; the other side of the family, while self-sufficient, is not rich. There is more than money involved because the acquisition of nonpastoral property has begun to change the dynamics of economic mobility and to stratify the *qishloq* to wealth.

The Arabs ascribe large herds to skillful herding and luck. Equally, fate may bring the largest herd owner to nothing. Families with thousands of sheep have been at times reduced to a few hundred. On the other hand, the richest Arab in the valley started with only a small herd. As long as animal wealth was unsecured by anything else, social mobility up and down was common. The purchase of agricultural land and urban property has put a buffer into this direct relation between herd growth and wealth. Wealth in stable investments means that even a large loss of sheep will not bring automatic destitution. It also provides an outside source of income that can be used to rebuild a damaged herd. Finally, multiple investments have a synergistic effect on each other. The ability to take cash from the pastoral, agricultural, or urban sectors and put it where it is needed gives one a tremendous competitive advantage over individuals whose money comes from only one sector. In an area where credit is available only at high rates of interest, the Arab who has money flowing in at different times from different investments becomes insulated from pressures felt by others.

In the case of the family discussed above, as one branch of

the family grew rich and was able to consolidate its position, the distance between rich and poor relatives increased. In contrast to the past, the wealthy are far less likely to fall in status today. They can lose their sheep and still remain rich, while, for reasons connected to the organization of the cash economy, poor Arabs have far less opportunity to rise today than they did in the past. Chapter 5 will discuss this in detail, along with the reason why wealthy nomads who own land not only remain in the pastoral economy but have come to dominate it.

The strategies for dealing with the economic growth of the region have obviously varied, but in general risk takers have been the big winners. This has led to a schism between those who took advantage of new opportunities and those who did not. The schism is deepest within those families who had the resources to invest. Poor individuals never had an opportunity to diversify because they lacked the resources. But those with one hundred to three hundred sheep had potential, and those who made the decision not to diversify find their present options more restricted. The degree of separation is directly related to the issue of choice. Failure as the result of God's will is no one's fault. Failure because one did not make the right decision—and being constantly in the presence of a cousin who did—is not conducive to harmony.

Because of the divisions between close kin, cooperation within the lineage takes place on the basis of common economic interests. The closeness of a patrilineal relationship is not a good indication of how those groups are formed. Malang Bai refers to his brother Momat Khan and his other nephews, Nuri, Buri, and Imam Khan, as "rotten people." His nephew Juma Khan is "not just a nephew, but a friend." As a result, Juma Khan and Malang Bai herd cooperatively in the winter and help each other in selling cotton. They also cooperate with Kassim Marat and Hussein, whom they call *bacha amuk*, or patrilineal first cousins. These people are in fact second cousins, but the real first cousins are ignored because of the differences described above. Thus anyone within the lineage with whom one has good ties is referred to as a *bacha amuk*. There is no attempt to falsify genealogies as a rule, just an attempt to relate the accepted responsibilities of close kin to the people who actually provide cooperation.

While land ownership divided the descendants of Rahim Bai, it has in other cases unified sets of brothers by giving them a common interest. Such is the case of the brothers Hussein and Kassim Marat, who inherited one hundred jeribs of land from their father. Like many Arabs who have inherited agricultural land, the brothers work it in common. Sheep are invariably divided at the death of the father, but agricultural land is different. The great risks associated with sheep raising make profit and loss in a herd an acrimonious affair should a dispute arise—for example, about decisions to sell *tokhalis* or wait until the sheep become *charis*. Land, by contrast, is easy to work in common no matter how many owners there are. There can be little dispute about procedure and sales—the crop is simply divided equally among the owners. In most cases there is no actual work involved because a sharecropper grows and harvests the crop. Brothers who run their own herds can still usefully keep the land in common. Whether land can be held in common by cousins, who may have little to unite them or who may want to sell their share, is not yet clear because the Arabs have not had agricultural land long enough for it to pass down to groups of cousins.

The *Qishloq* and Arab Social Life

Private property and changing political and economic conditions have reduced the *qishloq*'s effectiveness for any type of collective action. Nevertheless, the *qishloq* is home for the Arab nomadic pastoralists who spend much of the year there. Socially it plays an important role that supersedes much of the divisiveness. Because of the dispersion of people during the spring and summer, interaction between Arab families is limited. When I explained to an Arab in his summer camp that I was writing a book about their way of life, he laughed and told me that the *ailoq* was no place for that. "Here all we do is sleep. Go to the *qishloq*, and you will get enough to fill four books!" After the dispersion that characterizes the spring and summer, the return to the *qishloq* with its nucleated settlement is looked upon with relief—much the same relief that is expressed at leaving it in the spring. In many ways dispersion was traditionally a way in which tensions built up during the winter were eased by time and distance.

The winter is the slack economic season, and because of free time and proximity it is a time of celebration and feasting. Winter is the social highpoint of the year with a series of engagements, weddings, and circumcisions. These life-crisis events provide the year's major entertainment in feasts and gossip.

Arabs have few ceremonies, and even ritual occasions tend to be conducted in an offhand manner. While considering themselves to be good Muslims, the majority do not take religious obligations too seriously. Arab social events, no matter what the occasion, are very similar. They are staid affairs with no musicians, singing, or dancing, in contrast to those of their neighbors, who have all of these, especially for weddings. The only musical instrument the Arabs use is a *daira*, a tambourine-like instrument beaten by the women. I was sitting in the courtyard with an old Arab woman when we heard the sound of a *daira*. "It is a *tui* [celebration]," she remarked, and then sarcastically imitated it, "Bang! Bang! Bang! That is all we ever do," she complained, and said there was never music or *bazi* (play) at Arab weddings. "Tajiks, Uzbeks, Larkhabis, Sinjanis, all have music and *bazi* at their weddings." She was somewhat disgruntled at this fact and claimed that it was more fun to go to other people's celebrations than to Arab ones. Indeed Arab celebrations have a reputation for being dull, consisting mainly of eating. The introduction of battery-powered cassette players has improved the situation at more informal affairs, but traditional events still lack entertainment.

Bride-Price and Marriage

The family is the basic unit of Arab society. As explained in Chapter 2, the family is economically independent, and the need for cooperative groups is small. Basic decisions are made at the family level. Arranging marriage and paying the bride-price are events so important in a family's life that they provide very good evidence of changing social relations. The divisions within the *qishloq* and variations in status are most visible in these transactions.

A family is created by marriage, but because the inheritance of animals occurs at the death of the father, marriages do not automatically create independent households. Therefore, the family herd is kept intact for a much longer time than among many other nomadic pastoralists, and a man's wealth is not drained by anticipatory inheritance. A marriage is still a major expense for a household because of the necessity to raise the bride-price. There is often a large age gap between husband and wife because of this. On the average, women are married at sixteen or seventeen to men in their mid-twenties and thirties.

The groom's family must raise the necessary bride-price and be able to cover entertainment costs before a marriage can take place. The bride's family provides a certain amount of household goods, but very little by comparison. For the Arabs, bride-price (*qalin*) is a two-tiered system: 30,000 Afs. for the daughter of an average herd owner, 70,000 Afs. for the daughter of a wealthy *bai* or large herd owner. Men find preferred marriage partners, in order of preference, within the (1) clan, (2) tribe, (3) Uzbeks, (4) Tajiks. Marriage to patrilineal first cousins is relatively rare, in no small part due to the lack of cohesiveness in those minimal lineages. A marriage outside immediate kin is seen to bring more useful alliances. The only absolute rule is that Arab women are never given to Tajiks, although Arabs marry Tajik women freely. This appears to mark a bias that the Arabs picked up from the Uzbeks, who now do intermarry with Tajiks, for they are recorded as having the same prohibition in Qataghan during the 1830s (Wood 1872: 141).

Engagement negotiations determine the exact amount of the bride-price. It must be paid in cash unless otherwise negotiated. The most common length for engagements is one year. The engagement usually takes place in the winter and the marriage the next winter. This interval is used to pay the bride-price, but even if a man has the money on hand, a year's wait is considered proper. If the family does not have the money ready, the delay may be more than a year.

The bride-price is only part of the total cost of a marriage. The engagement and wedding feasts are open to all and in many cases run for three days. The size of these affairs can be gauged from the requirements of an engagement feast. The groom's family is expected to provide food for two feasts, one at each household. This involves twenty seers of dried fruit and nuts which are given to the guests to take home, between fifteen and twenty seers of rice, and two sheep for meat. The wedding feast is slightly larger. The total cost of a feast this size would be about 7,000–8,000 Afs. if the requirements were purchased on the open market. Thus the feasts connected with a wedding and engagement can cost half as much as the bride-price itself on many occasions. Most young Arab men work from five to ten years to get the necessary funds together.

Bride-prices vary considerably among ethnic groups. At the low end of the scale are the Tajiks, Uzbeks, and Arabs. The Tajiks in the poor mountainous valleys of Badakhshan have the lowest bride-prices, in some cases only 10,000 Afs. But in most places these three ethnic groups stick within the same range, there being a larger difference between average and elite bride-prices within a group than between groups. The Pashtuns and Turkmen have high bride-prices, often between 100,000 and 200,000 Afs., with Turkmen on the whole asking more than Pashtuns. The Pashtuns refuse to marry their women out, though they marry women of all ethnic groups. Unlike the cash payment demanded by the Arabs, a Pashtun bride-price is often kept artificially high by accepting goods and livestock at an inflated value. The "sticker price" remains high, but negotiation reduces the actual cost. In addition, marriage between patrilineal first cousins is common and leads to a reduced cost. Turkmen bride-prices reflect the high value of female labor in carpet production where a wife has a skill of direct cash value. The Turkmen have far more polygyny than other groups.

This bride-price differential has an effect on interethnic marriage. Men from groups with high bride-prices are in a dilemma as to whether they should wait the extra years to save enough to make a marriage within their own group, or negotiate with another ethnic group, where the cost would be less. One of the major topics of conversation among Arab shepherds is the advisability of making a "cheap" marriage in the mountains.

It should not be assumed that negotiating a bride-price is like haggling over a carpet. Differences in bride-price reflect status within ethnic groups; it is the range that differs. Thus an important Arab would reject out of hand a proposal by a poor Pashtun to whom even the elite Arab bride-price might seem comparatively low. Among important families the bride-price should be at the high end of the scale, whatever it is, since more than a bride-price is being fixed: an alliance is being made.

Among the Arabs it is important that families contracting a marriage be of similar status, mostly defined in terms of wealth. Since great differences in status appear even among close relatives, and since their cooperation is not vital to the family's pastoral economy, the tendency is to marry out for the sake of new connections rather than reinforce immediate kin ties. In one situation an Arab married one of his many sons to the daughter of a Tajik merchant from Badakhshan. He paid the elite-level bride-price, gaining important ties in the *ailoq* region. It was far more advantageous to ally himself with an important Tajik family than to find an Arab bride.

The woman's family is actively concerned about their daughter's welfare when negotiating a marriage. Though bride-prices involve a large sum of money, the family is expected to consider the marriage on its merits and not in sheer monetary terms. A *daukhtar foroush*, "daughter seller," is subject to much scorn. When the richest Arab in the valley was looking for a new wife, his previous wife having died, he was refused by some of the poorest households in the *qishloq* on the grounds that a man in his mid-sixties with grown sons should not be taking a new wife. Although he offered 70,000 Afs., it took quite some time to arrange a marriage, and he was subject to much criticism.

Polygyny is rare among the Arabs today. The only case I ran across was a man whose first wife was childless. Genealogies revealed that the practice was more widespread fifty years ago. The Arabs stress that one advantage of Islam is that it permits a man four wives (seven according to some Arabs, though orthodox mullahs are aghast to hear them say it). Yet the large herd owners are all monogamous, and divorce is rare. Certainly women do not consider polygyny a good thing. One surviving second wife roundly condemned the practice. Arab women are very strong-willed, and their opposition, in terms of keeping peace in the household, is an important factor. Sedentarization may be in part responsible. When the Arabs lived in yurts it was far easier to create an independent household for each wife. It is far more difficult to have two mistresses in a single compound in the permanent *qishloq* of today.

These marriage links, which often cut across *qishloqs* and ethnic groups, give the Arabs a wider social universe. Because Arabs in Imam Saheb have traditionally exchanged women with the Uzbeks of Rustaq, they have very strong ties with that region. Affinal ties also provide an entrée outside the *qishloq* that is useful in obtaining work. Just how useful these links are hinges on personal relations. Even more than with patrilineal bonds, affinal and matrilineal ties are activated to justify a relationship; they do not necessarily create one.

Summary

Historically the Arabs have been nomads who were willing to pay the price of political subordination for access to dependable resources. The pasture areas of Qataghan were very similar to those in the Zarafshan Valley. The major difference was that in the late nineteenth century Afghan political control of the region was far less organized than in Bukhara or the Russian-administered territories. The Arabs who had inhabited "fixed districts" in Bukhara became more nomadic in Qataghan. This fifty-year period of indirect state control and increased nomadism gave new strength to the Arab clan organization. The settlement and development of Qataghan in the last fifty years has in one sense restored the status quo ante of the Arabs' Bukhara position. But because it is now feasible to govern areas directly, the tribal organizations that facilitated control in the nineteenth century are seen as obstacles to administration in the twentieth. The changing nature of economics and government, which guarantees access to dependable resources that are privately owned, has led to the decline of the clan as an effective unit. The idiom of kinship has lost much of its force of persuasion. While residence and kinship are still coterminous, they are no longer organically related.

The wealthy have the strongest interest in genealogy. Descent is still important in validating status. Ironically the wealthy Arabs are least restricted by clan affiliation. They often visit members of other ethnic groups and are visited by them. Their knowledge of the region is expanded, and they are in a position to make profitable transactions. The poor Arabs, unable to trace their descent, are far more bound by their kin network. Visitors to their camps will invariably be relatives or perhaps Arabs from other clans. Their world view is more restricted. Since kin and neighbors are the same people, even if clan and lineage bonds are weak, the poor Arabs still work within the same network of people because they can change neither.

The description of the rise of individual self-interest and the fall of the corporate clan should not be looked upon as some sort of deculturation. Kinship structures that were highly adaptive in solving problems of organization and defense but that have ceased to be relevant can naturally be expected to lose their force. The process among the Arabs has been accelerated by private property, a money economy, and a more powerful centralized government. The social aspects of traditional organization still survive and are likely to continue to do so. The main problem the Arabs face, after loosening kinship obligation in favor of self-interest, is that they have left themselves vulnerable to individual attack. The Arabs have not yet put together groups that can provide for collective actions that work within the present system. The Arabs, in Benjamin Franklin's words, need to hang together lest they hang separately.

4. The Role of the Arabs
in the Provincial Economy

Pastoral nomadism is a well integrated part of the economy of
Qataghan. Arab and Pashtun nomads alike are dependent on the
farmers of the mountains and valleys for their grain and on
artisans in the bazaar for manufactured goods. The migration
schedule is as much in tune with the sedentary agricultural cycle
as it is with the cycle of seasonal changing pastures. The specialized pastoralists in Qataghan, who depend on the sale of live
sheep to an urban market, are more integrated into the money
economy than most of the region's subsistence farmers. This
chapter will focus on the links between the pastoral sector and
the bazaar economy as well as sketch the relationship of pastoralism to the agricultural economy. In order to understand the
place of pastoralism in this system, something about its
complement—farming—must first be explained.

For purposes of analysis, the regional agricultural system
may be divided into two components. The first is that of the
irrigated lowland valleys. Here is the nomads' winter home, an
area of irrigated agriculture on a large scale, roads and motorized
transport, large populations, and urban markets. The second
component is the mountainous region where farmers engage in
unirrigated agriculture and small-scale animal raising in an area
devoid of roads with poorly articulated marketing facilities. In
this area nomads have their *ailoqs* and spend the summer. They
have vested interests in both regions and in many ways serve as a
link between them.

An outline of the ecology and the history of development in
the river valleys was given in the first chapter. Here the focus will
be on how the Arabs have adapted to the agricultural economy
which has developed around them in the last thirty years. The
valleys of Qataghan are the most productive in Afghanistan,

growing wheat, rice, cotton, melons, sugar beets, and other minor crops. Imam Saheb itself is a major cotton producer. Wheat is grown on the same land to provide a subsistence crop. Although Imam Saheb is not a major rice producer like Khanabad, it does produce enough to meet local demand. The large melons of the valley are famous throughout Afghanistan and today constitute a major export.

Cotton is king in Qataghan—but its rule is not complete. Because of the nature of the pricing structure of the cash economy and the lack of a reliable market system, there is today a dual economy in the river valleys, with cotton, the major cash crop, competing for acreage with wheat, the major subsistence crop. Cotton has made the valleys rich, but, because the price paid for cotton is fixed by the government, its profitability compared to that of other crops varies considerably. The key equation is the price ratio of raw cotton to wheat. A high ratio in favor of cotton puts more land into production. The difficulty is that the government monopoly has kept its purchase price depressed in order to make a larger profit on export sales. In Qataghan the turning point is reached when the ratio is 2 : 1—that is, when raw cotton sells for twice the price of wheat. At this price and above, production is widespread; below this price farmers refuse to grow cotton, or grow only enough to raise a certain amount of cash. In developed countries the cotton/wheat price ratio is around 3 : 1. In the late 1960s the ratio in Qataghan fell to .91 : 1 in 1966–1967, and .85 : 1 in 1967–1968. As a result, the government forced the farmers to put 25 percent of their land into cotton for sale to the cotton company (a form of taxation). Things improved somewhat with price increases the next year that allowed the ratio to rise to almost 2 : 1, but then came two years of drought in which the price of wheat skyrocketed, making its production on irrigated land very profitable (Etienne 1972: 122–123). In 1973 a Republic was declared, and the new government raised prices considerably in order to encourage production which was needed for export. The ratio from 1974 to 1976 ranged in the vicinity of from 2 : 1 to 2.2 : 1, and cotton production was once again very important.

Farmers are critically sensitive to price fluctuations, but they are careful to plant a mix of crops. Even if the price of cotton were to rise, it is unlikely that wheat farming would be completely abandoned because there is no alternative dependable supply. Fry has shown that wheat prices vary randomly from province to province in Afghanistan, indicating a lack of articulation within the national economy (1974: 58) and also indicating that no province can afford to specialize solely in a cash crop because there is no evidence that grain could be imported cheaply with enough regularity to assure farmers that the system would not break down. Thus farmers divide their land between cotton for its high cash value and wheat for subsistence. In the mountains these problems do not occur—the people grow only grain.

From the Arabs' point of view the development of cotton cultivation has had many positive aspects. To a large extent they have been able to integrate sheep raising with many aspects of cotton production. This integration has increased the viability of pastoralism in Qataghan. There are four major ways the Arabs have benefited from the cotton economy.

The first important factor is that cotton as a cash crop fuels the economy of Qataghan. Since the Arabs depend on cash sales in the bazaar, the strength of the money economy is important to them. For example, in Imam Saheb alone the Spinzar Cotton Company paid more than $2 million for the cotton crop of 1975. In a country defined by the United Nations as a "least-developed" nation, the economy of Qataghan not only is much richer than average, but probably has more liquidity than any region in the country.

Second, the cycle of cotton growing can be worked easily into the nomadic schedule. Cotton is harvested from November to January. It is handpicked, which requires much labor. This labor is in part supplied by Arab women who receive 8 Afs. for each seer picked, or one-sixteenth of the cotton they pick if they want to be paid in kind. This labor provides cash wages for the women during the slack season of the pastoral cycle. This reserve army of women is important to the economy as a whole, since handpicked cotton brings a higher price on the world market.

After the cotton is picked, pastoralists use the cotton fields for grazing in late winter. The sheep eat the dried leaves. Cotton stalks provide a plentiful source of fuel in the winter. It is quite common for the nomads to move their sheep out of the swamp and onto the cotton fields after harvest. This schedule provides grazing at a time of scarcity. The fields then benefit from the sheep dung.

Perhaps the most important integration of the cotton economy with pastoralism has been the increasing use of cotton by-products as winter fodder. These by-products are of two varieties: the hulls of cotton seed, called *postak*, and the pressed seed, called *kunjarat*. Using these by-products as feed, the Arabs are now able to stable some animals during the winter and stall-feed them. The price and availability of these commodities is a major source of concern in the winter. This is especially true for the use of *postak* as emergency feed. For example, one Arab moved his sheep to the steppe a few weeks earlier than usual because it had been a warm winter and the grass was growing. A week later a sudden storm buried the grass in snow. In the past this would have had dire consequences, but the owner was able to purchase seven tons of *postak* and rent a truck to transport it to his sheep. He kept his herd intact and in good health until the snow melted. Small herd owners use cotton by-products only occasionally, but families with over a hundred sheep have become at least partially dependent on it. As a result, sudden weather changes have less impact than they used to. The high price of sheep encourages the cash outlay needed for the supplementary feed. Arab herds are thus in good shape throughout the winter even before the spring grasslands become available.

The integration of commercial cotton and pastoralism has created two new problems which will be discussed in the next two chapters: (1) the supply of feed has become a complex affair because of the relationship of the state-owned cotton company to the free market, and (2) the use of purchased fodder has turned subsistence pastoralism into a commercial operation.

The Bazaar

The economic focus of the valley is the bazaar in Imam Saheb. Containing over five hundred shops and seven caravanserais (G.A.B. 1972: 80), it is laid out along regular streets that converge on a large circular park. It took its present form as a result of town planning in the 1930s and in outline is similar to those of other towns in Qataghan that were constructed on the same pattern. It is the major market for the region. In addition to the bazaar proper, the Spinzar Cotton Company has a cotton ginning plant in the western part of town that controls the buying of raw cotton and the sale of the by-products from the ginning process. For the moment the discussion will focus solely on the bazaar and reserve for later the complex relationship between the market economy of the bazaar and the state-controlled monopolies like the Spinzar Cotton Company.

The bazaar is the marketplace for locally produced and imported goods. While many shops remain open on a daily basis, the economic life of the town centers around two bazaar days held each week on Monday and Thursday. The days have their origin in Uzbek custom and are the same for every town in the region. On these days people from the surrounding villages throng to the town to buy and sell goods, or in many cases just to look around. Mid-morning is the high point of the day; toward noon the crowds thin, and, while shops continue to do a brisk business, those people who have brought their own goods to sell in town usually conclude their business. The rhythm of the bazaar varies with the seasons. Winter and spring are far more active periods than the summer, when the nomadic population and their sheep are off in the mountains. Bazaar day is as much a social event as it is an economic convenience. It is a chance to have one's fortune told, perhaps see a snake charmer and buy his snake oil, or at the very least eat fresh bread from the town bakers.

From the perspective of the Arab nomadic pastoralists the bazaar may be divided into three major components: (1) the caravanserais, (2) the specialized shops, and (3) the sheep bazaar (*bazaar-i-gusfand*). In addition, at the edge of the bazaar, on the roads leading away from Imam Saheb, are cars and trucks which provide transport to neighboring towns.

Caravanserais

The various caravanserais in Imam Saheb link the urban market with the outlying *qishloqs*. The many functions of a caravanserai make it an ideal bridge between the relative complexity of town life and the simplicity of the *qishloqs*. One always patronizes the same caravanserai on market day, comes to know the owner and manager, and feels at home by having some kind of personal link within the urban context. Three of the caravanserais in Imam Saheb are owned by Arabs and stand adjacent to one another. Almost every Arab coming to the bazaar patronizes one of them. These caravanserais are perceived by the Arabs as a link with their own social world—something familiar in the strange and kaleidoscopic world of the town. This feeling is reinforced by the fact that the owners of many caravanserais live in their *qishloqs* and not in the town. While they are not urban people, as owners of urban property these people have stronger ties to and a better understanding of the bazaar scene.

The Arab caravanserais and their owners are quite visible social links between the town and its hinterland. On coming to town, Arabs take their horses or donkeys to their regular caravanserai, where they can be parked for the day for 2 Afs. One is then free to wander about town. Regular customers leave their purchases under the watchful eye of the manager of the caravan-serai, who controls the day-to-day operation.

The caravanserai is more than a link between town and country; it is an integral part of the bazaar itself. As a result of town planning, caravanserais occupy city blocks and are divided by regular streets. The average size of a caravanserai varies from three to five jeribs. This marks a sizable investment in land alone. Urban property in the town proper is valued at approximately 100,000 Afs. per jerib.

Serai Imam Khan is typical of the caravanserais found in Imam Saheb (Figure 3). It was rebuilt in 1974 at a cost of 820,000 Afs. It is traditional in form but makes use of concrete foundations. Unlike some, it lacks a second story. The caravanserai's

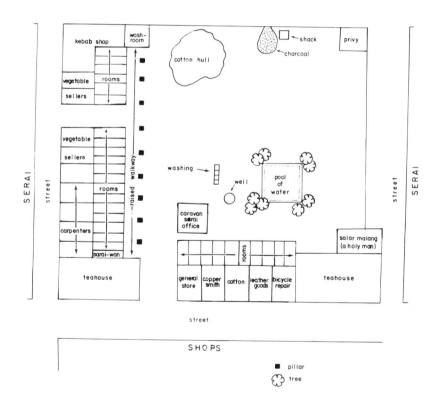

Figure 3. Serai Imam Khan.

income is derived from two teahouses and one kebab shop, rents from about fifteen shops facing the street, and rents from about thirty rooms inside the caravanserai. The caravanserai also sells charcoal and some cotton by-products. The rooms inside rent for 100 Afs. a month and are used by local high school students, low-level government officials, or itinerant traders, or are taken simply as storage space. On the outside of the caravanserai are commercial shops. Rents average about 300 Afs. a month. Artisans and merchants with similar goods locate next to each other so that parts of a caravanserai often contans shops of the same type. The caravanserai's interior acts as a receiving area for visitors and goods and as cheap residential space. The outside is devoted to commercial space. The series of caravanserais and their shops are the economic cells that create the bazaar itself.

Income from Serai Imam Khan amounts to approximately 120,000 Afs. annually. Part of this figure is derived from rents and services, the rest from the teashops. Teashops are an integral part of the caravanserai. The caravanserai owner contracts with someone to run a teashop on an individual basis. The owner and contractor split the profits after subtracting operating costs. Teashops face the street and are part of the public caravanserai. Traditionally, transients can spend the night in the teashop if they eat there. After dark the caravanserai itself closes its large metal-plated doors to the world. Outside shops are locked individually.

The caravanserai and particularly its teahouses act as information centers. Teashops are always filled with people exchanging gossip and price information, or comparing conditions in nearby places. The chance to socialize with other Arabs from different qishloqs is welcomed. It would not be an exaggeration to say that many Arabs are more interested in finding out what has been going on than in buying or selling anything. At the end of the day they can be seen returning to the qishloq with a bottle of kerosene or other small items that were bought to justify the trip.

Specialized Shops
The Arabs are dependent on the bazaar for all the manufactured goods they use. With only a few exceptions all the equipment a nomadic family needs can be purchased in the bazaar. This was made evident to me when I had to equip myself for the migration. In the company of an Arab I went from store to store until I was completely outfitted. The nomad market is important to the

town merchants. They stock goods particularly for the nomad trade from shepherd staffs to camel bells.

The goods in the Imam Saheb bazaar, as in most bazaars in Afghanistan, represent a wide range of products from all over the world. Afghanistan's liberal import policies allow people to purchase goods that in price and quality are unmatched in neighboring countries. Afghanistan has never been chauvinistic in its trade, a reminder of its former history as a trading center for East and West. Indeed, the wide range of goods found in the bazaar today is matched by Alexander Burnes's detailed account of the Kunduz bazaar in 1837 in terms of diversity and country of origin (1839: 122–146).

At the center of the bazaar are the many cloth shops. Cloth of all types—cotton, synthetics, silks, velvets and satins—is available. Shops cater to the tastes of different ethnic groups. Thus velvets and satins are for a Pashtun market, Russian prints are popular among Tajiks and Arabs, and Uzbeks and Turkmen prefer different kinds of silk robes. Purchased cloth is taken to a tailor because the Arabs do not usually sew their own clothes. Other items are purchased from the "used clothes bazaar," a collection of used Western clothes imported into Afghanistan in large lots from Western Europe and the United States. These clothes are usually in good shape and very cheap. Most popular among men are suit jackets worn over traditional clothes. Because of the variety of used clothes it is possible to find a shepherd wearing Italian hiking boots or a nomad in a full-length overcoat of camel's wool. In the latter case the nomad asked me if I thought it was really camel's wool, saying that cloaks of camel's wool were very expensive in Afghanistan and he had paid so little. I assured him it was, but agreed that at 500 Afs ($10) it was a bargain. Through these imports Afghanistan has one of the best-dressed populations in Asia at a cost far below the production cost of the imports; and these "used clothes bazaars" reach all corners of the country.

Other imported manufactured goods like razor blades, matches, kerosene lanterns, and unbreakable glasses are found in every household. Modern goods, if useful, are immediately incorporated into the traditional lifestyle. Chinese aluminum trays are purchased because they do not rust. Cassette tape recorders allow for local music to be recorded in the village and replayed at will; people rewind the cassette tape by spinning it on a stick because they do not want to waste the batteries. Matches, for example, are vital to any household. When I was traveling through the mountains with a salt caravan, we came upon some shepherds who had been without tea all day because they had forgotten to bring matches to start a fire. My companions later commented that only fools travel without enough matches. Hardened glasses from France have replaced porcelain cups because unbreakability is a real asset to nomads. Nomads even shop for brand names, preferring Russian matches to Indian or Chinese. They examine them suspiciously since the Indians now counterfeit the Russian trademark.

More traditional imports like tea and sugar are in great demand. Throughout Afghanistan tea drinking is a constant activity. Crates of every kind of tea of various qualities are for sale everywhere. Sugar is both produced in Qataghan and imported. Tea and sugar are bought in large quantities before the migration, since these staples in the lowlands are luxuries in Badakhshan.

These examples of imported manufactured goods show that the Arabs draw on a worldwide source of supply, but they also support many of the traditional crafts in the bazaar. These locally produced goods depend on local demand. In the cities most crafts have disappeared, but in places like Rustaq or Imam Saheb that serve a traditional hinterland, artisans still have a market. The loss of traditional crafts has been due in part to imports but also to the fact that the most artistic of the craft productions traditionally served a small elite market. This elite now spends its money on expensive foreign luxury goods like automobiles rather than on traditional objects of wealth.

Metalworking crafts are important to the nomadic population. Blacksmiths produce all kinds of products used by nomads: horseshoes, chains, locks, hobbles, shears, knives, and so on. Coppersmiths produce cookware and a distinctive water boiler designed specifically for open fires. Leatherworkers produce tough shepherd boots, fine riding boots, and saddlery gear. One part of the bazaar is devoted to village handicrafts like wool and cotton cloth, locally woven and made into large sacks. Without the large nomadic market many of their crafts would be in dire straits.

In many ways the bazaar is as adapted to the needs of the region's nomadic pastoralists as they are to the urban market. By turning from what the Arabs buy to how they market their sheep, we shall see that they are as integrated into the sedentary economy as any farmer in the valley—perhaps even more so.

Bazaar-i-Gusfand

The caravanserais are both gathering places for Arabs coming to town and an integral part of the bazaar itself, together with their specialized shops. But the most active place on bazaar day is the *bazaar-i-gusfand*—the sheep bazaar. More than just a market for sheep, this bazaar handles all the grain and animal trading for the whole valley. It is the institutional link between nomadic pastoralists and the urban meat market. One always pays a visit to this bazaar, regardless of whether one is interested in buying or selling anything. It is only by a trip through this market that accurate information about prices of all the basic commodities can be obtained. The activity in this bazaar is highly sensitive to seasonal demands and supplies.

Physically the *bazaar-i-gusfand* is twice as large as the average caravanserai. It has shops and teahouses facing one street, but the whole inside area is devoted to trading. There are no rooms inside, just a vast enclosed space. In the center are two concrete platforms with reed roofs. Each platform is divided into a number of stalls which are rented by the permanent grain traders. On non-bazaar days the place is quite deserted, with only the permanent grain traders in residence. Business is slack, and a premium is charged for any grain purchased. The grain traders are able to extract this extra money since they know anyone buying on a non-bazaar day must be in real need, hence the surcharge.

On a bazaar day this sleepy place comes alive. The entrance-way is crushed with people entering and leaving simultaneously. Just after dawn sellers from the *qishloq* arrive. They pay a few Afghanis for the privilege of selling here. Buyers of livestock and grain arrive throughout the morning. Purchasers of animals pay a small fee upon leaving. These charges are modest, but the turn-over is great. By noon most of the business is finished.

The *bazaar-i-gusfand* is divided into specific areas for each type of livestock. Half the bazaar is devoted to livestock, the other half to grain, reed products, and firewood. Animal sellers take their stock to the appropriate section of the bazaar. Individual sellers of grain, especially rice, simply line the path next to the permanent grain sellers. The owner stands next to his grain or animals and waits. Sellers do not initiate action but wait until interest is expressed by a buyer. Buyers walk through the area, comparing price and quality. Haggling is confined to the animal section. Grain prices, once established, are rarely bargained over, but animals have a uniqueness that invites long debate over virtues, defects, and price. Though many of the men in the bazaar are acting as agents, there is no institutionalized brokerage.

The activity within the bazaar reflects the seasonal variations in the agricultural and pastoral cycles. An Arab suddenly dropped into this bazaar could probably guess the exact time of year within two weeks.

The section of the bazaar that deals with sheep and goats is most important to the nomadic pastoralists of Imam Saheb. Although goats can be found here, Imam Saheb is sheep country, and the market reflects this. Every pastoralist pays a visit there to find out who sold what and how much was paid. The kinds of sheep for sale change with the yearly pastoral cycle. Spring, for example, brings very young lambs to market. These animals are sold by some nomads to raise ready cash for the migration and summer supplies, and are bought up by other nomads on speculation. If the lambs survive, a hefty profit can be realized on their return from the *ailoq* in the fall. Summer finds the sheep market all but deserted. With the vast majority of the sheep at the *ailoq* and with temperatures of 40° C in Imam Saheb, good meat is hard to come by throughout the summer. The return of the nomads with their sheep in the fall brings new life to the bazaar. *Tokhalis*, the six-to-eight-month-old castrated sheep, newly returned and fattened on the pasture in the mountains, are sold in large numbers. The sale of these animals provides the money needed to buy grain for a family's winter needs. During the winter wealthy nomads dispose of their *charis*. These huge fat-tailed sheep are the specialty of Qataghan and bring the highest price of any sheep on the bazaar. Owners carefully consider the market before selling. They may choose to sell off only a few at a time in order not to glut the local market. Those with large numbers of *charis* often find it worthwhile to rent a truck and ship their *charis* to Kunduz or Mazar-i-Sharif, where their sheep can be sold at a premium price at these substantially larger markets. Old ewes are also disposed of on the meat market during the winter.

Despite the great rise in sheep prices from 1965 to 1975 (see Figure 6), all nomadic pastoralists complain about the market—either that it has been such a good year that prices did not rise as expected because of the large number of sheep, or that it has been a bad year and they have lost sheep. If meat prices are good, then they complain about the price of wool or skins. Casual conversations are always biased toward the negative, giving the impression to the unwary that nomadic pastoralists are always on the brink of ruin, even when they are doing well.

Sheep are sold not by weight but as individual animals. It is up to the buyer to estimate the weight of the animal and the amount of useful meat and fat it contains. In an attempt to control rising meat prices the government has tried to fix meat prices and thus indirectly the price of the live animals. This policy is looked upon with disfavor by pastoralists and butchers alike, and the sheep owners have been able to effectively subvert the program. In order to rationally set the price of meat, an animal is purchased and the meat sold at a fixed price. When all the meat is sold, the money taken in is compared to the cost of the live animal and the figure obtained is adjusted up or down to establish a ceiling price for meat sales. In theory this system is admirably adjusted to regional differences. In practice it is a failure because when a government buyer appears in the bazaar, the sheep sellers are forewarned. So the government buyer is never able to purchase a sheep for the price-fixing experiment at anything less than 500–1,000 Afs. more than the usual market price. The ceiling price from this purchase satisfies both pastoralists and butchers.

Next to the sheep and goats, referred to as *maida poi* ("little feet"), are the cattle, *kata poi* ("big feet"). The largest place is reserved for the oxen. One part of this area is crammed with cattle; the rest is an open field on which potential buyers try out a yoke of oxen. Oxen are expensive, about 15,000 Afs., and are used as the traction animals for plowing. No one will consider buying an ox without first seeing how well it plows. This market is most active in early winter when plowing begins in the valley. Next to the oxen are cows. They rarely constitute an active market except in early spring when they have calved. Cows and young calves are sold together; older calves are sold separately. Sale of calves is in the hands of young boys because their fathers consider it undignified to stand over a little calf waiting for a sale. Purchase of cows is ordinarily confined to sedentary villagers, including pastoralists who no longer migrate. Cows are not considered fit enough to make a long migration, though I observed a few nomads who took them into the mountains. Cows provide not only future oxen, but milk. Sheep's milk, even when available, is not sold on the market because the nomads themselves consume it all. Cattle are not sold for meat except as a last resort. There is a cultural preference for mutton to beef that has strong empirical foundations—the quality of mutton raised specifically for the meat market is significantly better than that of beef from cattle that reach the butcher's block after a lifetime of hard work.

The middle section of the bazaar is devoted to the sale of transport animals. Loud braying focuses attention on the donkeys. The donkeys of Qataghan are admired by the people of Badakhshan for their size and endurance. Of particular interest are very large donkeys, the size of a small horse, that are considered to be a Turkmen specialty. They cost between 5,000 and 6,000 Afs. and carry a large load at a quick walk. Smaller donkeys, especially well adapted to mountain travel, cost from 3,500 to 4,500 Afs. Poorer-quality donkeys may be had for less. The Arabs depend on donkeys for regional transport of things like salt and wheat. Even the Pashtuns, who disdain donkeys, find they must have a few for jobs their camels cannot do in the mountains. Despite their economic importance, real capacity for work with little care, and even intelligence, donkeys are the butt of much humor in Afghanistan. This attitude makes donkey trading somewhat disreputable. Even the word *khar* (donkey) is enough to produce laughter. It is the standard animal prefix to modify grosser insults. Nevertheless, the donkey bazaar is usually active, especially in the spring when donkeys must be purchased before the migration. Donkeys are not as easily obtained in Badakhshan, where transport animal prices are in general higher than in Qataghan and the animals of worse quality. The need for wheat and salt keeps caravans of donkeys moving throughout the summer even though camps are stationary.

Camels are the pride of nomads who engage in long-range migration. According to informants, the number of camels in the region has been declining for years. This is confirmed by government figures (Grötzbach 1972: 186). There are usually only three or four camels for sale on any particular bazaar day. They cost 10,000–15,000 Afs. and are mainly traded by Pashtuns. Camels in Qataghan are large-boned, one-humped transport camels. They are used by nomads to move households on migration and still transport much of the cotton crop to market in the winter. One danger in buying a camel is that the owner may be selling it because it has a nasty temperament, for which camels are justly famous.

An open space full of mounted riders marks the horse-trading section of the bazaar. Famed for pack horses and fine riding animals, men in Qataghan have a strong interest in horse-trading.

Most nomadic families have at least a couple of horses. The bazaar trading is confined mainly to pack horses and average . riding horses. Work horses, used to transport people and goods, sell for 6,000–8,000 Afs., riding horses for 8,000–12,000 Afs. A low price for quality is admired, and bargaining is sharp. An open section in the bazaar is used to try the horse out.

The sale of prestige horses used to play *buzkashi* is outside of the bazaar confines. They cost 15,000–100,000 Afs. and are often famous throughout the region. Unlike the haggling in the bazaar, the sale of prestige horses is a personal matter; who is selling the horse is often as important as the horse's pedigree. Bargaining is diffident—the buyer wants a good price but does not quibble over small sums, as is almost always done in the bazaar. In part this is due to the fact that a prestige animal's value is enhanced by the high price paid for it, as long as there is no obvious cheating. Thus an Arab who bought a horse for 17,000 Afs. went back to the *qishloq* and told the story of the purchase, the pedigree of the horse, and people's admiration of it in the area. When another man asked how much he had paid, the new owner responded, "Well, I paid high for it—17,000 Afs." (Only for a prestige animal does one ever admit to having perhaps paid too much.) "No, that is a good price!" replied the questioner, who had no idea of what an expensive horse should cost; his agreement merely confirmed that the horse was in a high-status category. Except for the elite, who can actually determine value in the prestige market, the mass of people only know that such horses are phenomenally expensive. Just how expensive is learned by listening to rich men boast.

Grain Sales

At the center of *bazaar-i-gusfand* are the platforms that house the permanent grain traders. On bazaar day independent producers line the path with their own grain. The major commodities for sale are rice and barley. Imam Saheb is not a major rice producer like Khanabad, but enough is produced to make rice cheap in the valley in comparison to other parts of Afghanistan. Rice farmers bring sacks of rice to sell each bazaar day. Rice has a good price-to-weight ratio compared to other grains, making it worthwhile to bring relatively small quantities to market. Buyers are also interested in buying small lots. Barley is grown mostly on unirrigated fields outside the valley and wholesaled in the bazaar. It is used for horse feed. Wheat, except during planting season, is noticeable for its absence as an important commodity. There are, however, some flour merchants who serve an urban market.

The unimportance of wheat in the bazaar at first sight seems strange, given that wheat bread is the staple food for everyone in the valley. But the contradiction is not hard to explain. Wheat is a subsistence crop that is not integrated into the cash economy, at least not through the bazaar. For many land owners, surplus wheat is considered better than cash. Surpluses, above the need of immediate consumers, rarely enter the bazaar. The United Nations has estimated that only 20 percent of the annual wheat production ever reaches the bazaar (U.N. 1971).

There are a number of factors that help perpetuate this practice. Transport difficulties even within the valley discourage taking wheat to market. Whereas it is easy to take ten or twenty seers of rice to the market, where it sells for about 100 Afs. a seer, it is much more trouble to move enough wheat, which sells for only 40 Afs. a seer. A ten-seer purchase of rice would be big, but fifty-to-one-hundred-seer purchases of wheat are common. A buyer does not buy wheat except in big lots. As a result, it is easier for the Arabs in the valley to personally contact farmers with a wheat surplus and buy directly. The sellers do not have to transport the wheat, and the buyers can move it at their convenience. Thus wheat transactions throughout the valley bypass the bazaar. This observation is readily confirmed by the location of the many mill houses where the grain is converted into flour as needed. Almost all of them are in outlying districts and not in the town itself. They work constantly. Most are powered by diesel engines, with the exhaust connected to a whistle that announces the location and operation of each mill. They mill far more wheat than is ever seen in the bazaar.

Beyond transport difficulties and private sales there are strong economic reasons for holding wheat. First, agricultural land is divided between wheat and cotton. Most landholders devote some land to each, and cotton meets their cash needs, wheat their subsistence demands. This mix allows a wheat surplus to develop without a need to sell it. Because of government "anti-hoarding" laws, there is no class of middlemen that attempts to extract this surplus for sale elsewhere because the government prohibits the private commercial storage of grain. Grain may be stored in large quantities in the villages, where it remains relatively isolated from market forces, but the government refuses to buy grain itself, depending on foreign aid to make up deficits. It is able to prohibit commercial storage of wheat by that small percentage of merchants who could potentially enter the trade, in part because the government owns the only modern silos in the country (Fry 1974: 51, 58, 116).

The best reason to hold wheat is as protection against the great fluctuation in wheat prices. As Figure 5 shows, the deviation of wheat prices is extremely erratic and encourages wheat accumulation. Sitting on wheat enables the holder to maintain a good standard of living—regardless of what happens to the market price. Although, as with sheep, there is an inflationary trend, the volatility in price is so great as to make taking cash risky in surplus years because its replacement cost may be double or triple that price the next year. The weather is such an unpredictable element that it makes sense for wheat farmers to store a surplus for their own consumption to smooth out the large imbalance in the pricing structure. For the farmer, wheat is a safer investment than cash, but for the pastoralist cash is far more stable than live sheep. The sale of sheep to the bazaar is therefore far more regular than wheat sales. From this analysis it would appear that the Arab nomads are far more integrated into the market economy than are the subsistence wheat farmers. Ironically, it is the Arab nomad who is far more dependent on urban markets for survival than the farmer, who in many ways is insulated from the money economy.

Relationship of the Nomadic Pastoralists to the Bazaar

One's overwhelming impression after watching the *bazaar-i-gusfand* for some time is that the nomads are tied far more closely to the market economy than are many of the valley's farmers. This is certainly true for wheat farming, although cotton cultivation is completely market oriented. The reason has to do with the nature of production and the storage of surpluses in the agricultural sphere. A farmer can store a grain crop almost indefinitely with little loss and low maintenance costs. Afghanistan is a very dry country, so rotting grain is not a problem. The nomadic pastoralist cannot store surplus sheep in a similar manner. Until they are sold, sheep are risky assets. There is always the possibility that the stock may die or be stolen. In addition, "surplus" stock must be actively watched over and fed at a cost to the owner. The farmer can lock a wheat surplus in a room and leave it; the nomad cannot do the same.

In Qataghan a pastoralist must sell sheep to raise money for basic needs. Whereas the farmer has a stock of wheat that can be drawn upon for daily needs, a pastoralist cannot draw on sheep directly to meet these needs, except for milk. It matters little whether one is selling *tokhalis* directly from the *ailoq* or full-grown *charis*—the Arabs raise sheep to sell, not to eat. Until the money is in hand, the pastoralist has no assured surplus. The price structure of the market encourages sheep sales because within the past ten years sheep have become quite valuable. Unlike the fluctuations of wheat prices, this trend upward has been far more stable. Within any year the deviation of sheep prices downward is small. Theoretically a pastoralist might save stock to sell at higher anticipated prices the next year—but the risk of losing the animals is so high that no one finds this worth the risk. What is worth the risk is holding a sheep until it becomes a *chari*. The increase in price each year justifies the risk:

Bara	800 Afs.
Tokhali	1,500 Afs.
Shishak	2,000 Afs.
Chari	3,000 Afs.

While these figures vary depending on the time of year and condition of the animals, the increases are large. A *tokhali* brings almost double the price of a spring lamb, while a *chari* is twice the price of a *tokhali*. Pastoralists who need money sell their *tokhalis*, thus making a large profit and avoiding future risk. Wealthier pastoralists try to hold onto their sheep and make the maximum profit by selling *charis*. As a result, *baras* and *shishaks* are not usually sold at the bazaar; if possible, the owner will hold them until they have reached a more profitable age. These increases are certain and worth aiming for; holding out for some future market is not, for the risk of stock loss would far outweigh the benefit.

The farmer, by contrast, does not put stored grain at risk by holding it. Conditions that hurt next year's crop have no effect on the stored surplus. Variation in wheat prices makes this a good conservative strategy. A farmer can wait to see how next year looks before making a decision. A pastoralist must act more quickly.

A chart of wheat prices from Kunduz shows just how much fluctuation there is (Figure 4). Whereas the price for sheep, when it drops, varies by about 10 percent, wheat prices vary by hundreds of percentage points. Within any given year animal prices normally fluctuate little, but the annual fluctuation of wheat prices would give even a hardened commodities trader an ulcer. We lack similarly detailed data on sheep prices, but some sketchy national data for a twenty-three-year period shows the different pattern (compare Figures 5 and 6).

In the 1960s the price of sheep skyrocketed in Qataghan. The reasons for this will be discussed in the next chapter. Here we need only note that meat prices have been rising steadily and year-to-year fluctuations are minor compared to those of wheat. This trend is continuing. While wheat has dropped from the drought-induced highs of the early 1970s, meat prices have stayed high. Although sheep raising is a riskier business than irrigated agriculture, in one respect it is more stable—the value of stock has risen constantly (with only minor declines) while wheat prices have risen at times to great heights only to fall to new lows. It might also be pointed out here that cotton prices—fixed by the government—have traditionally been set far below the world market rate and thus, while dependable, do not yield the kinds of profits farmers desire. The one exception to this generally rosy picture of sheep raising is the drought in the early 1970s, which destroyed animals in many regions and caused prices to fall as nomads sold animals at giveaway prices in some places. But this did not apply to Qataghan, where adequate water supplies protected nomadic pastoralists from major loss. In fact, some evidence indicates that Qataghanis bought up cheap sheep from drought-stricken areas.

The Arabs in Qataghan are integrated into the bazaar through the sale of live animals to the urban meat market. Since they buy wheat and other goods with the cash they obtain, they can be said to have a symbiotic relation to the agricultural valleys. But this observation is not adequate—all nomads in Afghanistan have some sort of symbiotic relationship with farmers. It is the differences that are important. The distinction between pastoralists who sell live animals and those who derive their income from the sale of pastoral by-products like wool, butter, skins, or cheese is not often made. Those selling live animals have very different problems in marketing, storage, and maintenance. Because they cannot subdivide sheep, they must find a place to sell them in numbers. Even here there is a difference between nomads who market their sheep through agents and those who sell directly in the market. In any event these pastoralists are part of the cash economy. Trade in butter, cheese, and wool, on the other hand, is more amenable to barter and piecemeal exchange.

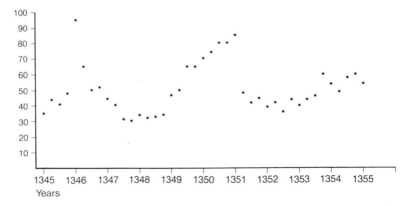

Afghanis per seer

Figure 4. Quarterly wheat prices in Kunduz from 1345 A.H. (1966–
1967 A.D.) to 1355 A.H. (1976–1977 A.D.). *Source*: Afghanistan Bank,
unpublished figures.

These products can be stored without great danger of loss. A third
type of pastoralist engages in selling *qarakul* skins—a cash
activity par excellence. Here trade is dependent on international
fashion, government regulations, and various wholesale buyers.

The relationship of a nomadic pastoralist to the market in
Afghanistan is varied. The Arabs, and later the Pashtuns, in
Qataghan have developed an urban-oriented pastoralism that
takes advantage of permanent winter villages close to urban
centers. Their strategy has not been applicable to all nomadic
pastoralists, but in their adaptation to ecological conditions,
marketing opportunities, and choice of pastoral specialty, they are
engaged in a larger range of activities than is often suspected.
This is not a recent phenomenon, as was demonstrated in
Chapter 1. An old Arab woman described to me how her father
had taken sheep to Bukhara for sale before there was a market in
Qataghan, and had returned with a bag of silver tangas, which,
she remembered, he used to jingle to the delight of his children.
Traditionally sheep have been perceived by the Arabs as "cash on
the hoof." Their traditional market connections and attitudes
toward their sheep laid the groundwork for a change to the
completely commercialized production of livestock in Qataghan.

Afghanis per seer

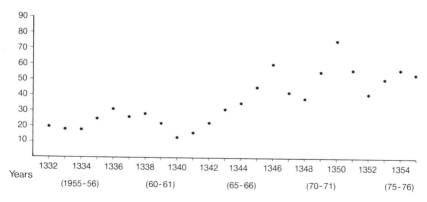

Figure 5. Afghan wheat prices: national averages from 1332 A.H.
(1953–1954 A.D.) to 1355 A.H. (1976–1977 A.D.). *Sources: Survey of
Progress, 1960–1961* (Kabul: Ministry of Planning); *Survey of Progress,
1961–1962* (Kabul: Ministry of Planning); *Survey of Progress, 1964–1965*
(Kabul: Ministry of Planning); Etienne 1972: 276; U.N. 1978.

Afghanis per seer

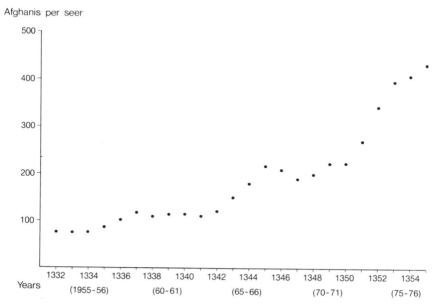

Figure 6. Afghan mutton prices: national averages from 1332 A.H.
(1953–1954 A.D.) to 1355 A.H. (1976–1977 A.D.). *Sources:* Same as for
Figure 5.

The Migration

When the nomads of Qataghan leave for the mountains, they all
go together. Masses of sheep followed by strings of camels move
into the mountains of Badakhshan. Nomads from Imam Saheb
head for Darwaz; those from southern Qataghan move toward
Lake Shiwa. There are only a limited number of trails and passes,
so the nomads move as a fluid stream on a predictable course.
Although the migration lasts for only three weeks, a profitable
relationship is established between the nomads and certain
villages through which they pass.

There is a certain amount of conflict between villagers and
nomads over potential or actual damage to crops. The amount of
this damage is actually quite small because the nomads are
careful to keep their animals out of fields. The problem is most
often caused by farmers who insist on planting over what they
know is the main trail of the migration and then complain about
their wheat being trampled. The nomads maintain, justifiably,
that the hill farmers continually try to expand their fields into
any open space, making transit, let alone camping, difficult. The
other conflict is over pasture. The nomads push their animals
through as fast as possible in the spring, and each herd does very
little grazing until it reaches the mountains. Nevertheless,
hundreds of thousands of sheep are moving through, and farmers
have a litany: "You are only here for a day, but we have to use this
pasture all the time." They then try to convince the nomads to
move on by claiming that a better spot is just above, or that no
nomads have camped here, ever. The nomads usually ignore this.
If they are Pashtun nomads, they just look mean and the farmers
disappear. Arabs have a less fierce reputation and will generally
give the complainers a cup of rice, which satisfies them.

In spite of these small disputes the Tajik farmers service the
migration. The main business at places where nomads usually
stop is selling fodder. The Tajiks go and cut a donkey-load of
fodder, which they sell to the nomads for 15 Afs. The nomads are
pleased that they don't have to worry about grazing their transport animals and find it a bargain. The Tajiks make some money
and keep the nomads from running their animals all over the
place. Some Tajiks even rent fallow fields in the spring for
grazing. In the fall everything is harvested, and nomads move
where they please at no cost. After the fodder sellers come the
petty traders. They trade dried fruit or cooked chick-peas for
equal weight of camel's wool. This trade is especially popular

with children, who often take a knife to their father's camel and trade the wool they cut. Some camels get completely plucked in this manner. The traders also sell things like needles, iridescent bobby pins, and jew's harps. In the morning, when the nomads leave, small children often come to sweep up dung to take home for fuel.

At major mountain passes where nomads must camp together there are temporary bazaars. On the trail to Darwaz the first is at the entrance to Manzel Dasht near Shahr-i-bozorg, the second at Yobun in Rogh. These bazaars last only about two weeks. These temporary bazaars are like great fairs. At Yobun the space is extremely limited, so the nomads are camped quite close together. Next to them are four white tents housing Tajik traders. They sell shepherd staffs (a specialty of the region), eggs, candy, fresh and dried mulberries, tea, kerosene, medicine, sewing stuff, cloth, oil, shoes, boots, and condoms (used mostly as balloons)—everything in fact that is needed to re-equip a nomad family. The nomads enjoy these fairs, drink a lot of tea, and visit. The next day they leave and are replaced by a new set of nomads. Two weeks later there is not a sign of this trade. After leaving these temporary bazaars the nomads enter their *ailoqs* in the high mountains.

Highland Badakhshan

The economic structure of the valleys, with their irrigated agriculture, export crops, roads, and markets, stands in sharp contrast to that of the mountainous areas. These mountain areas depend on rainfall agriculture (*lalmi*), lack roads and markets, and are almost completely subsistence oriented. Villages are isolated; in some cases it is a week's walk to the nearest bazaar. Cash is a scarce commodity, and barter still plays an important economic role. This is the *ailoq* region, the summer pasture area for the nomads of Qataghan.

The nomads are an important, if only seasonal, force in Badakhshan. They act as links between the lowlands and highlands, and so are able to take advantage of regional differences. In the mountainous districts of Badakhshan the nomads have entered into a symbiotic relationship with the hill farmers which economically benefits both groups. Socially, however, there is a wide gap between the mountain Tajiks and the nomads. While much of this discussion will be applicable to either Pashtun or Arab nomads, the specific cases will view the interaction from the Arab perspective. The Arabs dislike the Tajiks, who usually return the sentiment, and yet it is necessary to reach some kind of modus vivendi. As we shall see, this balance is struck situationally, and in the course of an afternoon I observed everything from complete hostility to an open welcome. The focus of this section will be on the social interaction and its economic roots.

Arabs in the Ailoq

The Tajiks in the mountains of Badakhshan are a transhumant agricultural people. They raise mainly wheat and barley on their land along with goats and cattle. Extremely isolated even by Afghan standards, they cannot easily dispose of what surplus they do produce. The nomads, moving into the heart of this region, thus provide an important market to the Tajiks as major consumers of wheat. Unlike the lowland pattern, transactions are personal and take place outside the market structure. If in the winter nomads are involved in complex market-mediated exchanges, in the summer they engage in personal nonmarket transactions.

In preparing to go to the *ailoq*, the Arabs buy enough rice to see them through the summer. Rice is comparatively cheap in Imam Saheb but unavailable and still a luxury item in mountainous Badakhshan. The Arabs do not carry wheat into the mountains but rather purchase it locally. The large numbers of nomads in the mountains create a large demand, and this is a boon to the wheat-growing areas. In a year with good or average rainfall the Tajiks manage to produce large surpluses because they cultivate as much land as possible on the theory that if it is a poor year their extensive planting will yield an adequate return. The Arabs from Imam Saheb spending the summer in Badakhshan depend on the subprovince of Rogh to supply them with wheat. Darwaz is traditionally a grain-deficit area, so nomads summering there often travel two or three days south into Rogh to buy grain. If the harvest has failed, the nomads have the baggage animals to make the long trip to Rustaq, where grain is always available.

Wheat, bulky to transport, is virtually unexportable over the rough mountain trails. Since the nomads buy on the spot and have the animals to carry the wheat away, the Tajiks are able to sell their wheat despite the lack of markets and transport. In exchange for the wheat the nomads supply a valuable commodity—cash.

A wheat transaction is conducted on an individual basis. A nomad takes his donkeys and goes to a village that is known to have a surplus. This information is obtained by asking other nomads or Tajiks or just going from village to village. The nomad and the farmer haggle over the quality and price until they reach an agreement. This transaction, though personal, is not necessarily a friendly one. Arabs and Tajiks have little good to say about one another but do have a mutual interest in seeing that a transaction is made. Both sides are likely to do small things that indicate lack of respect. Two Arabs went off to a village to buy wheat and purchased fifty seers at 37½ Afs. per seer, which they felt was a remarkably good price. However, one of the Arabs complained that the good-for-nothing Tajik had not even offered them tea.

Large quantities are bought at one time so that wheat buying has to be done only once or twice a summer. The Arabs clean the wheat of dirt and stones and take some of it to a local water mill near their summer camps. The Tajiks do the milling as well as supply the wheat. Usually about ten seers at a time are milled so that the wheat flour will be fresh until baked. The miller receives one-twentieth of the flour as a fee. The process of wheat buying and milling keeps someone from camp moving fairly regularly between the *ailoq* and the villages. Relations with nearby villages having mills is much more cordial and friendly than with the more distant villages from which the nomads buy wheat.

The mountain villages of Badakhshan engage in subsistence agriculture. They are not tied into the money economy. Yet there are goods like salt, ironware, tea, and cloth that must be purchased with cash from a distant bazaar. Villagers make the long trip to the major bazaars of Rustaq or Faizabad once or twice during the summer. The nomad market is cultivated because it easily supplies the cash to take along to these markets. That is, surplus grain gets converted into money which can be used in the bazaar. The nomads, knowing of the Badakhshi's desperate need for cash, bring enough money—in small bills—to meet their summer expenses. For the nomads, coming from Qataghan where cash is plentiful, this presents no problem. The result is that in mountainous Badakhshan one can buy almost anything for cash, which is especially valued by the Badakhshi, but one can *sell* almost nothing to the Badakhshi for cash. They are willing to barter, but not to buy. They do not want to waste money's transferability on a nonbazaar transaction. This was brought home to me when some Arabs told me I could make a big profit selling my shotgun to the Tajiks. I complained that the Tajiks were too poor to have the money to buy it. Ghulam Sakhi, who did a lot of business with Tajiks, corrected me. "Some Tajiks are very rich, but they don't like to buy with cash; they like to trade." Being poor and not having money were not the same thing.

Selling wheat to the nomads for cash is the most important aspect of the Arab-Tajik relation in terms of the number of people involved. Also of importance to the Tajiks is the barter trade for sheep and goats conducted in the mountains. Unlike the Pashtuns in the Hazarajat, the Arabs are not trading nomads (Ferdinand 1962). They are not unmindful of the potential gain but prefer to barter as a sideline. They do not extend credit for goods; a barter transaction is complete in itself.

The bartering market centers around the Tajik goats and sheep. The Tajiks raise many animals, but because of harsh winter conditions the number they can maintain is severely limited. Some of the animals are for household use. Cows provide milk and replenish the supply of oxen for plowing, but are of no interest to the nomads. Goats in large numbers and some sheep are the mainstay of the Tajiks' animal trade with the nomads.

The Arabs take advantage of two things in their trade with the Tajiks: the expensiveness of all goods imported into the province and the cheap prices of Tajik livestock. Most Tajiks lack the means to sell their livestock in lowland markets because the few stock they have to sell would never justify the long journey. Thus an Arab buyer can quickly buy up goats from many individual households and collect a sizable herd. Part of this trade is conducted in cash. A particular Arab buyer from Imam Saheb brought 100,000 Afs. into the mountains to buy Tajik sheep and goats. Although goats are small in comparison to Arab sheep, he paid 300–400 Afs. per goat and expected to sell them in Imam Saheb for 1,000 Afs. apiece. Most of his herd was "door stock," goats raised by the women of the household. To show me, he called out a few common names for goats and many of them responded.

A larger profit can be made in barter deals than with cash. Typically the Arab brings an expensive item from the bazaar and strikes a deal with a wealthy Tajik. In one such transaction a .22 caliber rifle was exchanged for seven sheep of various types. The rifle was valued at what it would cost in Badakhshan, which is considerably more than it had cost in Imam Saheb, and the number of sheep exchanged were also valued at the lower Badakhshan rate. Thus the nomad makes an initial profit from the first trade which is then easily doubled by selling the sheep at

Imam Saheb prices. Other Arabs trade horses and donkeys to the Tajiks. Tajik horses and donkeys are considered inferior to those from Qataghan. Tajiks pay up to 50 percent more for the same animal in Badakhshan than an Arab pays in Imam Saheb. Payment is taken in sheep or goats, which are sold in the lowlands at a high profit. While much of the trade is in the hands of large buyers, small herd owners and even shepherds engage in buying or bartering for a few sheep as a quick way to make some money. Because of this shepherds demand some of their wages in advance so that they can speculate on Tajik livestock.

The nomads are able to engage in this trade because their own herds are nearby in the mountains. They can easily accommodate the sheep they have obtained and fatten them up in their *ailoq*. At the end of the summer when the nomads return to the lowlands, it is no extra work for them to include the Tajik animals in their own herd. The Tajiks, although aware of the large profits the Arabs make, are satisfied to trade their surplus animals for which there is no other easy market.

Arab *ailoqs* lie directly above Tajik villages. The Arabs as owners of these *ailoqs* try to maintain cordial relations with the closest villages because they are constantly passing through and use village facilities like water mills. In spite of general animosity between villagers and nomads, individual Tajiks and Arabs often become "friends." A village friend (*rafiq*) relationship is initiated by the Tajik, who approaches the Arab with an invitation for tea and bread. As a rule, both Tajiks and Arabs only grudgingly extend each other hospitality, and may even refuse altogether, and this invitation marks an exception to the rule. The Arab from that time on stops at the *rafiq*'s house for the night on the way to and from the *ailoq*. This relationship is personal and not transferable. I was in the company of an Arab who had a village friend at whose house we stayed the night. Traveling with us were five other Arabs, who spent the night on the outskirts of the village where we rejoined them at dawn. They were not welcome at this house. A Tajik who initiates a *rafiq* relationship must have a surplus of bread and tea and a guest house to accommodate people. The Tajik we stayed with had entertained my Arab friend for over thirty years. In return the Arab does favors for the Tajik. Because nomads make a number of trips to Faizabad during the summer and have many baggage animals, the Tajik will ask his friend to bring him some small things like cloth or a suit of clothes for which he gives money. The Arab provides the goods at cost and makes delivery on his return. Although favors done on both sides are rather small, they are highly valued. The Arab has an assured place to sleep and eat near his *ailoq*, which may still be a half day's walk away, in an area noted for its lack of hospitality, and the Tajik gets small goods that would otherwise require a major trip. As a result most Arabs have a village friend in one place or another.

Relationships established in the mountains also link the Tajiks to the lowland economy. The winter in Badakhshan is quite harsh, and villagers are trapped in their houses for months on end. Many young men leave the mountains before the snows to seek work in Qataghan. Having a friend who lives in a village there is a good way to find work. Many Arab herd owners hire Tajiks for winter labor, and the Tajiks get these jobs by means of such a friendship. The Arab friend not only introduces the Tajik to the employer, but also negotiates the wages to make sure that the Tajik is not cheated. Close connections between Arab and Tajik families are sometimes reinforced by marriage connections, although only in one direction—the Arabs will marry Tajik women but refuse to marry Arab women to Tajiks.

Wealthy Tajiks play host to many Arabs who have large flocks in the region. They store provisions for them and feed their shepherds when they pass through. At this level information and prestige are the most important considerations. These Tajiks make frequent trips to the lowlands and want to have the friendship of men with influence there. In addition they can order luxury goods from the lowlands which the nomads can deliver during the migration. In one case a rich Tajik ordered a large carpet from the lowlands which, when duly delivered, provided a large profit to the Arab who bought it for him.

Salt Trade

Both Arabs and Tajiks must buy salt for themselves and their animals. It is the salt trade that is the catalyst forcing people to make the long and difficult trip to Faizabad. As explained in Chapter 2, salt is quite expensive in Badakhshan. It is also hard to transport because only pack horses and donkeys can use the narrow mountain trails. Consequently, nomads may make two or three trips to Faizabad in order to obtain all the salt they need. Some Arabs specialize in this trade and act as regional wholesalers to other Arabs. Although they may occasionally sell to Tajiks, the Arabs cannot possibly meet their requirements, so the Tajiks themselves must also go to Faizabad or Rustaq.

The salt trade is the backbone of the Faizabad bazaar. Salt

imported by truck from Taloqan is sold in large blocks or coarsely ground. The Tajik farmers are basically self-sufficient. Were it not for their need to obtain salt, they could avoid the market entirely—or at least for long periods of time. Once in Faizabad they use the opportunity to buy cloth, kerosene, matches, iron tools, and other goods available only in the bazaar. The nomads buy only salt, since they consider everything there overpriced. As noted earlier, it is for the bazaar transactions in Faizabad that cash is necessary, and this produces the great interest among the Tajiks in trading with the nomads.

The Faizabad bazaar is by the standards of the mountain Tajiks the epitome of the money-oriented world of the market. Food is bought and sold, items are available only for cash purchase, and there are trucks to be seen. But the Faizabad bazaar betrays its subsistence orientation and lack of articulation with the rest of the Afghan economy. First, a whole sector of the bazaar is devoted to salt. Salt is sold in all Afghan bazaars, but in Faizabad it plays a dominant role. Second, there is no equivalent to the *bazaar-i-gusfand* of Imam Saheb. Very little livestock is marketed in Faizabad. It is difficult to buy or sell animals there. The overwhelming impression is that very little of the hinterland's products come to Faizabad. The market there caters only to the needs of people who have very little cash to spend. A survey of business conditions in Afghan towns revealed that the only place which "appeared less prosperous than reported in the past and whose inhabitants indicated that business conditions had deteriorated" was Faizabad (Fry 1974: 48).

5. The Commercialization of Pastoralism and Its Impact on the Arabs

In 1965 the Arabs and other nomadic pastoralists in Qataghan made a major structural change in the organization of the pastoral economy. This was to replace the traditional in-kind payment for labor with cash wages. The change was made within a single year by all ethnic groups as a response to the sudden doubling of sheep prices. Payment in kind had been a major bulwark in maintaining familial subsistence-oriented pastoralism. Its abolition had a profound impact on the economic and social organization of Arab pastoralism. In the ten years following this change, many families stopped migrating and yet were supported by the pastoral economy; sheep raising became commercialized to the extent of supporting absentee sheep-lords; the value of women's labor declined; and economic stratification became more rigid.

To understand these changes we must look in two directions. First, there were factors outside the Arabs' control that created and maintained the sudden price increases that caused the Arabs to reorganize their traditional labor relations, based on the family, into a commercial enterprise, based on hired shepherd teams. These exogenous factors involve political and economic developments within Afghanistan, international political conflicts, and increased trade within the region, all of which not only were beyond the Arabs' control, but also were largely unknown to them. Nevertheless, the Arabs responded to these pressures, which were measured by something they were extremely conscious of—sheep prices. In part these changes were the indirect result of various development projects with results that were more profound than the planners realized, especially when changes were disguised in traditional nomadic garb and were not recorded by econometric surveys.

A second set of factors was internal. The structural response to the outside pressures was logically to change from in-kind payments to cash wages because wages were the last major noncommercialized feature of the pastoral economy. Having made this change, the system itself dynamically responded to the new factor. Decisions that had been made by rote were remade in light of the new situation. The importance of the in-kind payments to the traditional familial pastoralism was highlighted by its absence. Its abolition triggered much that had been latent in a system which preadapted pastoralism in Qataghan to commercialization. The Arabs gradually became the sheep ranchers of Qataghan.

Background

Qataghan has always been a fertile region, but it had no way to effectively market its surpluses:

> As for grain its production in this country is limited by its being all but unsaleable. Any man who choses may have ground to cultivate on the condition of paying one-eighth of the produce to the Amir. A rupee buys a large bag of wheat weighing more than two cwt English, and in many places two bags can be had for the money. Barley is still cheaper, rice two rupees a bag. Flour ½ cwt a rupee. There is probably no country on earth in which life can be supported cheaper and better. Though money is scarce there is no absolute poverty. I have now been here for three months and I have never seen a man in rags. (Burnes et al. 1839: 131)

By comparison, prices were much higher in Kabul at the same time:

For one rupee	Kabul	Turkestan
Wheat	8 seers	20 seers
Barley	9 seers	24 seers

(Burnes et al. 1839: 28)

This price differential between Kabul and Qataghan continued, with Kabul prices two and one-half to three times greater from the 1830s until the opening of the Salang Pass in 1964 (Vavilov and Bukinich 1929: 609; Schurmann 1962: 405–410). After this time grain prices varied randomly with no region having consistently higher or lower prices (Fry 1974: 58–59). Obviously transport was a critical restraint on the economy of Qataghan.

In spite of this restraint, a period of spectacular development had occurred in the twenty years between 1935 and 1955. As described in Chapter 1 during this period development was financed by private Afghan capital, and the swamps of Qataghan became the major cotton producing region in Afghanistan. Export of this cotton to the Soviet Union did not require good roads. Despite an unpaved road through the Hindu Kush via the Shibar Pass, Qataghan during this period was not closely linked to Kabul. This provincial development gave Qataghan a light industrial base that became the economic focus of the region. But development in Qataghan was striking in large part simply because it occurred nowhere else in the country. The province grew rich, but its economy was not integrated into the national economy, nor was its full agricultural potential exploited.

This first phase of development produced few changes among the Arabs. Pastoralism did not benefit greatly from the regional growth. The increased immigration of Pashtuns and increased land cultivation were in fact viewed negatively by the Arabs. It was a second stage of development that created a transportation infrastructure that had an impact quite as large as the creation of private pastures in the 1920s.

In 1953 the Afghan government took control of half the stock in the Spinzar Cotton Company, which had developed Qataghan (Fry 1974: 88–89). This action marked the beginning of state capitalism in Afghanistan, often defensively referred to as "socialism" by the government. This action gave the state the profits of a completed enterprise, for no real effort was put into the region by the government after that. But after 1955 foreign aid began to come to Afghanistan. These projects, while often spectacular failures at producing internal development, as in the case of Hilmand Valley, provided a transportation infrastructure that benefited Qataghan more than any other region outside of Kabul itself. It was through these projects that Qataghan became more integrated into the Afghan national economy, and this drew pastoral production out of its subsistence orientation and into the cash economy in a big way.

Reasons for the Rise in Sheep Prices

Also critical to the economy were the increased sheep prices in Qataghan and the strong impact they had on nomadic pastoralists there. Four factors were responsible. (1) The economy of Qataghan was more commercially oriented than that of other provinces even before the arrival of international aid projects. (2) Road building projects linked Qataghan with the rest of Afghanistan and the Soviet Union. (3) There was an increase in disposable income in the country as a result of foreign aid. (4) International sheep smuggling to meet foreign demand kept prices high.

It is not possible to completely separate these factors except for ease of discussion. In reality it was their simultaneous application to Qataghan that caused the sudden increase in the value of sheep. These factors were external to the Arabs, but, like the Treaty of 1895 that allowed the Arabs to exploit the pastures of Darwaz, they had a direct effect on the Arabs. While the Arabs were concerned only with sheep prices, a barometer of the economy, we must look at the changing market patterns that created this new climate.

Preadaptation of Qataghan to Commercial Development

The first stage of development in Qataghan made it the most commercially oriented of all Afghan provinces. It was the major exporter of cotton and domestic producer of rice. In the pastoral economy the large number of Qarakuli sheep in the province was important because their lamb skins were the major export item of Afghanistan to the world economy. By today's standards production was not large, but it made both farmers and pastoralists far more commercially oriented than those in other parts of the country. Qataghan was part of the cash economy when most of Afghanistan depended on subsistence farming and barter trade.

The Arabs in Qataghan traditionally marketed their sheep in urban markets. This meant that they, and later the Pashtuns who followed their example, were tied into the market economy even when the returns on sheep were rather low. Any change in the market, therefore, had a direct impact on the Arabs. Qataghan was an area of surplus, and sheep prices remained quite low. By the 1930s the Arabs' traditional market in Bukhara was closed to them by the Soviet Union, and internally the Afghan economy did not provide adequate replacement. Sales on the bazaar provided adequate income, but at low prices sheep were like a subsistence crop. If the demand increased and marketing facilities became available, it was only natural to assume that the same sheep might begin to more closely resemble the other cash crops of Qataghan.

Road Building

A basic problem facing Qataghan, as well as the rest of Afghanistan, was its poor roads. The roads built in the 1930s had been mere graveled tracks. This was a tremendous improvement over the donkey trails that had existed before, but these roads were often impassable due to rain and snow and did not permit large-scale commerce. Describing the economic conditions up until the early 1960s, one analyst noted, "The economic organization of Afghanistan resembles a wide sea dotted with islands of economic activity, each more or less limited to its own local market primarily because of inadequate transportation" (Wilber 1962: 62).

This state of affairs might have continued indefinitely had it not been for the Cold War competition between the Soviet Union and the United States. Afghanistan, in a familiar role as a strategic neutral state, played on the fears and ambitions of both power blocs. In the twenty years following 1953 Afghanistan collected over a billion dollars in various types of aid. Of greatest importance, Afghanistan acquired a fine paved-road system including, in 1964, the Salang Pass, which made traffic over the Hindu Kush a year-round affair.

Admittedly the routes and capacity of the system were greatly affected by the strategic interests of the Great Powers. The Soviet Union was interested in north-south links, the United States in east-west links. Afghanistan therefore got a complete road circling the country except between Herat and Maimana, where neither the United States nor the Soviet Union was interested. An unfortunate side effect of this massive aid was the unwillingness of the Afghan government to invest its own funds in building secondary roads that would link the hinterland with the main roads (Fry 1974: 58). The road to Faizabad was one of the worst in Afghanistan, often closed and dangerous when open. But in 1976, when a Ministry of Planning official was asked when a new road would be constructed to connect Faizabad with a new Soviet-built road terminating in Kishem, he replied, "As soon as the Russians or the United Nations want to build it." Even in Imam Saheb, a dirt road to the port of Shir Khan, situated at one end of the valley, was not constructed until 1975, and then as an adjunct to a Soviet project to stabilize the banks of the Amu River.

Despite a lack of interest in secondary road development, Afghanistan was for the first time directly linked internationally and internally. Between 1959 and 1968 import prices fell 40 percent, while export prices rose 15 percent (U.N. 1971: 37). The transport bottleneck that had been strangling Qataghan was loosened. The effect on internal prices was dramatic: "In 1961 wheat prices in the most expensive towns were 150% higher than the cheapest towns. Thanks to improvement in transport facilities price differentials fell to about 30% by 1966" (U.N. 1971: 24).

Qataghan also increased its competitive advantage over more remote areas like Badakhshan, which the roads bypassed. These more remote areas suffered as traditional forms of trade and transport became noncompetitive. Fry even argues that the famines in 1971 and 1972 were due not to a lack of grain but to a transport cost structure that did not encourage wheat exports to the remote, hard-hit provinces (1974: 58).

Transport to remote places was discouraged, but from Qataghan bulky and perishable commodities were now shipped easily. Melons, famous all over Afghanistan, became an important cash crop. They were bought by the truckload and shipped to Kabul and Pakistan within forty-eight hours. In the past they had been unexportable; in 1975 three plane-loads were shipped to Kuwait to open up the lucrative Persian Gulf market. This ease of transport has even affected sheep marketing. Large numbers of *charis* are shipped by truck to regional centers so they can be disposed of in large lots, at premium prices.

Foreign Aid Money

Along with the road building and other projects came money. Thus, just as Qataghan was finally able to export its surpluses, the Afghan economy was more than ready to absorb them. Residents of Kabul and other fortunate areas found their disposable incomes rising. Imports increased drastically, fueled by the inflow of foreign aid (Fry 1974: 215). Internally this increased disposable income was put into a higher standard of living by upgrading the diet with more rice and meat—both exports of Qataghan. This trend, especially with ever higher demands for meat with higher disposable incomes, is a continuing feature of the Afghan economy. The Republican seven-year plan issued in 1976 explained:

> Demand for animal products is elastic and the magnitude of this elasticity in Afghanistan has been estimated at unity. In other words demand for meat and other animal products goes up in the same proportion as increase in per capita income. Furthermore, the population expansion and increase in income have raised the level of this demand and have enhanced the level of consumption of animal products. (Ministry of Planning 1355 A.H.: 87)

The increased demand and the ability to easily ship goods from Qataghan did not cause prices in Kabul to fall, but raised the prices of surplus regions to parity. This bonanza to the producers in Qataghan was marked by the sudden doubling of sheep prices in 1965, shortly after the completion of all-weather Salang Pass. The result was dramatic. Sheep worth 500–1,000 Afs. were now selling for 1,000–2,000 Afs. Sheep, the Arabs said, had become "very expensive." Nor was this the end. Prices in the next ten years continued to rise another 50 percent—not as dramatically as in 1965, but enough to make sheep a "growth stock," so to speak.

Export Demand

The initial rise in sheep prices may be explained by better transport and increased internal demand. The continuing rise of sheep prices, at a rate far faster than that of inflation, was due in large part to external markets, especially Iran. Technically the export of livestock was forbidden, but this did not prevent a lively export trade involving millions of sheep. Even official trade figures showed that trade in livestock commodities, 90 percent sheep-related, accounted for 30 percent of all foreign exchange earned by Afghanistan (Ministry of Planning 1355 A.H.: 86). As large as this recorded trade was, smuggling to Iran, and to a lesser extent Pakistan, has had a much greater effect on maintaining high sheep prices. Exports to Iran rose at an ever increasing rate:

> In 1970–71 the number of sheep on the hoof coming into the country from Australia and South America rose to between 250,000–300,000. Experts claim that for every live sheep legally imported in 1970–71, two or three were being unlawfully brought in from Afghanistan and Turkey . . . (Black 1976: 403–404)

This substantial demand leveled off for a while only to rise to greater heights when

> . . . between 1971 and 1975 rapid growth of Iranian cities and urban per capita income caused prices paid to the producer for mutton to progress by more than 150%. (Ibid.)

This external demand kept prices high even in areas like Qataghan, where no smuggling occurred. It is difficult to estimate the present size of the illegal export trade, but it is clear that the Arabs and other nomadic pastoralists in Afghanistan benefited indirectly from the rising price of meat in Iran.

The Change to Cash Wages

The response of the Arabs to increased sheep prices was to stop paying for pastoral labor with ewes and to pay cash wages instead. This response is not hard to understand. In many ways pastoralism in Qataghan has been "rationalized" to a remarkable degree for quite some time. Pasture was privately owned, and sheep were sold to an urban market for cash. The only nonmonetarized sector of pastoralism was labor. When prices rose, the impact was immediate because the Arabs were already tied closely to the bazaar. The remaining part of the traditional system that came under strain was labor payments. The sudden rise in the price of sheep brought forth the contradictory aspects of sheep as units of value in themselves and sheep as commodities for sale. The Arabs had in fact long viewed sheep as commodities, but as long as the value of the sheep in money and the value of a shepherd's labor remained equivalent, the system stayed intact. When the value became disproportionate the rich pastoralists used the opportunity to destroy the old system, which had ramifications beyond the equivalency of a money wage to a certain number of sheep.

The Arabs felt the problem more deeply than other pastoralists since they paid for labor with ewes, whereas Pashtuns paid in lambs. But pastoralists throughout the region switched over to cash wages because they all agreed that sheep had become "too expensive" to be used as payment for labor. Underlying this was a market-oriented strategy of the wealthy pastoralists who wanted to make sure that the increased surplus value in the sheep went to them.

The change came about quickly and without much protest for several reasons. First, the number of herd owners employing shepherds was not very large, since the only labor hired was whatever the family could not supply. Because they all made the decision at the same time, each herd owner argued that everyone else was changing too. In justifying this change herd owners used a "fair price" argument. They maintained that a shepherd under the old system had been paid so many ewes for a six-month contract. Now, they said, in only one year the price of sheep had doubled, and the shepherd could expect only the "fair price" for his labor. This would be the cash value of the traditional number of sheep based on last year's prices, and thus the shepherd would make the same as the year before. Finally, this argument was successful because Qataghan in general and the Arabs in particular were highly monetarized by Afghan standards. Sheep had been perceived by shepherds and owners as money before the change took place. Money and sheep were equivalents, and money was the universal scale of conversion. Even when bartering, the Arabs translated first into money and then back into goods to determine the rate of exchange. Seeing sheep as commodities also emphasized the Arabs' local reputation as stingy people. An Uzbek pastoralist once bragged to me about the large number of sheep he had slaughtered to entertain guests. He contrasted himself to a rich Arab herd owner who, with three thousand sheep, had slaughtered only six, while he, with a herd of six hundred, had slaughtered sixty. An Arab who heard this story later admitted Arabs were stingy, but commented sarcastically that it was better to sell a sheep at the bazaar for a couple of thousand Afghanis, and then on the way home to buy a couple of hundred Afghanis' worth of meat from the butcher to feed guests. The equation of sheep and money was accepted by both shepherd and herd owner. It gave moral justification to a change that was in any event inevitable with the rising price of sheep and the greater economic power of the herd owners vis-à-vis the shepherds.

Changing over to cash wages was not seen as a strategic change in the nature of pastoralism, only as a tactical solution to an immediate problem. Since the rate of pay was the same as in the previous year, there was no real difference between cash and sheep. Or was there? In fact, ewes were quite different from money. They were the pastoralists' capital. In taking payment in ewes, a shepherd not only got paid for his work; he acquired the necessary capital to build his independence from his employer. With cash payments a shepherd remained in the wage labor market with only a remote chance of acquiring the necessary ewes to become an independent herd owner. Cash wages were the means by which a pastoral proletariat came into being.

The shepherds accepted the new conditions because there was little they could do about the rapidly changing nature of the sheep market. In addition, many of them did not seem to grasp how fundamental a change had been made. In the short term, the number of shepherding jobs increased as large herd owners replaced their families with teams of hired shepherds to do the herding.

Commercialization of the Pastoral Economy

The move to cash wages removed the last obstacle to the commercialization of pastoralism in Qataghan. Pastoral investment was open to anyone with money—pasture, labor, and sheep could all be acquired with cash. Tribal affiliation or previous experience as a pastoral nomad was not required. Familial subsistence-oriented pastoralism now came into direct competition with a form of profit-oriented commercial ranching. Within ten years after the change to cash wages, the commercial enterprises had come to dominate pastoralism in the region.

Familial subsistence-oriented pastoralism differs qualitatively from commercial ranching even though both depend on market sales. Although the subsistence-oriented system depends on cash sales, it uses family labor to the utmost and takes full advantage of pastoral by-products like milk and wool. Hired labor is only an adjunct to this system, and "profits" from sheep cannot be usefully measured. Like Chayanov's peasant producers (Sahlins 1972: 87–92), the family's labor has no monetary cost, and even when a sheep dies the family gets to eat it. This traditional system is still maintained by owners of forty to two hundred sheep. With private pasture and good prices they survive as a sort of middle-class nomad, but in importance they have been replaced more and more by commercial operations.

Commercial ranching is raising sheep for sale on the market to make a profit, using teams of shepherds to take care of the sheep. It is a business in which subsistence activities are ignored because owners are interested only in the cash value of their sheep. Milk production in a commercial operation serves only to feed the shepherds and thereby reduce the food costs of the owner. If the shepherd shears the Turki sheep of a commercial herd, he can keep the wool. The owner is not interested in it. Finally, a commercial operation demands much more from its hired labor, with a longer time in the mountains than families spend there and with no tents provided. Shepherds live under conditions far harsher than those to which a family would be subjected. In commercial pastoralism the notion of profit is explicit and can be calculated because everything has a money cost.

Before cash wages, specialized shepherd camps were rare among the Arabs because of the high cost in ewes and consequent capital drain. The larger the herd got beyond the capacity of the owner, the slower the herd's growth rate. Changing over to cash wages profoundly altered this situation. First, the absolute cost of wages was reduced in terms of sheep. The price of sheep doubled while wages remained the same, thereby reducing the effective cost of labor. More important, when payment was not in ewes, the relationship between hired labor and capital loss was eliminated. Labor costs were now money costs that were subtracted from profits like any other cost. The herd owner's capital remained untouched. Large herd owners got a double benefit from the decline in the cost of labor relative to the value of sheep and the ability to separate labor costs from capital gains. The previous brake on the growth rate of large herds was no more. Wealthy pastoralists quickly understood this, switched over completely to shepherd teams, and stopped migrating with their families. On the other hand, shepherds not only lost ground on a percentage basis; they lost the means of acquiring ewes. In the past the system of payment in ewes taxed the rich pastoralist for the benefit of poorer pastoralists, keeping both within the bounds of the system. After cash wages were instituted, the relation between labor and capital was profoundly altered. Shepherds were now stuck in the wage labor market, and wealth differences became more pronounced.

The new state of affairs quickly began to permeate all aspects of Arab economic and social life. Payments in kind had stabilized Arab pastoralism and had made the family the unit of production. The basic goal of pastoralism was to satisfy a family's needs rather than to maximize profit, if profit could really be measured in subsistence pastoralism. The rise of commercial ranching destroyed the guts of the traditional system in only a short time. The sheep and the people were the same, so the traditional garb of pastoral nomadism disguised the fact that it was undergoing a profound change. If the emerging sheep capitalists had suddenly started wearing three-piece suits, the change would undoubtedly have been noticed.

By the time of my research ten years later, commercialization had had five major effects on Arab life:

1. Wealthy pastoralists had stopped migrating and had replaced their family's labor with hired shepherds, thus effectively running a commercial operation.

2. The value of women's labor and the social status of women had declined significantly with the end of migration and their separation from the productive economy.

3. The Arabs had become more economically stratified, with an increased gap between rich and poor.

4. Greater emphasis was now put on the care of sheep by building barns and obtaining fodder in order to get the highest prices in the market.

5. Urban investors had entered the pastoral economy and were a major force in hiring shepherds and supporting commercialized families.

At the time of my research I was able to observe families that continued traditional practices, so I was able to compare them to the newly commercialized sectors of the pastoral economy. One interesting result was that, even as commercial pastoralism was facilitated by private ownership of pasture, private ownership also protected many marginal pastoralists. The cash economy has in part created what might be termed pastoral involution, whereby many traditional forms are actually possible only because of the resources and options provided by profit-oriented commercial pastoralism. A definition of what it takes to support an Arab family gets quite complex, but one need not own sheep to stay in the pastoral economy.

End of Migration

Migration to the *ailoqs* ended for many Arabs after sheep prices doubled. The end of migration did not mean these families left the pastoral economy. Rather it pointed up the fact that though it was necessary for the sheep to migrate from one seasonal pasture to another, it was not axiomatic that families must do the same. With changing economic circumstances, cheap wage labor made it feasible to hire shepherds to care for the flocks. The families of poor Arabs that supplied this labor also became sedentary because wages and food were provided for the shepherds only. Despite a continued dependence on the pastoral economy, rich and poor families now stayed in Imam Saheb the year round, the wealthy by choice, the poor by the conditions of the wage labor market. At the present time only middle-level nomads owning from forty to two hundred sheep and poor families working as part of the commercial economy migrate in the traditional manner.

Contrary to many stereotypes about nomads, the Arabs were not fond of the migration. Like many Western families, they enjoyed the cool mountains in the summer but looked upon getting there as a troublesome burden. The trip was not satisfying in itself, just a means to an end. Until labor conditions changed in 1965 wealthy Arabs had little choice in the matter; they could not afford the luxury of replacing family labor with hired labor and still be viable pastoralists. When it became possible to hire shepherds cheaply, wealthy nomads immediately switched to shepherd teams. What was lost in milk production was compensated for in increased sheep prices. The abandonment of milking and family migration became one of the major features that distinguished this new commercial pastoralism from the traditional type. Considering how important these activities had always been, it was obvious that a profound change had taken place.

The use of shepherd teams created a greater demand for pastoral labor. A shepherd team consists of four men—one *chopan* and three *chakars*. Replacing families with these teams opened up more jobs, especially for young men as *chakars*. As an increased number of wealthy households became sedentary, they created a larger sedentary class of poorer households whose men took on shepherding jobs. This number was further increased when urban investors entered the market and also hired shepherds. Due to wage labor, among the Kata poi, the poorest Arab clan, presently one-third of all households are sedentary. Sedentarization has gone largely unnoticed because the Arabs have had fixed *qishloqs* with their own land for sixty years, but now an increasing number of people live in the *qishloq* year round.

The creation of an internal airline has also encouraged the trend toward shepherd camps. It would take an Arab family three weeks to migrate from Imam Saheb to Darwaz. A man on horseback could make the trip in a week if he moved in long stages. The airline can deliver passengers to the mountains in forty-five minutes. It is now possible for herd owners to fly into the mountains to supervise their shepherds for a few weeks in the middle of the summer. By this means the owners maintain direct control over their sheep and can make decisions, solve problems, buy Tajik livestock, and see that the shepherds do not mistreat the sheep. Even though their families no longer migrate, most absentee herd owners fly to the mountains at some point during the summer. They fly first from Kunduz to Faizabad and from there make a connecting flight to a dirt airstrip high in the mountains. They can choose from Shughnan (access to Shiwa), Nesay (to Darwaz), or Khawan (to Dasht-i-Ish and Rogh), which puts them within a half-day's walk of the high pastures. Flights are very cheap and always crowded with nomads who complain of constant overbooking and cancellations of flights. Air travel has become so common that when I first proposed to migrate with the Arabs to the mountains, an Arab *bai* assured me there would be no problem: "We will go to Kunduz and buy you a ticket on the airplane to the *ailoq*." When I protested that I wanted to see the "real" migration, he laughed and exclaimed, "Only poor people walk!" As a result of this development, air travel is one of the standard ways to make the migration, and nomads exchange tips on packing to stay within the twenty-kilogram baggage limit.

Change in the Status of Women

The commercialization of pastoralism in Qataghan had a direct and negative impact on the role of Arab women in the economy. Women's labor, vital to subsistence-oriented pastoralism, became marginal in commercial herding strategies. Increased sedentarization has also affected women more than men.

In Chapter 2 the description of traditional pastoralism revealed that, though men took care of the sheep and the women handled both the milk processing and the care of the camp, these activities were integrated, with the family as the core of production. In this system women's labor was vital. The new commercial system of shepherd camps severed the link between supporting a family and taking care of sheep. Herd-owning families were supported by the profits from the sale of sheep, shepherd families through wages. Milk processing, the primary economic task of women in the summer, was abandoned. Women's work was sacrificed because it was only of marginal value to men, who were now only interested in the cash value of their sheep. Women's important work in pitching tents, packing animals, and cooking was also rendered unnecessary by the commercial system. Shepherds have no tents to pitch, have very little to pack, and do their own cooking. The cost of replacing women's labor, by an extra *chakar* who cooked, for example, was nominal.

The choice to stop migrating rested with the men, who invariably referred to the great difficulties of migration. They claimed that they were doing their families a favor. Women agreed that the migration was exhausting, since they did most of the work on it. But one advantage was that the summer was spent in the mountains and not in the steamy swamps of Imam Saheb. When we left on migration with an Arab family, some Arab women came out to wish us good luck. They told the Arab women packing that they were lucky to be going to the mountains: "You are escaping; we have to stay here." While the men claim to have ended migration for altruistic reasons, the real cause seems to have been their own dislike of the work required during the migration and the unexciting nature of the mountain tops. Their decision to give up migration when it became a feasible option sedentarized not only their own families, but the families of their shepherds.

With the loss of their major economic activities centered around milk processing, women's contribution to the economy was perceived as much less important. Women still cleaned wool and made felt and other items used even in commercial pastoralism, but now their contribution was removed from the direct care of sheep. In one sense economic specialization resulted in less social integration. Sexual division of labor that in the past was only analytically divisible had now been separated in fact. Women's labor was no longer part of the close cooperative public enterprise that traditionally gave nomadic women higher status than their sedentary sisters in Afghanistan.

This change in status and work roles has caused women to be viewed as dependent, irresponsible actors whose contributions are now confined to the household. With much of their traditional work abolished, and unable to travel, sedentarized Arab women have become profoundly bored.

Both nomads and farmers preferred sons, but a daughter in a nomadic family took an important part in the work, especially during migration. Discussing the "frontier days" of the 1920s, an Arab woman described to me how she had taken a rifle and driven off some Tajiks who were chasing her father. "Nomad women know how to use a rifle," she explained, comparing herself to "useless" village women. Yet earlier this same woman had watched her young grandson going off to town to do some errands and had turned to me in an offhand manner to say, "Thank God for a son; daughters just sit and eat shit!" Their household was now sedentary and offered very little constructive work for the family's many daughters. This woman's granddaughters obviously fell into the category of useless village women she disdained.

Because of their permanent *qishloqs*, Arab women traditionally changed behavior patterns from conservative village practices of the valley to a far freer mode on migration and in the mountains. Sedentarization has increased the outward appearance of women's modesty. But these same women grew up riding on camels and staring haughtily at the villagers they passed. So while outward forms of modesty are observed, sedentarized nomad women have not internalized these values and thus feel free to mix and talk in any situation if an excuse can be found. While outwardly trying to act in an appropriate manner, they often show that they have adopted the form but not the substance of a social custom.

The full veil is not used in villages, but some women own one, a sign of sophistication. Once when I was eating dinner with Hussein, he told me he thought the veil was a good thing: "I was in the bazaar yesterday when a woman in a veil came up to me and said hello. I was surprised; I didn't even recognize her until she started talking—it was Ahmad Khan's wife. She told me Ahmad Khan was out of town and the baby was sick, so she came to buy medicine. Those veils are very good because a woman can walk around and not be recognized or bothered." Neither Hussein nor Ahmad Khan's wife, close neighbors, seemed to see the contradiction of a woman in a veil striking up a conversation with a man in the street. A veiled woman is supposed to be invisible, but seeing a neighbor, this woman could not resist the opportunity to discuss some problems. Having followed the rules of modesty by wearing the veil, she then acted as she pleased. Hussein himself also put more stock in form than substance; for him it was just a good protective disguise.

Interestingly, Ahmad Khan would have been furious had he known of the incident, for he had picked up town values on the modesty of women and used to give me lectures on the subject. But his wife was still a nomad, and although she wore the veil, she never understood or accepted the value system behind it.

While older sedentarized women adapt to different cultural conventions without internalizing their underlying values, there may one day be a generation gap between them and their daughters, who have no experience outside the *qishloq*.

Economic Stratification

Pastoralism is a risky business with the potential for great gains as well as spectacular losses. The Arabs tell many stories that illustrate the rise of poor shepherds to great herd owners and the downfall of families that have lost thousands of sheep. Rapid mobility up and down the economic scale was considered the norm. In fact, the fluid system described in these stories no longer exists. Wealthy pastoralists owning over five hundred sheep or their equivalent in other investments make up about 5 percent of all families. They are now firmly established and are unlikely to lose their position, while cash wages have made the possibility of becoming rich an impossibility for a growing percentage. This is particularly true since the Arabs never recovered from large stock losses in the 1950s. At that time a number of families owned over a thousand sheep, the traditional definition of a *rama*, or herd. Today, as an old Arab complained, "Men with two hundred or three hundred sheep go around calling them a *rama*."

The traditional system was never fully open to movement because gains and losses of animals were not the total picture. Private ownership of pasture gave an advantage to the descendants of large herd owners who claimed extensive pastures at the turn of the century. These families, often the very ones who lost thousands of sheep, are still independent herd owners and not part of the wage-earning shepherd class. They had the resources to rebuild that came with good pasture, the excess of which they rented out. The poorer pastoralists who lost sheep and owned marginal *ailoqs* risked not only the loss of their sheep but the permanent loss of their *ailoqs* to Pashtuns if they could not occupy them. Without an *ailoq*, chances of becoming self-sufficient were remote.

Nevertheless, the traditional shepherding contracts greatly slowed the growth rate of the largest herd owners and funneled ewes to impoverished pastoralists. This transfer of capital gave stability to the economic system. As long as one could hold on to an *ailoq*, a few years of shepherding would generate an independent herd. Although described as equivalent to wages, ewes were not sold to raise money. Instead, the shepherd waited until his ewes had lambed and sold the offspring. The ability to acquire ewes gave the *chopan* an important social position far above that of the wage-earning *muzdur*. Histories of famous *chopans* who earned enormous numbers of sheep and were skilled in all aspects of sheep raising were told to me with pride.

This fairly fluid system was at the point of solidifying at the time of my research. The major factor, cash wages, had only been in operation for ten years, so people's sense of fluidity was still based on the evidence of the old system, but the old system was no more.

Cash wages destroyed the distinction between poor wage laborers and *chopans*, who were paid in ewes. The new system made it impossible for a shepherd to rebuild his herd, since he did not have enough money to both feed his family and buy sheep. While ewes provided the nucleus of a herd and lambs to sell, cash was static. Shepherds working today cannot hope to become independent, and without a herd of one's own, one cannot get rich. The ability even to get started again, which was built into the in-kind system of labor payment, no longer exists. A man without sheep remains a pastoralist, but keeps other people's sheep.

The wealthy have become more stable than in former times. In the last twenty years, and especially since the increase in sheep prices, these families have been diversifying their investments. They now own land and urban property as well as sheep. Should they lose their sheep for any reason they would still remain wealthy. This safety net makes their pastoralism tremendously profitable, since they can move profits from one sector to another and are in the advantageous position of having a steady cash flow in an area where credit is available only at high rates of interest. Their sheep flocks now grow at a much faster rate, since they keep their ewes and pay low wages. Their ability to expand is far greater than in the past.

As might be expected, the gap between rich and poor is great —and widening. Those independent pastoralists who are self-sufficient have the potential to rise, but it is unlikely, even if they do increase their number of sheep, that they will be able to diversify their holdings as easily as the present top stratum, because both land and urban property values have risen tremendously.

The more the pastoralists in Qataghan have become an integral part of the market economy, the more the distribution of wealth has begun to resemble the sedentary sphere of disproportionate wealth in the hands of a few, with fewer and fewer structural ways to break out of the cycle. It is unlikely that this will be recognized at large until rich herd owners show their ability to weather crises that were devastating in the past. Ten years of the new system has not yet provided these long-run tests.

Increased Care of Sheep

Commercialization of sheep raising has encouraged an increase in capital investment for improving the care of sheep. Just as the increase in sheep prices reduced interest in sheep as milk producers, it increased interest in maintaining flocks in good condition and minimizing herd losses so that sales in the market could be maximized. Traditionally, sheep were kept on open pasture year round. Low prices for sheep and a scarcity of fodder made it unprofitable to put extra investment into sheep if the return was only marginally greater. High sheep prices made such additions profitable.

Many Arabs now have a sheep barn (*gusfand khana*) in which they keep their *tokhalis* over the winter. The *tokhalis* are fed a mix of pressed cotton seed and hull (*kunjarat* and *postak*) which is highly nutritious. Since castrated fat-tailed sheep are the major sale item of the Arabs, they try to keep them fat over their first winter so that during the following spring they will gain more weight instead of having to make up lost weight from winter grazing. The commercial nature of this feeding is emphasized by the fact that ewes are not stabled during the winter but are out with the older castrates. *Charis* are also stall-fed before they are sold. The amount of winter feeding varies from owner to owner based on the ability to acquire feed at low cost (a problem discussed in Chapter 6) and the condition of the winter pastures. The swamps of Imam Saheb provide far more natural winter pasture than other regions of Afghanistan but cannot always maintain the animals' weight at their summer maximums.

Spring pastures are often left partially ungrazed in lush sections in order to provide hay for the winter. Some nomads have the hay harvested by tractor; others cut it by hand. Private ownership of spring pasture encourages this type of delayed use, since the nomad who foregoes exploiting a section of spring pasture does so only with the assurance of being able to hay it for winter fodder.

Even more important than winter feeding to maintain weight is the use of cotton by-products as emergency fodder after snow falls. Chapter 4 discussed the ability of herd owners to support large flocks of sheep with cottonseed hulls when pasture was frozen over. In one case an Arab delivered seven tons of this *postak* to his sheep during a week when there was no grazing. In addition to being able to move large quantities of feed to his sheep, he and other nomads with rented trucks took the opportunity to cull sheep suffering from the cold and return them to the sheep barn to help them recover. Buying fodder and trucking it to the sheep costs money, but because sheep ranching is a commercial venture, sheep owners are willing to sink substantial sums of money into protecting their investment. Truck-loads of *postak* for sheep are the most obvious manifestations of this, but even owners of a small number of sheep now purchase fodder and transport it on camels to their sheep. With the rise of sheep prices, pastoralists at all levels have become more and more integrated with the major cash crop of the region—cotton. While profitable for all concerned, it ties even subsistence-oriented pastoralists into the money economy to obtain this feed. This integration not only is important in terms of requiring more cash transactions; it also forces nomads to deal with a bureaucratic state industry which is far more complex than the bazaar.

Influx of Urban Investors

The changing nature of pastoralism in Qataghan began to attract sedentary investors into sheep raising. The sudden rise in sheep prices made livestock an extremely profitable investment, especially for those people whose extensive cotton holdings generated a great deal of cash. Before 1965 the relatively low price of sheep made outside investment less attractive because the profits had to be measured against the risks of livestock loss. More important, investors were faced with proportionately higher costs of labor resulting from payments in kind to shepherds.

Monetarization of labor removed the last obstacle to outside investment. Land, labor, and sheep could all be purchased with cash. Private ownership of pasture was a preadaptation that facilitated commercial pastoralism. Since one's rights to pasture were not tribally based, urban investors had no difficulty in obtaining access to good pasture by renting it from a nomad who had extra. This also had a beneficial side effect in preventing overgrazing, because private owners forestalled any attempt to move more sheep onto the pasture than had been contracted for. It is the running of urban investors' sheep that has created a large number of shepherding jobs. Their quiet entry into pastoralism showed that sheep raising was not the exclusive preserve of nomads, though they provided the labor and pasture to make the investment possible.

Let us examine a case in which a merchant family entered the pastoral business. This family is Pashtun and belongs to the Hazarbuz clan, which specializes in the tea trade from India. The patriarch of this family arrived in Imam Saheb just after World War II, established a cloth shop, and invested in cotton land. Later, with the improvements in the road system, the family bought a truck and engaged in trade with Pakistan. In 1971, during the drought that crippled many parts of Afghanistan, word spread that for lack of water and fodder nomadic pastoralists in Maimana were in a bad way and losing sheep rapidly. The old man instructed his son to go to Maimana with the family truck and buy sheep. He gave his son Nik Momat 15,000 Afs. with which he bought thirty sheep. Nik explained that he was able to get them for only 500 Afs. a head because the nomads there were starving and needed money to buy wheat. He trucked the sheep back to Imam Saheb, which—being in the Amu River swamps—had no water or pasture problems that affected livestock.

This family had no pastoral background or experience, but they bought sheep on speculation since they knew it would not be hard to support them in Imam Saheb. They made arrangements with a rich Arab, a *bai* who owned urban property and was acquainted with them, to take care of their sheep along with his own. In four years this flock grew from 30 to 120 sheep. The investment of 15,000 Afs. was now valued at 250,000 Afs. Admittedly, they bought the sheep cheap, but such returns have led many people to finance investments in sheep. Nik declared that sheep rivaled cotton in Imam Saheb as a cash investment, "and sheep multiply!"

Cotton farming encourages speculation in sheep. The cash brought in by the sale of cotton finances the purchase of sheep, and since sheep are also raised for the market, money can be moved from one sector to another. This high profitability is also coupled with a lack of suitable investment outlets in the Afghan economy for cash surpluses. Investment is seen as so precarious that many wealthy people in Imam Saheb still bury their money. One man and his sons reputedly put paper notes worth millions of Afghanis out to dry once a year so they would not mildew.

People wishing to invest in sheep but having no background or experience in pastoralism have three basic alternatives for taking care of their herds. The first way is to do as the family described above did and make an arrangement with a nomadic pastoralist to include one's sheep with his. In the case above, the Pashtun family provided the wages and food for one shepherd in exchange for the care of their sheep. The Arab, who ran his herd with shepherds, thus had his costs reduced by one-quarter, since his 700 sheep would have obligated him to hire four shepherds anyway. The 120 extra sheep were no extra work. There was no fee for use of the pasture because the sheep were grazed on the Arab's own pasture. This method usually requires a previous friendship between the two parties.

The second method is to pay a fixed rate to have one's sheep taken to the *ailoq* where summer grazing is the best. The owner of a few sheep may be able to furnish them with pasture during the winter but has no access to summer pasture, and sheep get fat only if taken to the *ailoq*. This arrangement is made with what I will refer to as "commercialized" families. They have some sheep and their own pasture. They sell their labor and pasture as a unit to sedentary sheep owners. One Arab charged 50 Afs. a head for use of his high pasture in Darwaz and 20 Afs. a head for grazing in his low pasture in Rogh. In addition, he had rights to wool and milk produced by the sheep. This method is most attractive to investors who own only a few sheep. They can have them grazed on the best mountain pastures for a nominal cost, more than offset by the increased market value of a fat sheep. Sheep fattened in the mountains are also thought to be far better able to survive the winter in Imam Saheb.

The third means of providing for commercial herds of sheep is for the owner or the group of owners to obtain all the requirements themselves. The urban investors rent a summer pasture and hire a team of shepherds to look after the sheep. If they rent the pasture from an Arab they invariably hire Arab shepherds on the theory that their investment will be safer. Such herds usually average 800 sheep and are often owned by two or three people who have pooled their sheep to make the investment. In the winter these investors also hire shepherds but do not have to rent a pasture, being subject only to the illegal exactions of the border commissar like everyone else.

Urban investors try to take care of their sheep for the least cost per head. In commercial pastoralism costs and profits are explicit, so investors can calculate which type of care is best for their own interests. Running sheep with a commercialized family is most advantageous to those investors with few sheep; renting pasture and hiring shepherds is possible only with a lot of sheep; and splitting the labor costs with a nomad falls between the other two.

Each of these three strategies has a different cost structure. The data in Table 3 show the cost of pasturing sheep in Darwaz during the summer of 1975. Strategy A, running sheep with a commercialized family, is cheapest for herd owners with fewer than 100 sheep. Since the owner pays only a fee for each sheep, this strategy has the lowest overall cost for a small number of animals, although it has the highest cost per head. Strategy C, renting pasture and hiring shepherds, involves the lowest cost per head for large herd owners who can put together 800 sheep. Usually two or three large investors combine their animals to obtain a herd of this size and split the costs among themselves.

Table 3. Costs of Sheep Pasturing: Three Strategies

A. *Paying commercial family*
Cost per sheep: 50 Afs.

B. *Investor runs sheep with Arab herd for percentage of labor costs*

1 *chakar*	4,000 Afs.
¼ of food supply	1,200 Afs.
Equipment	300 Afs.
Total	5,500 Afs.

Number of sheep: 120
Cost per sheep: 46 Afs. (approx.)

C. *Investor rents pasture and hires shepherds*

1 *chopan*	6,000 Afs.
3 *chakars*	12,000 Afs.
Pasture	4,000 Afs.
Food	5,000 Afs.
Salt	4,000 Afs.
Equipment	1,500 Afs.
Total	32,500 Afs.

Number of sheep: 800
Cost per sheep: 40½ Afs. (approx.)

This strategy therefore attracts investors who own more than 250 sheep. Strategy B, sharing labor costs with an established nomad by providing a shepherd, falls between the two extremes and is most profitable for investors who own between 100 and 250 sheep. Here the cost per head varies; it becomes less as the investor's herd grows, up to the point at which the nomad partner demands an additional shepherd as compensation.

Shepherds

Shepherd camps are the most visible edge of commercial pastoralism. They are immediately identifiable because they are camps without tents. Sometimes perched on a flat rock on a steep mountainside or else within low rock walls that used to shelter an Arab tent, they symbolize the change that has occurred within the pastoral system.

The contract system is organized around two six-month contract periods, the spring/summer season and the fall/winter season. As in the traditional shepherding contracts, no risk is assumed for losses. Cash wages are paid partially in advance, with the balance received at the end of the contract period. Food and shepherd boots (*chambuz*) are provided by the herd owner, together with heavy felt robes (*kaybanaks*) that the shepherds sleep in. The average shepherding crew consists of a hired shepherd (*chopan*) and three assistants (*chakars*). In the absence of the owner the *chopan* makes all the decisions.

In 1975, wages for a six-month contract among the various nomads were as follows:

	Arabs	Uzbeks	Pashtuns
Chopan	5,000 Afs.	7,000–8,000 Afs.	6,000 Afs.
Chakar	3,500 Afs.	5,000–6,000 Afs.	4,000 Afs.

The substantial difference in wages is due to two factors. First, shepherds are hired from one's own ethnic group by and large. Arabs are therefore excluded from the Uzbek labor market, where wages are higher, although many Uzbek herds migrate only locally. The discretion of these labor pools was illustrated when, in the company of some Arab herd owners, I questioned some Uzbeks about their wages. The Uzbeks were astonished to hear that the Arabs paid so little and asked how it could be so; the Arabs replied that this was just what they paid. Arabs under contract to Pashtun merchants were paid at the Pashtun rate. The merchant herd owners always hire Arab shepherds when they rent Arab pasture as insurance on their investment. The second reason for the differential is that the Arab wage was in fact under acute strain and during the next year (1976), it was raised to 7,000 Afs. for a *chopan*, 5,000 Afs. for a *chakar*. This large jump was due mostly to the beginnings of a labor shortage in the pastoral sphere. Young men attracted by high wages in Iran (where wages were ten to fifteen times those paid for similar work in Afghanistan) were leaving Imam Saheb to work abroad. Wages are still extremely low compared to the value of sheep, but labor problems connected with the cash economy have only now begun to make themselves felt. Labor mobility is extremely high in commercial pastoralism. A shepherd never works for the same herd owner for more than three consecutive contract periods, and many change employers each contract period. The end of the relationship may come from either party; it is simply a matter of not entering a new contract obligation. If a shepherd must leave for some reason during the contract period, he will obtain a substitute, usually a relative, to take his place.

The major reasons for refusing to rehire a shepherd are incompetence, dishonesty, and laziness. The major reasons for refusing to work for herd owners are subscale wages, poor food, and personal dislike. Perhaps the greatest reason for fluidity is the belief of shepherds that no one can stand to work more than eighteen months continuously with contract sheep. In this case a shepherd "sleeps" for a contract period: he stays home with his family and picks up odd jobs in the bazaar to bring in some money.

Commercial Families and Pastoral Involution

The migration from the lowlands in Qataghan to the mountain pastures in Badakhshan, now consisting mostly of Pashtuns, is one of the most spectacular and colorful events in Afghanistan. Dust clouds raised by thousands of sheep fill the sky as strings of camels decorated with beads, tassels, and cowrie shells move along in a stately manner, the bells around their necks clanging out the rhythm that soon subconsciously becomes associated with nomadic movement and caravans. Women sit atop the camels, Pashtuns in satins and velvet rich in gold brocade. The loads themselves are topped with carpets or some other piece of finery. This mass of people and animals temporarily engulfs the roads and trails. On main roads trucks may be stalled in a sea of animals. In remote mountain villages the migration is like a week of constant parades. Not a patched tent is to be seen. These nomads, one might suppose, surely epitomize the purest and most classic tradition of nomadism in Afghanistan.

In fact, they do not. The finery and display, especially among the Pashtuns, is made possible by the close integration of the pastoral sphere with the money economy. This wealth allows them to move and live in a style the nomads themselves see as "classic"—how it ought to be done. The nomads in Qataghan are one of the few groups that have the money to care about such things and do them properly. This traditionalism, which casual observers often describe as "timeless" or at least rooted in "millennia," involves nomads who have been in the region for a hundred years in the case of the Arabs, or thirty to fifty years in the case of the Pashtuns, who make up the majority of nomads in the region. The nomads would be pleased to know that their nomadic performance is rated so highly. The migration of sheep owners to Badakhshan by airplane is invisible to most observers, as are their complaints about being unable to acquire cotton by-products for feed or their outrage at the "bastard clan" of truck drivers who demand a fortune on snowy days to move feed to the sheep. The elaborate traditional garb of the nomadic migration, though made possible by the money economy, effectively disguises the nomadic pastoralists' integration into the market and the major changes brought about by commercialized pastoralism. At the national level this results in a "nomad problem." Nomads must be settled and educated because they give the country a bad image. In Qataghan close inspection shows that the nomads do own land, but they are not about to give up sheep raising.

This situation can probably best be understood as a case of "pastoral involution." Even while the economy in Qataghan becomes more and more monetarized, the effect on the pastoral system is to reinforce, elaborate, and perpetuate some of the most classical elements associated with nomadic pastoralism. While similar to involution as described by Geertz (1963), the situation I am describing does not encompass the whole pastoral economy but impinges on two very specific aspects. The first one is the use of profits derived from the monetarized economy to fund traditional cultural aspirations. In Qataghan this is found basically among the Pashtuns, who are pragmatic entrepreneurs in terms of their investments and marketing strategies, but indulgently nostalgic with the money they invest in the trappings of nomadism—large black tents, many camels, fancy baggage, and expensively clothed women. The Arabs, having never been really enchanted with nomadism as movement, are far less concerned with these forms. It is this first form that is most visible and lends an air of elegance to pastoral nomadism which it lacks south of the Hindu Kush. The second and economically more important aspect is that commercialization has created a new niche for pastoralists with few sheep. With the influx of merchant money in pastoral investments, these families have been able to maintain a high standard of living within the pastoral economy without having to own sheep. The process that has proletarianized shepherding has in this instance been a key factor in keeping familial subsistence-oriented pastoralism alive and healthy.

The very forces that put an end to the family as the basic unit of labor in Arab pastoralism paradoxically also created a niche that enabled some families to continue as pastoral nomads that previously would have been economically unable to do so. These families, which I have called "commercial," are able to operate as a family unit in what outwardly appears to be a very traditional manner, but owe their position to a specific adaptation within the commercial economy. In the mountains some of the most traditional-looking encampments fit this description— pastoral nomads who own comparatively few or sometimes no sheep living very well by taking care of sheep owned by urban investors.

This commercial niche was created by the entry of urban investors into the pastoral sphere. Wealthy pastoralists switched over to hired shepherds, as did large-scale urban investors who could afford to hire shepherds and rent *ailoqs*. This left open a niche for nomadic pastoralists who could meet a demand created by investors who owned few sheep and who lacked the means to really take care of their investment. In the winter this is a minor problem because, with available swampland, cotton by-products, or fallow fields, an owner in this position can come to many different ad hoc solutions, but for summer pasture more formal arrangements are necessary to obtain labor and pasture.

In a changing situation many families were attracted to taking other peoples' sheep to their *ailoq* because it allowed them to maintain a better economic position than a family supported by wage labor alone. By selling their pasture and labor as a unit, these families were able to maintain a traditional lifestyle although they lacked their own capital. By acting as retailers of a service that was otherwise available only at the wholesale level, they were easily able to attract customers. It is these investors outside the nomadic pastoral system who benefit more from this familial strategy and are responsible for keeping it alive. An example of one commercial family will explain how a traditional subsistence-oriented pastoralism is grafted onto the market economy.

Ahmad Khan is the patriarch of an extended family. He owns a low *ailoq* in Rogh and a high one in Darwaz. This pasture is far in excess of the needs of his own herd of 100 sheep, but these 100 sheep would not easily support him and the families of his five sons, a total of twenty-three people in six tents. When I visited him in Zerendaw he was herding 250 sheep in the lower pasture and 500 in the upper pasture. Most of the ewes were in the lower pasture, and the castrates were in the higher one. This provided superior grazing for the meat animals and allowed the ewes to be milked daily by the women in the lower pasture.

Because a family does not own enough sheep to support itself does not mean that this family must leave the pastoral sphere, but that in some manner it must supplement the income derived from sheep to make ends meet. We have seen that shepherd contracts are one such way. But this yields only a cash wage. Taking other peoples' sheep to the mountains enables Ahmad Khan to equal the wages his sons could earn as shepherds plus gain pastoral products like milk and wool.

From the sedentary Uzbeks who own the sheep Ahmad Khan receives 50 Afs. per head from sheep in Darwaz, 20 Afs. per head from those in Zerendaw, plus the rights to wool, milk, and any dying sheep. In return he provides pasture, salt, and pastoral labor during the six-month contract.

The standard wage for an Arab shepherd that summer was 5,000 Afs. Ahmad Khan received about 30,000 Afs. for taking care of the Uzbek sheep. When the money paid out for salt, probably about 3,000 Afs., is subtracted, the remainder is approximately equal to what his sons could have earned as shepherds. The family's advantage over shepherds (who have their food provided) is that in addition to receiving the money wages, it could milk the ewes and shear the sheep. Since most of the wool and milk are consumed by the family, they cannot be assigned a market value, but they definitely allow a standard of living above that of shepherds, who support their families only with cash wages. The number of sheep that die in the *ailoq*, though unpredictable, also provides the family with meat. In this way members of the family—working as a unit—are able to extract the maximum in milk and wool as well as make money, though their own capital is not enough to support them. By selling family labor and pasture as a unit they are able to take advantage of what to them is free (labor of family members and their own pasture) and use it to maintain a traditional way of life through commercial sheep raising.

6. The Arabs and National Institutions

The previous chapter presented evidence that national and international factors caused an increase in sheep prices to which the Arabs adapted by commercializing pastoralism. This had ramifications in many other areas of Arab life. Here I will examine the Arabs' relationship with the monopoly cotton company as well as with the provincial and national government. The type of links the Arabs have established with these institutions is of fundamental importance. The provincial or subprovincial level of government is the arena for the implementation of national laws and policies. Its agents, and not officials in Kabul, make up the Imam Saheb resident's everyday experience with government. On the economic side, state industries and monopolies are the most important organizations of the modern economy.

The Spinzar Cotton Company is an economic giant in Qataghan. With the increased use of fodder, the Arabs have become more dependent on Spinzar and its policies to obtain cotton by-products. The discussion in this chapter will begin by showing how Spinzar is linked to the bazaar economy and the Arabs. Little has been written on how these state-owned industries fit into the economy at the local level (Fry [1974] analyzes the role of these industries in the national economy). By illustrating just a small part of the cotton company's many activities it is possible to show how this occurs and to raise a larger question that cannot be fully answered here—that is, to what extent the abysmal inefficiency of Afghan state industries is an artifact of inappropriate measures.

Second, there will be a look at the administration of the subprovince of Imam Saheb from the Arab perspective. This is purposely a parochial point of view. But it is the pattern of government actions at this level, replicated at the local level all over the country, that makes up the experience of the vast majority of people in rural Afghanistan. This level has for many reasons remained opaque to outside observers, falling between the grand systems—usually centered on the capital—studied by political scientists or economists, and the small-scale systems—usually centered on a village—that are favored by the anthropologist. In fact, this gap is also reflected in the real world: the articulation between the lowest government unit and the villages in its purview is quite weak and fuzzy. Certain structural characteristics can be identified, however, which shed some light on an area that has puzzled many observers: "Le problème des forces et factions politique locales est particulièrement difficile à analyser en Afghanistan" (Etienne 1972: 110).

Finally, the chapter will conclude with a historical overview of the relations between Qataghan and the national government of Afghanistan.

A National Industry and Its Local Markets: Spinzar and the Sale of Cotton By-Products

The Arabs have historically been tied to urban markets. The impact of the commercialization of pastoralism in Qataghan has been to increase the complexity of the market itself as well as the opportunities it offers nomadic pastoralists. Thus far the bazaar has been treated as a self-regulating market where prices are set by supply and demand. The other part of the economy has not been discussed in detail—the state-owned industries whose production, buying, and selling are done by administrative orders that fix prices and lay down rules for the disposal of finished products and by-products of the company as well as rules and prices for acquiring raw material.

By 1975 the Republic of Afghanistan had either nationalized or claimed large interests in every sector of the modern economy. Popularly referred to as "socialized" development, in organization and policy it was in reality a form of state capitalism. The immorality of capitalist profits and exploitation of labor was remedied by making the state the capitalist. The Afghan state has traditionally used its political power to claim equity in profitable enterprises, or to give itself a monopoly in the sale of profitable commodities (Fry 1974: 52–53). Afghan capitalists have claimed with some justification that any enterprise that succeeds becomes a target for government acquisition, for the government itself shows little initiative in establishing new enterprises. This policy pits one segment of the Afghan elite against another, since foreigners may not own land in the country and there is no private foreign capital of any importance invested in the country.

Qataghan was the center of development activity in the 1930s. In sharp contrast to the failure of the Hilmand Valley projects financed by the Afghan government, Qataghan's development was so profitable that everybody in the region benefited. Cotton was responsible for the growth, and Spinzar, as the monopoly cotton company of the region, became the most profitable enterprise in Afghanistan. It was so successful that when Daud Khan became prime minister in 1953, he demanded 51 percent equity for the government as part of his "etatist" development philosophy (Fry 1974: 88–89). In 1973, when Daud became president of the new Republic of Afghanistan, one of his first acts was to completely nationalize Spinzar and throw its president in jail, charging him with corruption—for, among other things, receiving large kickbacks from German textile firms and paying the expenses for the king's lavish hunting trips, particularly one tiger hunt in India.

The arrest of the president of Spinzar shook the company and pointed up some important features of Spinzar that made it different from other Afghan companies. Spinzar had its roots in the development of Qataghan, where it owned large tracts of land. It was the only important industrial enterprise centered outside of Kabul. With its headquarters in Kunduz and branches in every town of the region, it acted like a feudal lord over Qataghan. When Daud arrested the president, seized his assets, and padlocked his mansion, it was more than economic change—it marked the end of the dynasty founded by Shir Khan, who started the development. As one Spinzar official told me, "We didn't think of him as the president of a company; we thought of him as a king." Indeed, one was more likely to end up in jail in Kunduz for treason against Spinzar than for treason against the government.

The shake-up dismissed much of Spinzar's elite. This opened up important jobs to men who would otherwise have never gotten an opportunity. While some of these men were incompetent political appointees, others gave hope that the company might again become a model for Afghan development. Although the company was now nationalized, Spinzar officials still maintained a different relationship with the people of Qataghan than did government officials. The company's center of operation remained in Kunduz, and Spinzar officials were locally recruited, often from families with regional ties established in the 1930s. Transfers were made within the system and competition was for jobs in Kunduz. Thus, unlike government officials who wished to be transferred to Kabul, Spinzar employees spent their lives working in Qataghan. They had very strong ties to the region and a personal stake in the province's welfare, which was rarely true of government officials sent out from Kabul. Second, Spinzar rivaled, even overshadowed, the central government in Qataghan. In most of Afghanistan the government was the only bureaucratically organized institution; in Qataghan Spinzar was organized along the same lines, but it paid its officials more, provided them with housing, and had more employees than the local government. A branch manager in the Spinzar system was often perceived as an equal in status to the local subgovernor. In terms of the cash economy, Qataghan was a "company province."

Spinzar, as the monopoly buyer and processor of raw cotton, is the major force in the cash economy. The fixed prices at which it buys cotton are the major determining factor in how much of Qataghan will be planted in cotton. While these prices are important to those Arabs who own land, the availability of cotton by-products produced by ginning process is of consuming interest to all pastoralists. During the winter, conversations in an Arab *qishloq* always turn to the subject of the availability of *postak* (cottonseed hull) and *kunjarat* (pressed cotton seed). As described in earlier chapters, these products are used to stall feed animals to maintain their weight and as an emergency feed supply in the event of snowstorms. With the increased value of sheep, the urgency of obtaining fodder has increased. Whereas in the past it was uneconomical to invest money in this commercial fodder, it has now become not only profitable but absolutely critical in emergencies. Spinzar produces the only supply, and the Arabs as well as other stock breeders watch its actions carefully.

Spinzar is organized with its main plant in Kunduz and branch plants in each town in Qataghan. Each branch has a manager who is responsible for purchasing raw cotton, ginning it, and disposing of the by-products not committed by contract. Spinzar is a bureaucracy in which each manager, despite powers that are circumscribed, is basically in charge of every facet of his branch. He oversees both the production and the disposal of the product, subject to a continually changing set of instructions sent out from Kunduz.

The pastoralists are interested only in *postak* and *kunjarat*. These by-products are produced in large quantities by the ginning process and are therefore cheap enough to serve as fodder. This is first-rate fodder, too, used in many parts of the world, including the United States.

If the pastoralists had their choice, they would prefer to purchase these commodities at the bazaar, where there are no formalities: a buyer pays cash and carries off the purchase. This is the easiest way but unfortunately also the most expensive because the bazaar charges whatever the market will bear. Therefore the cheapest way to obtain the product is to go to the company, which sells it at a fixed rate. But all Afghan state industries, though they have fixed prices and may be obligated to dispose of their product locally, require the potential purchaser to obtain a permission slip, an *ejaza*, signed by the manager, that authorizes the sale of a specific amount of the product. The branch manager can authorize sales of products only at that branch. Obtaining this *ejaza* may require the payment of an extralegal fee, but to obtain one, in any event, a buyer has to deal with the Spinzar bureaucracy in order to get the manager's signature. This is not an easy task for an illiterate Arab sheep owner in search of a ton of *postak*. Indeed, at many plants, depending on the manager, such a man is not even admitted to the office of the branch manager. A class of middlemen has therefore grown up around this process. They use their familiarity with the bureaucracy and real or supposed influence in the right places to obtain *ejazas* for their clients. They demand a fee for this and stress their unique abilities for the job. It is to their advantage that the process remain difficult. The Arabs often prefer to use these middlemen because they are easier to deal with than the company employees with their mystifying paperwork.

The reason that pastoralists go to the trouble of getting an *ejaza* is that the company price is significantly lower than the bazaar price. Permissions would be just a bothersome formality if the price for the product sold by the company reflected its true market value. However, the products of most state industries are sold well below their market value, at times even below their production costs, because the price is arbitrarily set by a ministry in Kabul or by the president of the industry. These men are usually political appointees with no knowledge of how, in processes like ginning cotton, to apportion production costs to various by-products. While they sometimes so overvalue a product that no one buys it, more often the price is deliberately set well under its known market value.

There is an important reason for this. In a state-controlled industry where prices are arbitrarily fixed, a low price for a desirable commodity will create a demand much greater than the supply. Part of the manager's job is to sell the product, but because of the large demand the manager can choose who receives an authorization to buy. When the difference between the free market price and the company price is great, the *ejaza* itself takes on monetary value. People are willing to pay for an *ejaza* as long as the company cost and the price for the *ejaza* together are cheaper than the bazaar price. While the managers often take money for writing permissions, an *ejaza* is not just a simple bribe because its price is beyond the control of the branch manager. If the price difference is large, the *ejaza* has a market value of its own regardless of whether the manager gives it freely or not. In fact, an *ejaza* most closely resembles an option on a commodities futures market. It is a promise to sell, at a future date, a fixed amount of product at a fixed price.

Ejazas, although made out to a particular individual, are transferable. They can be bought and sold on the bazaar with the buyer taking the *ejaza* to Spinzar to obtain the commodity. These papers are like a futures market in that the amount paid for an *ejaza* is determined by the market demand. The company price is fixed, so that the higher the bazaar price, the more an *ejaza* is worth. Conversely, if the bazaar price falls, so does the price offered for an *ejaza*. The market can be manipulated, since Spinzar is a monopoly supplier, and officials have been known to stop sales in order to drive the bazaar price up and increase the value of *ejazas*. It must be emphasized that *ejazas* are a structural device linking the bazaar and government industries. At a national level this is one way bureaucrats in Kabul amass large sums of money just in the course of doing their regular business. Officials cannot demand more money for their signatures than the current market rate for *ejazas*, which fluctuates. A corrupt official has to send a messenger to the bazaar to find out how much a permission is worth that day. Conversely, although an honest official may give his permissions freely, they have the same value. This makes the signatures of certain officials intrinsically valuable because the holder of the permission has the right to buy from a state industry at an extremely low fixed price.

The permission can be used in three ways. First, if the holder is a merchant, the permission will be used to acquire cotton by-products for resale on the bazaar at the much higher free market price. Second, if the holder is a nomad, the permission will be used to buy needed fodder directly from Spinzar and thus avoid the high prices demanded for the same fodder in the bazaar. Third, a holder who has no direct use for the permission can simply sell it to a merchant or nomad who is unable to get a permission directly. Since Spinzar is the sole supplier of cotton by-products there is some rivalry between merchants who would like to monopolize the resale business and the nomads who want Spinzar to sell to them directly.

The complexity of this market is one of the reasons why Arab pastoralists discuss the problem so much. Middlemen who can obtain *ejazas* wield a great deal of power. The *ejaza* may cost them nothing, but they can collect from their clients at the going rate. This is still less than the cost on the bazaar, and, equally important, a good source of supply in emergencies is invaluable. During my time in Imam Saheb *ejazas* were distributed freely to pastoralists, which the Arabs said was very unusual. Nevertheless, because of the demand and because pastoralists might not get enough of the product by going directly to the manager, there was still a large market for *ejazas*, pointing up the fact that the system is a structural mechanism to adjust supply and demand rather than a case of simple corruption. Rates for *ejazas*, of course, increase if a manager restricts their distribution, but a market for *ejazas* exists regardless of who is distributing them. As long as the price spread between the state industry and the bazaar is large, the market for *ejazas* remains active.

Following the actual market will make its dynamics clearer. In the winter of 1975 the market structure for *postak* and *kunjarat* looked like this:

	Postak	Kunjarat
Spinzar price	5 Afs./seer	25 Afs./seer
Ejaza price*	2 Afs./seer	7 Afs./seer
Bazaar price	12 Afs./seer	40 Afs./seer

Ejaza cost is unaffected by quantity.

Spinzar was the monopoly supplier of these two commodities, and both nomads and merchants competed for the same supply. It was the merchants who set the *ejaza* price, since it was they who were most willing to buy permissions in order to acquire cotton by-products from Spinzar and resell them in the bazaar. The *postak* market was active because *postak* was used both as animal feed and as a cheap heating fuel. If the free market price for *postak* was 12 Afs. per seer, then a nomad who could acquire an *ejaza* to buy from Spinzar at 5 Afs. per seer would save

5 Afs. per seer even if he paid 2 Afs. per seer for the *ejaza*, and more if the *ejaza* was obtained free. Equally, the merchants' profit was the difference between the price set by market demand and the fixed Spinzar price, plus the cost of the *ejaza* and other expenses. From such figures we can see why there was a lively trade in *ejazas* and why middlemen who could obtain them, even at a price, were important.

Ejaza prices are elastic, and it is possible for the *ejaza* market to collapse. This happened to the *kunjarat* market within a few weeks after the above data were collected. The government decided that the bazaar rate of 40 Afs. per seer for *kunjarat* was "excessive" and ordered merchants to sell *kunjarat* at no more than 30 Afs. per seer. Looking back, it is apparent that the Spinzar price of 25 Afs. per seer plus the cost of an *ejaza* at 7 Afs. per seer put the break-even point for a merchant at 32 Afs. per seer. At 30 Afs. per seer, merchants would lose money on all sales of *kunjarat* stock. The supply of *kunjarat* on the bazaar immediately dried up because no merchant wanted to sell at a loss. With the new ceiling price at 30 Afs. per seer, bids for *kunjarat ejazas* dropped to between 2 and 3 Afs. per seer, bringing the new bazaar wholesale price to 27–28 Afs. per seer. This brought about some sales in the bazaar because of this new supply of cheaper *kunjarat*, but the profit was so low and so many *ejazas* had been purchased at 7 Afs. per seer that *kunjarat* remained unavailable. Within a few weeks merchants and buyers began to ignore the ceiling price, and *kunjarat* again appeared for sale. As usual, the local government lost interest in the matter soon after it had fixed the price and took no action when the price eventually moved above the official ceiling to 35 Afs. per seer. The government's action had put fear of intervention into the merchants' calculations, and although the *ejaza* price later rose to 5 Afs. per seer, the *ejaza* market for *kunjarat* remained depressed.

Government intervention in the bazaar is quite common and creates much market instability. The fixed prices are rarely effective, since they treat symptoms rather than causes of rising prices. The futures market in *ejazas* integrates fixed, and unrealistically low, company prices with provincial demand. When the company price exceeds market values, *ejazas* cannot even be given away, as happened in one branch where demand for *postak* was low. The market price of the product determines the *ejaza* price, not vice versa.

Price fixing of other commodities and services is also common, but producers and consumers are willing to ignore it because otherwise there would be no transaction. Posted prices in most areas are only sporadically enforced. This led the owner of a local bath to explain to me that fixed prices existed only to provide extra income to the police on holidays when they needed money. He said that only at these times did they officially check compliance, and then they received bribes to ignore the violations, but he declared that "After all, they have to make a living too!"

Here some of the difficulties of national policy at the local level are evident. The government does not have the interest or the capability to run a planned economy, nor is it willing to allow the bazaar to develop on an unrestricted basis. Because of this, not only must a merchant in the bazaar balance potential supply and demand, but one can never be sure when the government will step in and interfere, making planning extremely risky and almost any business a hazardous venture. In such a climate there is a bandit approach to investment; that is, to make as large a profit as possible and get out. Because future conditions are unpredictable and investments are insecure, a small profit is not worth the risk. At the local level in Imam Saheb, in the midst of the cash economy, there is a proliferation of trade and a lack of capital investment.

This "permission complex" is common to all Afghan state industries and government storehouses, and as such deserves attention. It is often assumed that the requirements for permissions to buy are a sign of lack of responsibility which necessitates that every decision, no matter how minor, be approved by the highest possible authority. The delegation of authority is seen as a goal of the modernization process that will enable Afghan industries to operate as efficiently as Western ones. This assumption posits that Afghan industries are abysmally inefficient (as measured by their balance sheet) and that this *ejaza* complex is culturally based and economically irrational.

This and other inefficiencies reduce the profitability of state industries because they serve another purpose by providing extra revenue for the operators of the enterprise who earn fixed salaries. In many cases the system is quite efficient in mechanical terms, but is reported to be producing at a low level so that goods can be diverted without arousing suspicion. Managers who show surpluses are put under great pressure to hide them lest this level become the norm. As shown above, fixing low prices increases demand for *ejazas* and payment for signatures while reducing potential revenue for the company. Even slowness, for which

Afghan bureaucracies are infamous, may often be the result of planning rather than laziness. For example, the plant in Imam Saheb worked efficiently, and farmers got their money within two days, but at other plants it took weeks. An Afghan engineer explained, "Who would pay to go to the head of the line if there were no line?" The longer the line, the more certain people will pay to be processed first. But before this can happen, a long slow line must be created and maintained.

Middlemen

As we have noted, the complexities of dealing with the various bureaucracies have led to the creation of a middleman role which is quite lucrative. These middlemen help buyers from the *qishloq* obtain various products. Alternately, many of them use their knowledge of the *qishloq* to help government officials with extortion schemes. The role is therefore highly ambiguous. An Arab needs a connection to help in dealing with Spinzar but despises the middleman's cooperation with corrupt officials.

Personal ties to Spinzar and government officials are crucial for a middleman. Entertaining officials in lavish style, organizing hunting parties, and paying social calls are vital elements in this process. The reputation of a middleman as an effective broker is based on his perceived ability to make good on his promises or threats. One famous middleman held elaborate feasts for Spinzar officials, using his neighbor's carpets, with borrowed money. To outsiders it looked as though he had access to these officials and could obtain their cooperation. He also entertained a corrupt commissar who provided personal protection when he strayed into legal difficulties. Despite outward appearances, this man was out of favor with the Spinzar manager and many government officials, but the appearance of influence could be used as readily as influence itself when dealing with uninformed Arabs.

Middlemen dealing with Spinzar engage in relatively simple transactions to obtain cotton by-products for their clients. Besides obtaining *ejazas*, the middleman can exploit inside information to make large profits. Knowing such things as how much of a product is committed to export, which products are being deliberately withheld from the market by the company president rather than the branch manager, how large a stockpile of product is available, and whether better or worse quality will replace it are all of vital importance in predicting future market prices. The better the information, the bigger the profits from insider trading.

On the more disreputable side, a minority of middlemen

reverse their traditional role of guiding the villager or nomad through the complexity of the urban scene and instead guide corrupt officials through the opaqueness of the village scene. Because the residents of *qishloqs* render themselves inconspicuous, a corrupt official needs a guide to find which families behind the similar mud walls have more money than their neighbors. Middlemen who have such information about the *qishloqs* can, though they are urban based, pick out targets of opportunity. For example, when a new commissar arrived, his predecessor having been exiled to Darwaz, he was anxious to collect money from those pastoralists using the swamp. Since it was near the end of winter, the new commissar knew he had to hurry, yet he was in ignorance about who to get the money from. So he arranged with an Uzbek middleman to be guided to the wealthy herd owners. For the next few weeks his jeep began to appear in the *qishloqs*, always parked at the door of a wealthy herd owner. There was an early exodus of sheep to the steppe soon after the news of the commissar's visits became known.

Arab Difficulties with Middlemen—The Case of Kungel Bai
It is not unusual for an Arab to be victimized by a middleman, especially a non-Arab one. The Arabs are particularly vulnerable since they are not politically united, so those who are cheated cannot call upon their kin or clan to help them get their money back.

Kungel Bai was a wealthy Arab who owned both sheep and land. He had two sharecroppers working his land. A middleman, nicknamed Gudomdar, often used Kungel Bai's house as a center for hunting parties of the local elite, through which Kungel was acquainted with a number of prominent officials. One day, one of Kungel's sharecroppers came to town with part of the cotton crop and took it to the cotton company to be weighed and sold. Gudomdar, upon seeing the sharecropper, offered to do the paperwork, stating that it was the least he could do for his friend Kungel. The sharecropper gave him all the papers except for the small numbered receipt which was needed to get the cash from the pay office. Gudomdar got the paperwork done but told the man to come back later. When he was gone Gudomdar went to the manager and explained that one of *his* sharecroppers had lost the receipt for getting paid. The manager looked at the papers, did not recognize the owner's name, and authorized payment. Gudomdar collected 21,000 Afs. The next day Kungel came to town and tried to find Gudomdar, who was nowhere to be seen—and at

120 kilos he was not easy to hide. After ten days the manager, who had gone to Kunduz, heard about the theft and investigated. The papers had been made out in Kungel's father's name (though he was long dead), a common practice in Afghanistan, so the manager had not recognized the name. He promised to help Kungel, in part because he, too, had gone hunting at Kungel's *qishloq*. Kungel at the time was in the company of a mullah who was a friend of Gudomdar. The manager asked why he had not warned Kungel. The mullah denied knowing Gudomdar, who was, he claimed, at best an acquaintance, and proceeded to explain those particular chance occurrences that had thrown them together constantly. This was not the first time Gudomdar had been accused of thievery, but the manager swore he would see him in jail for this one because he, too, had been deceived.

Gudomdar's father was contacted and told that he would be held responsible for the claim. He assured the manager that Gudomdar would return the money. Rumor had it that he had initially lost it gambling and had gone into hiding. When this became public knowledge, a rash of claims came from Arabs who said he had taken money from them too. Gudomdar continued to stay out of town. The manager asked if Kungel wished to press charges with the police. Kungel declined. He was afraid, because Gudomdar and his brothers also acted as middlemen for officials bent on extortion. Kungel explained, "If I reported it to the police, then in the end I would be put in jail for stealing Gudomdar's money!"

Now Kungel, after a month, was getting desperate. Perhaps the manager was not really interested in helping him. He learned from gossip that the chief engineer in Kunduz was an enemy of the manager and would probably act on any complaint against him. So Kungel went to the chief engineer and filed a complaint stating that someone had stolen his cotton money and that the branch manager refused to do anything to help him or to pay him. The complaint neglected to mention that he knew who had stolen his money or that the manager had promised to help. Kungel deemed this complaint safer than a criminal complaint because it involved only Spinzar officials, and with any luck he could use the fierce rivalry within the company to get his money back. The chief engineer was delighted to have the complaint. "What kind of thieves do we have in Imam Saheb that are so incompetent that they steal from the farmers directly?" he reportedly asked, and eagerly sent two inspectors to investigate the situation. To their disappointment the inspectors found that

Kungel's sharecropper had voluntarily surrendered the paper to Gudomdar, that ownership was not clearly indicated on the paper, that all forms were in their proper order, and that there was a notice explaining that money had been issued to Gudomdar, who had lost a receipt. The inspector railed at Kungel for causing them to travel so far for nothing. They were chagrined that their enemy had made fools of them and were not anxious to report back to Kunduz.

The manager was furious at Kungel for what he considered a betrayal: "When your money was stolen I was sorrier than you. I felt a personal obligation to get it back. But now I won't do anything more. Get it back yourself!" And he added, "Who does Gudomdar steal from? Just you Arabs. He can't steal from Pashtuns or Turkmen; they wouldn't stand for it. He must think the Arabs are very low that he can steal from them at will."

Kungel's inability to get his money back and the manager's description of the Arabs exemplified the difficulties Arabs have in dealing with the larger governmental structures. Arabs do not need political organization to protect themselves from raids or administer justice. This has been preempted by the government and their close proximity to it. However, there are real gaps in the articulation between provincial government and *qishloqs*, so that it is difficult to obtain a remedy for many problems. Kungel theoretically needed only to file a criminal complaint, but as shown, the government system would not have come to his aid, or if it had, he would have risked losing the money to corrupt officials. His loss also showed how little Arabs support each other in disputes. Had Gudomdar pulled the same trick with a Pashtun, he would have put his life at risk. Arabs prefer to seek out other patrons, and in Kungel's case he managed to alienate two of them. Collective action has become rare among the Arabs because their encapsulation by the national government has broken down tribal solidarity while failing to provide a structure which an individual can count on if in trouble. Because they no longer have collective resources to defend, most Arabs are not willing to take on someone else's problem.

Provincial Government in Imam Saheb

Imam Saheb is a major subprovincial division of Kunduz province and the local unit of administration in the valley. The powers of administration are divided between the commandant of police and the subprovincial governor. Because Imam Saheb is on the border, a third official, the commissar, has jurisdiction over the immediate border territory and is administratively independent of the local government. Provincial officials are mostly Pashtuns, or in some cases Tajiks. Turkic peoples have no part in the administration. These officials came from other parts of Afghanistan as only minor posts are given to local residents. Under the Republic, officials were frequently transferred to prevent them from building personal power bases and to stem corruption by presenting an official with unfamiliar territory. Links between government officials and the *qishloqs* are weak. Officials look upon the *qishloqs* as terra incognita; the people of the valley look upon the government as a powerful and dangerous force.

The local government represents the national state in the area, but because the people of the countryside are ruled by that government and not an organic part of it, the government depends on appointed village officials, *arbobs*, to act as middlemen between them and the *qishloqs*.

By custom, the *arbob* of a *qishloq* is chosen by the residents and confirmed by the government. In some cases, however, the government has appointed *arbobs* without consulting anyone. The *arbob* position is the structural link between village and government, but it is not an intrinsically powerful position. An *arbob* has the power of command only when acting at the behest of the government, when his order is implicitly backed by the power of the state. When acting on his own, an *arbob* can be safely ignored.

In general *arbobs* are literate, have some kind of link with the town (often urban property), and come from wealthy families. Links to the town are particularly important since the business of government is alien to the Arabs and since the ability to deal with government officials demands some experience with town life and values. The position is of dubious honor, in part because in the past the *arbob* had important tax collection duties, but mostly because the government is associated with trouble and corruption, which allows many *arbobs* to take advantage of their position.

There are two distinct role models for the *arbob*. One model is that of the traditional *bai* who takes on the obligation out of a sense of noblesse oblige to help handle the affairs of his local community. In this case, although officially holding the position of *arbob*, he will not use the title. One Arab *arbob* felt it decreased his status as a traditional *bai*, and although I knew him quite well, it was only when interviewing others that I discovered he was an *arbob*. The second type of *arbob* uses the position to make money by acting as an intermediary between the *qishloq* and the government. In contrast to the *bai* model, this type enjoys being called *arbob*. Publicly flattered, these *arbobs* are often privately despised. When I naïvely suggested that a certain man would be trustworthy because he was an *arbob*, I was quoted a proverb: "The pig is in the jungle; the *arbob* in the *qishloq*." This came from an old woman whose son was also an *arbob*, though on the *bai* model. Pigs in the jungle were considered unclean, avaricious, and dangerous.

In spite of their bad reputation, *arbobs* who use the position to make money are necessary. An *arbob* acting as a *bai* may help defend the *qishloq's* interests but he is unlikely to help anyone involved in a criminal situation. Criminal cases are the stock and trade of the money-making *arbob*, and people in trouble go to him. These *arbobs* actively solicit business and profit from their neighbors' troubles.

An example of how an *arbob* works is illustrated in a criminal case given below. Only the first part, how an *arbob* deals with his Arab neighbors, was observed directly; the action within the government office was derived second-hand from those familiar with the etiquette of bribery.

The Arabs are infamous in Imam Saheb as stock thieves. They say they began actively stealing livestock after large herd losses in the 1950s. Later, the increase in the price of sheep made stock theft a great temptation. From the description of wage labor given in the last chapter, it is readily apparent that the successful rustling of even a few sheep can be a large income supplement. Because of this Arabs often find themselves in trouble with the police.

One night two Arabs and two Turkmen lifted seven sheep from a Turkmen *qishloq*. Unfortunately, they chose to conduct the theft by the light of a full moon and were recognized. Police were sent to an Arab *qishloq* to arrest the thieves and bring them back to town. As is usual in these cases, the policemen, conscripts doing military service, spent the night at the suspects' houses. (Should a suspect attempt to flee the area, the police would continue to live in his house and eat his food until the family demanded that he return to get rid of them.)

The first Arab suspect came to Arbob Omar's house after dinner to discuss his problem, having left the policemen at his house. The young Arab made no protest of his innocence, but wanted to know how he could avoid going to jail. He was an obviously frightened man.

Omar said he would talk to the Turkmen who owned the stolen sheep to see if he could arrange something, but that it would cost a lot of money. (Arbob Omar's favorite solution to all problems was a lot of money.) The Arab said he was a poor man and didn't have any money. Arbob Omar ignored this protest and proceeded to describe the conditions of Afghan jails in minute detail, and told a number of frightful tales of people who had been imprisoned. The Arab began to go into a state of shock. Omar wound up his story with "It's all right if you have some other brothers. When there are four brothers, one can be imprisoned, one can do his military service, and there are still two to stay around and take care of things. But you are alone, aren't you, just you, your wife, your mother and sister, isn't it?" Omar silently let the implication of this fact fill the late-night air.

When the Arab talked again about having no money, Omar testily interrupted him and said, "Look—you have floor cushions, don't you? And a couple of rugs, a cow—sell them!" Visibly trembling, the Arab left as Omar promised to go talk the matter over first thing in the morning.

The next morning the father of the second Arab sheep thief arrived. An older man than the one Omar had dealt with the night before, he was one step removed from the problem. Whenever possible Arabs prefer to use agents to negotiate for them in any serious matter in which they might be at a disadvantage. The agent will present the case more forcefully and not compromise as easily as someone who is in direct need of assistance. This negotiation was quick and without scare tactics. Omar told the old man that this theft business was a serious matter and would require 10,000 Afs. in bribes. The old man said he could raise only 1,000 or 2,000 Afs. A crony of Omar sitting in the room disputed this. "What about the 5,000 Afs. you got for your cotton?" he asked. Middlemen have a good idea of the worth of their clients and how much they can extort. The older Arab was told to go into town, and Omar said he would see what he could do with the local government.

The next stage in a criminal process is in the hands of the government officials. The story continues here with the *arbob* now representing his client to get the police commandant to drop the charges. (This probably involved a previous deal in which the complainant agreed not to object.) If the *arbob* has taken 5,000

Afs. from his client he will go to the government and deliver a bribe of 2,000 Afs., declaring that the accused is poor and that no more money can be expected. In practice both the commandant and the *arbob* work within a system where the price of bribes is relatively fixed, unless an exceptional opportunity arises. Thus an *arbob* who collects 5,000 Afs. from his client knows that the bribe will cost 2,000–3,000 Afs. plus hush money for the complainant. The procedure is facilitated because it is routinized; the participants know each other and how the spoils are divided. A middleman is often required to give a bribe, since a sheep thief, for instance, cannot just knock on the commandant's door and hand over money. He lacks the status.

These transactions are, of course, illegal, but in a way provide rough justice. A sheep thief can get five years in jail if he is caught. Through the system of bribery the thief in effect pays a heavy fine for the crime and avoids jail. The bribe is heavy enough to be a real punishment and to act as a deterrent, but provides a flexibility that the formal system of criminal justice does not offer. Money is paid so routinely that a commandant can become almost impartial. There was a murder in Kunduz where a commandant demanded 20,000 Afs. in exchange for dropping the charges. The murderer's relatives tried to bargain with the commandant, but he reportedly declared, "For 40,000 Afs. you could murder forty men for all I care," but if the 20,000 Afs. were not forthcoming, then the man would surely go to jail. The commandant said he did not care which option was chosen. The man went to jail.

Unfortunately, the whole legal system is thereby corrupted through bribery even to the highest levels, which makes effective administration, civil or criminal, a difficult task. Moreover, taking bribes often merely whets the appetites of some officials, who then actively extort money from the population. While bribery as an alternative to jail allows for flexibility, its overall effect is to decrease respect for the government administration. Since the government does not provide local services to the *qishloq*, it has become associated with conscription of young men, criminal matters, and extortion. Likewise, in the view of the government administration, the *qishloqs* are very strange places, full of sheep thieves, quarrels, and potential bribe money.

In carrying out their duties most officials try to generate bribes for themselves. This used to be rationalized on the grounds that a large bribe was required to purchase the position, and therefore the official had to get a return on his investment. Later, officials were trained for jobs in the administration, but with the abysmally low salaries, most quickly succumbed to the lure of corruption. Once infected, very few have had the ability to stop or to limit their extortion to what they needed. Though the mass of the people pay for these practices, most people do not object to corruption per se, but only to the greediness of the officials. With fewer and fewer taxes and an unwillingness on the part of the government to pay its administrative officials a wage appropriate to their status, corruption has become an indirect tax that keeps the system going.

When the Republican government came to power in 1973, it condemned the open corruption of the monarchy. The severe character of President Daud made the threat of a wholesale cleanup a real possibility to government officials. One Afghan described the initial reaction: "When the people heard that Daud was in power, for the first week no one in the whole country took a bribe; they were too scared; but then they realized that the president's eyes couldn't see everywhere nor could his ears hear everything, and soon they began to demand money again." Ironically, when a man who intended to root out corruption came to power, conditions in the provinces actually deteriorated. I asked an Arab whether corruption was worse under the monarchy, and his reply was, "Under the king officials would demand 100 Afs. to do something; now they demand 200 or 300 Afs. for the same thing because they say now they are taking a risk of losing their jobs." So honesty at the top has resulted in a risk surcharge at the bottom and in complaints that officials now extort from everyone, whereas they used to bother only rich people. This complaint is based on the problems of getting identity cards. Every male Afghan has to carry a card, and because of the new government, new cards were issued. Local officials used the opportunity to extort money from whole villages to issue the cards. They used the threat of arrest as a weapon, since it was illegal to be without a card. The similar problem of the commissar demanding grazing rights has already been discussed.

The natural response of farmers and pastoralists alike is thus to avoid the government whenever possible. Informal arbitration of disputes is effective because the disputants fear dealing with the government more than they fear losing the dispute. It also means that government representatives are treated with uninformative coolness when they try to deal with a problem in a *qishloq*. Though the *qishloq* may be only a short distance from the town, it remains closed to official inquiries. A rather comic incident will illustrate the nature of being "unhelpful"—when cooperation is needed—without refusing anything.

A conscript serving in the police force was sent to a large *qishloq* to find a man and bring him back to town. The soldier went first to an *arbob*, who sent him to another, who told him to wait at the mosque, where hours later he was told that the man had not been seen for weeks. Dejectedly, he began to walk back to town in the late afternoon. At the edge of the *qishloq* he saw many people gathered. It was a wedding feast, and they invited him to have something to eat. The policeman sat down and ate, and ate, for the government does not serve army or police conscripts decent meals. He complained of having gone from one place to the next, of having been attacked by dogs, and of having waited hours for people. It also seemed impossible to find the right house. This was because his address was not specific, responded the Arabs; the name of the *qishloq* was applied to four different places covering a large area. It wasn't their fault the government had given him instructions that were too vague. It was obvious that no one was going to offer anything more than polite assistance. The conscript then declared "*Askars* [soldiers/ police officers] are treated like dogs!" No one disputed this, for most of the men had served in the army or police and fully agreed with him. Dropping the government business, the Arabs discovered that the man was a Tajik from Badakhshan and came from a village close to where a number of Arabs had their *ailoqs*. They exchanged news about various people; the soldier thanked them for the meal, and left in good spirits. He had not raised the issue of the government business again. The police commandant would hear at sundown that the Arab he wanted was nowhere to be found.

Although the *qishloqs* are encapsulated by the national government, the government finds it hard to use its power to deal with nonspecific types of autonomy that residents use in order to screen themselves from that power.

Despite this gloomy picture of the Arabs' dealings with national institutions, the success or failure of various Arab clans has in large part been based on taking advantage of new opportunities provided by these national structures. In sharp contrast are the Aw foroush clan, the richest Arab clan, and the Kata poi clan, the poorest.

At the micro level the local government seems predatory, but we must stand back and remember two things. First, the burden of taxes and corruption, the extractive feature of government, is probably far lighter in real terms today than it was in the 1920s. Second, although the Afghan government fails to provide services to its population, it did provide an environment of peace and relative stability that lasted for almost fifty years. Afghanistan's reputation as a wild and rebellious land is not usually seen in this light. The ability of the Arabs to come to grips with and accommodate the growing power of the central government has insured the success of the Aw foroush clan, while failure to do so has left the Kata poi clan vulnerable.

Ironically, many of the problems faced by Kungel Bai—lack of Arab support or collective action—were the result of the structural link between the Arabs and the government negotiated sixty years ago. The Arabs received villages and *ailoqs* on an individual basis, with titles that would be respected and protected by the Afghan government. We have seen from examples in central Asia that when a tribal society loses its tribal political rights and collective resources to the administration of a sedentary state, social organization and kinship no longer play such important political and economic roles. When the Arabs dealt with the Afghan government and received individual ownership of vital resources, their ability to act as a tribal unit began to wane. But the advantages of individual action within the structure of the Afghan state have left a gap. In disputes below the level of defending land titles or keeping the peace, the government does not provide reliable administration. These middle-level affairs are fraught with difficulties, but are nevertheless the result of successful arrangements of long standing about the most important problems the Arabs faced: stability of the region and security of property.

The ability to come to an advantageous accommodation with the Afghan government and the changing economic situation is the hallmark of the Aw foroush clan. Its founders claimed the best *ailoqs* in Darwaz and got them confirmed by the government. The Aw foroush took advantage of Amanullah's reorganization of Qataghan to get permanent land rights in Imam Saheb. Some Aw foroush invested in cotton land and urban property. Historically, when opportunities have arisen it has been Aw foroush who have taken advantage of them when it was cheap and easy to do so. Not all of them, of course, but enough for the Aw foroush to be considered the wealthiest and most astute clan of all.

The Kata poi (the "witless people," as the Aw foroush disparagingly call them) have traditionally taken just the opposite tack. They have always been extremely conservative, and have never taken advantage of any of the new opportunities exploited by the Aw foroush. Living in the middle of a swamp, they were content if the government left them alone, but conservatism proved to be a poor strategy in times of changing conditions. As we have seen, there have been massive changes in the basic ecology and economy of Imam Saheb since the Arabs first settled in an uninhabited malarial swamp. The Kata poi are now in difficulty because of decisions made by their grandfathers in the 1920s. The implication of these decisions and the difficulties of a conservative preference toward nonaction have threatened the existence of the Kata poi during the 1970s.

All Arab clans received title to their land in the 1920s except the Kata poi, who never tried to get the swampland actually deeded to their clan, apparently because everyone else considered it useless. It was thought that agriculture was impossible there because it was not possible to irrigate the land with the traditional water system. The Kata poi's right to use and graze the land had never been questioned by other nomads. The Kata poi encampment consists of sixty households and has no *arbob*.

In 1974 a rich man in Imam Saheb got permission to plant sesame on part of the land grazed by the Kata poi. Using a tractor, he planted an extensive unirrigated tract of land and made a large profit. The Kata poi were naturally alarmed at an encroachment on what they thought was their land. They had good reason to be, for that winter a diesel-driven water pump arrived from India, and plans were made to irrigate part of the plain that the Kata poi lived on.

The Kata poi had much more clan solidarity than other Arab clans, but they lacked both the contacts and the information that would have enabled them to press a claim to get title to the land they had occupied for a hundred years. Naturally enough, they approached an Arab middleman. He claimed to have a friend in Khanabad who had now graduated from the law faculty and could make out the papers. He also said that the governor in Kunduz was a "good man" and sure to act favorably. But, he noted, "Money makes proposals sweet," and recommended a hefty bribe: "If the Panjshiri [the man who planted the sesame crop] gives 20,000 Afs., you must give 50,000 Afs." There was murmuring about the large amount of money that would have to be raised, and that perhaps it was excessive. But the middleman had talked so convincingly about official papers and powerful people and seemed to know the process so well that the Kata poi believed he could handle the matter, which was of critical importance to them. He was an Aw foroush, after all. As the middleman left he asked for a complete list of all adult males and their sons so that he could draw up a petition with their claim of having occupied their land for the last hundred years.

There was but one problem—the middleman lacked the connections for a job of this importance. His glib talk of how the governor was a good man who would certainly act favorably masked the fact that he had never met the governor, nor had he ever had any business with him. Even if he had had the connections, the central government had decided to conduct a land reform program and soon banned all land transfers pending a national program. A few months later I saw the middleman again —riding a new motorcycle.

The Kata poi's trouble stemmed from the changed conditions that had come about over the last fifty years. In the frontier days of the 1920s land could be had for the asking. In the 1970s land was a valuable commodity. Even the swampland that the Kata poi used took on new potential with investments like tractors and water pumps to develop their land. When Shir Khan was governor of Qataghan he had wide powers to distribute land. It is unclear if present governors have any such rights. Certainly they are virtually powerless compared to the autonomy of Shir Khan in the 1930s. Governors can no longer strike deals with tribal people. The Arabs received *qishloqs* as clans, but the Kata poi as a clan have no standing now because the government recognizes only *qishloqs* and is linked to them through *arbobs*. The Kata poi today find that the clan is no longer a unit that can negotiate with the government. The opportunity to bargain as tribes and clans in Qataghan is over. The Kata poi, now isolated and without trustworthy representation, are discovering that the conservatism of their grandfathers is not easily remedied. The inability of the Kata poi to handle the new, more complex world around them suggests that many of the traditional aspects of Arab political and social organization are not well adapted to problems that they now face. Change is not an inevitable process, but the consequences of change catch up even to those who may have tried to ignore it.

The National Government and Qataghan— Historical Overview

The Afghan state has only recently been able to control all parts of the country from the center. This process began in the late nineteenth century when Amir Abdur Rahman crushed all internal opposition to his rule in a series of campaigns that put Afghanistan firmly in the grasp of the Kabul government (Kakar 1971). Until that time many parts of Afghanistan were semi-autonomous, ruled by local elites with shifting loyalties. After Abdur Rahman only Pashtun districts in the south and east kept some measure of autonomy, which did not end until Prime Minister Daud (1953–1963), with modern weapons acquired from the Soviet Union, was finally able to produce an Afghan state that could enforce a temporary monopoly on the use of force.

The Afghan Republic with Daud as president (1973–1978) reflected this struggle of the national government to effectively control the territory within its borders. Its organization was autocratic in form, with power spreading from the top of the hierarchy downward. The national structure, the creation of a powerful elite, encapsulated a large number of smaller political structures with which it had very weak organic connections. The national governmental structure and the tribal and peasant peoples it ruled had little in common. It is normal for a national political structure to have goals and aims different from those of the local structures it encapsulates (Bailey 1969: 12), but in Afghanistan there was a particularly large gap between them. The systems were discontinuous, and relations between the national representatives and local residents were fraught with difficulties because, with some justification, both sides looked upon the relationship as an adversary one.

In Qataghan the provincial government sat upon the province like an alien conqueror, which historically it was. The very word *government* was synonymous with trouble to local residents. The separation of government and people was even physically apparent. The government compound was in one part of Imam Saheb. Here officials could be found, and government business conducted. When one left this urban scene on any road out of town, the government disappeared. Here a man in uniform was out of place. This does not imply that the provincial government lacked control of the area; quite to the contrary, it effectively dominated it. Yet like oil and water, government was separated from the population, floating atop local structures.

There were a number of reasons for this. Perhaps most basic, subprovincial government was the lowest unit in the national administrative hierarchy. Its officials were part of that national system which was laid on top of the area it administered but which was not organically linked to it. The chain of command ended here; enforcement of decisions below this unit depended on force and power because the tribes and peasants did not see themselves as part of a national system—rather they felt they were the objects of administration. Afghan officials looked upon local residents as ruler to subject, not as public official to citizen.

Government officials were urban people who disliked service to the provinces. They constantly tried to arrange transfers back to Kabul. They felt little kinship for the local people with whom they dealt. Government officials always dressed in Western clothes, setting themselves apart from the traditionally dressed, turban-wearing residents of rural Afghanistan. Indeed, with a few exceptions, government officials were embarrassed by rural Afghanistan, which they felt was a backward place filled with backward people. They did not hesitate to express their feelings of superiority. Since their job was not to provide services or respond to local problems, but to keep the peace and collect revenue, idealistic pronouncements from Kabul about nationhood and justice were received with cynicism at the local level. Whatever faith there was in the national leadership did not extend to the overweight and overbearing officials who represented the government locally.

No matter how such a system was staffed, there would have been problems, but the national government's overt favoritism toward the Pashtuns reinforced strong feelings in non-Pashtun regions that the government was an alien oppressor. In Qataghan, as elsewhere, almost all officials were Pashtuns, usually Pashtuns from the south. For this reason *Afghan* still means "Pashtun" in the north, and *Afghan government* means "government by Pashtuns." Most non-Pashtuns felt that the wealth of the north was exploited for the benefit of Pashtuns in the south. They looked upon the large number of Pashtun immigrants as natural allies of the government. However, since the whole province was settled largely by immigrants, the Pashtuns were not the only ethnic group that benefited from the development of Qataghan. There was a separatist movement in Qataghan demanding that Turkestan be for "Turkestanis"—basically anyone who was not Pashtun. Anonymous leaflets occasionally appeared in Imam Saheb, in part a backlash to the national government's incessant propaganda about Pashtunistan. If the Pashtuns were entitled to self-determination in Pakistan, other ethnic groups in Afghanistan were not slow to think of their own rights. Remembering the Saqaoist period (1929), when large sections of the country supported the bandit king because he was a non-Pashtun, the Republican government was hypersensitive to separatists' threats.

There could be no doubt that the government encouraged the settlement of Pashtuns in Qataghan, but their relation to the national government demonstrated that the Pashtuns in Qataghan were also encapsulated by the central government. The Pashtuns in the north found it advantageous to identify themselves with the Pashtun elite that governed the province. However, Pashtuns in Qataghan were effectively stripped of the autonomy they had known south of the Hindu Kush. Starting with Amir Abdur Rahman, northern Afghanistan had been used as a place of exile for rebellious Pashtuns. To local residents they were seen as allies of the government, but this was due to their isolated position in ethnically alien territory rather than to any innate respect for the Kabul government. The government had adroitly turned rebellious Pashtuns into loyal supporters in the northern provinces while effectively destroying their independence. Evidence for this could be seen in the lack of tribal assemblies for decision making, politically weak khans, and liability for conscription and taxes like anyone else. Pashtuns still showed great pride in their heritage, but the rich land of the north and strong government control tended to switch the emphasis from politics to cultural traditions that did not affect the region's power structure. The force of the Afghan state encapsulated the Pashtuns in Qataghan as it did other ethnic groups, but the strategy of favoritism toward Pashtuns bound an important part of the population to Kabul when its objective interests lay with the other ethnic groups in the region.

There has been a slow change in the way rural Afghanistan has been administered over time. Almost unnoticed, the central government has moved from a dependence on rural production as its basic source of revenue to other taxes, leaving the countryside virtually untaxed. At the same time it has been claiming more and more political prerogatives in ruling the countryside.

In the nineteenth century and through the reign of King Amanullah in the 1920s, taxes were a major burden and involved a yearly confrontation between government tax collectors and farmers. Taxes of as much as one-fifth of the crop were not unusual, and considerable extortion accompanied tax collection.

After Amanullah began to change the collection of taxes from in-kind to cash, he increased the money taxes regularly, particularly those levied on stock breeders (Ghani 1921: 124–130). At that time more than 62½ percent of government revenue came from animal and land taxes. In 1972, by contrast, less than 1 percent of national revenue came from this source. This decline was due to the effects of inflation on a fixed money tax, the political power of landowners during the parliamentary period in resisting tax increases, and the increased tax money available from alternate sources (Fry 1974: 155–156). Nomadic pastoralists were not taxed at all after the livestock tax was abolished in 1964. Whereas extracting taxes was the major job of traditional administration, this important aspect was well in decline by the early 1950s (Schurmann 1962: 234–235). In 1975 taxes were not discussed much in Qataghan because they had for all intents and purposes ceased to exist.

As revenue extraction became less and less important, the government increased its political functions. When it was busy extracting important amounts of taxes, the government was content merely to keep the peace. If there was no complaint, there was no crime, and people could settle matters among themselves. In more recent times the government has claimed a wider jurisdiction. Theft, murder, and kidnapping now provoke government action even if the parties involved arrive at an acceptable settlement. Canfield (1973) has described this process in the Hazarajat, where a government official ferreted out a murderer despite the fact that the victim's kin had accepted compensation and considered the matter settled. Part of this change was due to officials who had a new code of values that was not shared by the more traditional population they governed. There seemed to be, in addition, some kind of historical trade-off whereby the government abandoned its oppressive tax collections but took on a more direct role in handling affairs at the local level in exchange.

As a whole the government in Qataghan did not effectively link itself to the region in a meaningful way that would integrate the various ethnic groups into a national state. This was in strong contrast to the Spinzar Cotton Company, which was intrinsically linked to the economy and people of Qataghan. The major plans of development in Afghanistan stressed that preservation of Afghan culture was an absolute requirement. But the government had no goals as to what Afghanistan should become, beyond those of technological improvement. This was because "Afghan culture" was also a code word for the status quo, and in many cases it was not cultural values that were at stake but the privileges of a small elite. Although the extractive machinery of government fell far more lightly on rural Afghanistan than in the past, it was evident that as the elite began to feel it could do without the traditional sources of revenue, there was even less reason to give the rural majority a voice in government. The relationship of government to people remained an adversary one. As long as officials were sent out from Kabul with no concern for the wishes of the provincial inhabitants, things would remain the same.

Conclusion

In previous chapters the distinction has been made between a pastoralism in which sheep are part of a subsistence economy and one in which they are a lucrative "cash crop." This distinction was shown to be the key in understanding the transformation of pastoral nomadism in Qataghan into a form of commercial ranching. It also helps to explain the seemingly contradictory models of economic processes among pastoral nomads espoused by Fredrik Barth and Jacob Black.

Barth's classic model of economic processes among the Basseri of southern Iran has been widely adopted in the study of nomadic societies throughout southwestern Asia because of its elegance. The Basseri maintain an egalitarian society because of the constant sedentarization of both rich and poor nomads. Among the wealthy, sedentarization occurs as a result of investments in land. Basseri families that find their livestock holdings growing beyond their immediate needs invest their excess income in land. Land is valued by nomads in Iran because it is a more stable investment than sheep, has a high rate of return using sharecropping arrangements, and carries high social status in the larger Persian society. As these landed interests grow, they begin to supersede sheep in economic importance, and at some point, perhaps after a year of heavy losses on the range, a landed family will decide to settle for good. This decision is also encouraged by the low rate of growth for herds of sheep let out under contract to shepherds. A more common route to sedentary life is the gradual impoverishment of those nomads who have small numbers of sheep. A minimum number of animals is required to support a family. Animals provide not only milk, but wool, butter, and hides that are traded for the grain which makes up the bulk of the Basseri diet. If a family falls below this minimum, it finds itself in a downward spiral of debt. Each year productive animals are sold to pay old debts, which makes it harder to break even the next year. Eventually all the livestock will be sold, and these poor Basseri are forced to join the landless peasantry. They would prefer to stay in the pastoral economy by shepherding other peoples' sheep, but there are few such contracts to be had. By ridding the tribe of any families that depart radically from the mean in either wealth or poverty, the Basseri maintain a balance in many areas. The population remains stable, the community-owned rangeland is not degraded, and the political structure remains egalitarian, producing no rivals to the princely family that rules the external affairs of the Basseri and links them to the national government (Barth 1961: 101–111).

Among the Lurs, who live northwest of the Basseri, a very different process is at work. Instead of an egalitarian set of self-supporting nomads, Black found pervasive inequality. Wealthy Lurs stay in pastoralism and own most of the sheep, which are herded by poor Lurs who are dependent on shepherding contracts for their livelihood. This situation had its origins in the forced settlement policies of Reza Shah in the 1930s, when it was made a crime to migrate. The strongest families among the Lurs seized what had been tribally owned agricultural land and claimed it as personal property. After the fall of Reza Shah during World War II, the Lurs began to raise sheep again but on a different basis. Families with land added sheep to their holdings to form "agro-pastoral combines" which employed poorer Lurs as a labor force. Later, when order was restored in provincial Iran and new roads constructed linking remote Luristan to the rest of the country, the Lurs found a new market for their sheep as meat animals. Land in Luristan remained valuable for subsistence crops, but sheep provided the region with a new way to make large sums of money. Wealth differences became more pronounced, and a patron-client relationship developed to such a degree that most Lurs in the pastoral economy became absolutely dependent on the contracts offered by a few rich Lurs (Black 1976: 191–215).

These two cases could not be more starkly opposed. Barth's model sedentarizes the extremes and leaves only an egalitarian set of independent nomads. In Black's model the wealthy form agro-pastoral combines and control the ownership of most live-stock, which are cared for by poor nomads, leaving very few of the independent producers that are the strength of the Basseri.

Thus, for Barth, the mean rejects the extremes; for Black, the extremes devour the mean.

The major structural difference between the two systems seems to hinge on the existence of herding contracts. If herding contracts were available, then nomads who had lost their stock could remain in the pastoral economy by herding sheep owned by wealthy nomads. On the other hand, if contracts were not available, then Barth's model would accurately reflect the process of sedentarization. Since among the Lurs the wealthy had refused to leave the pastoral economy, Black suggested that it was possible that the same thing had occurred with the Basseri but that it had not been recognized by Barth, and he raised three ethnographic objections to Barth's model. First, many nomads, including the Lurs, complained about the poor quality of contract labor but still employed it. Second, Barth's detailed descriptions of herding contracts suggested that they were commonly used. Finally, Barth had reported some Basseri who engaged in casual labor to increase their income and avoid sedentarization. For these reasons Black labeled Barth's model "plausible conjecture" (Black 1976: 17).

There is, however, a more profound difference between the Luri and Basseri cases that better explains why the two models differ. This difference is the profitability of sheep as cash investments in each system. The case of the Central Asian Arabs has shown that when the market price of sheep was low, sheep were valued for the wool, milk, and milk products they supplied as well as the money their sale brought in. Sheep were not seen as attractive investments because the risk was high compared to the possible profits. When the cash value of sheep rose sharply, this changed, and outside investors as well as rich Arabs began to invest in sheep for a cash return using contract labor. The changes that this brought about in the Arab economy suggest that Barth's model works best when sheep are raised for subsistence and have a low cash value, while Black's model is most appropriate for those nomads who have begun to raise sheep commercially for cash as a major economic enterprise. A closer look at the profitability of raising sheep among the Basseri, Lurs, and Arabs demonstrates this.

The Basseri engage in subsistence pastoralism. Sheep provide wool, clarified butter, and lambskins for sale or trade, together with milk, milk products, and meat which a nomadic family can consume directly (Barth 1961: 17). The nomads have a symbiotic relationship with the farming communities along their migration route. Most of the agricultural and industrial products they need are obtained from trading partners in these villages. Direct purchases in the bazaars of the region "represent only a fraction of the turnover of a nomadic household" (ibid.: 98). In this type of sheep raising, nomadic pastoralism provides an adequate, even superior, standard of living compared with that found in the region's villages. But the return on investment, while quite high for nomads running their own sheep, is very low for an outside investor who must run sheep on contract. The Basseri run ewes that are each valued at 80 *tomans*—which provides a 100 percent return annually, 60 *tomans* in exchangeable products and the remainder in food for household consumption (ibid.: 16, 99). If these same ewes are run under a Basseri shepherd contract, the return on the investment to the owner is much lower. Under the terms of a shepherding contract, the owner receives a cash payment of 10–15 *tomans* per ewe from the shepherd, who gets to keep all the products and is required to return a flock of the same size and age composition to the owner at the end of a year (ibid.: 13–14). Thus an investor gets a return of 12–19 percent on an 80-*toman* ewe and is entitled to no part of the herd's natural increase. Considering that pastoralism is a risky business, this is a very low return. It also explains why Basseri who have acquired land through profits on sheep that they have run themselves lose interest in maintaining flocks under contract.

This situation changes when the pastoral economy becomes oriented toward cash sales. The Lurs have an economy very similar to that of the Basseri except that they also sell yearlings to urban meat markets. Luri shepherding contracts are much more favorable to the owner. If a shepherd takes Luri ewes, he must split half of all the flock's produce with the owner and pay for any veterinary care and any winter fodder that is necessary. A more speculative shepherding contract for old Kermenshah ewes provides a forty-sixty split between the shepherd and the owner. The owner is responsible for veterinary care, needed fodder, and winter pasture, but the shepherd is liable for 40 percent of the cost of any ewes that die while under his care. Yearling shepherding contracts involve a division of profits on the sale of these animals to the meat market with a fifty-fifty or sixty-forty split between the owner and the shepherd (Black 1976: 161–171). Compared with the Basseri shepherding contracts according to which the owner receives one-fifth of the ewes' produce and no increase in stock, a Luri contract gives the owner half of both. This difference goes a long way in explaining why wealthy

Basseri leave pastoralism and wealthy Lurs do not. In addition to a larger percentage of pastoral products and a percentage of the flock's increase, Luri owners also raise yearlings for cash sale in the meat market, and the Basseri do not.

Although the Lurs are more market-oriented than the Basseri, their use of ewe contracts and in-kind payment does not begin to approach the commercial orientation of the Arabs in Qataghan. The Arabs, who were always tied to the market even when sheep prices were depressed, tended to abandon in-kind payments for shepherds and to lose interest in most pastoral products when the value of their sheep as meat animals eclipsed all else. Sheep became such good investments that urban merchants joined wealthy nomads in competition for shepherds to herd their sheep for cash wages. These labor costs and other expenses amounted to between 5 and 10 percent of the increased value of the sheep, even less if figured against the total cash value of the livestock. To these absentee owners, milk, milk products, and even wool were of such marginal value that the shepherds were free to take what they wished as long as the sheep got fat. In sharp contrast to a Basseri shepherd, who pays the owner a fee per ewe, a commercialized Arab family demands a fee from the owner to take the sheep—whether ewe or meat animal—and has rights to all the pastoral products of this herd. In this situation wealthy nomads stay in the pastoral economy using the labor of poorer nomads, but pastoralism becomes a business and not just a livelihood.

These three cases suggest a transformation of pastoral nomadism in parts of central and southwestern Asia over the past few decades. The Basseri, with their local village trading partners, weak links to urban markets, and poor opportunity for outside investment in pastoralism, undoubtedly follow a very old pattern, the dynamics of which are captured by Barth's model. But the construction of roads and the development of a profitable national market for meat have drawn previously marginal nomads like the Lurs into at least part of the cash economy. The traditional Luri economy changed in response to this new situation by encouraging the sale of yearlings in the new market, but it retained many features of subsistence pastoralism. Shepherding contracts were much more favorable to the owner than those among the Basseri, but the shepherd still got a share of the flock's increase, and the owner demanded a share of the milk products. The Arabs represent the transformation of nomadic pastoralism into a form of commercial ranching. They have strong links to urban markets, raise a breed of sheep particularly for that market, and can explicitly determine profit or losses in monetary terms. Payments for shepherds changed from ewes to a cash wage, and the owners of large numbers of sheep have abandoned interest in milk and even wool production in some cases because of their marginal value compared to the sheep's value on the bazaar. Sheep are popular investments not just for rich nomads but for urban merchants as well. Black's model, in which large-scale sheep owners hire poor shepherds so that both groups remain in the pastoral economy, works well here. The society becomes more stratified by wealth, and there are fewer middle-range nomads.

As the demand for meat has risen in southwestern Asia, subsistence-oriented nomads like the Basseri have come under new pressures. Barth made his study in the late 1950s, when the cash economy had had little effect on nomads, who were only marginally connected with the national economy. In the last twenty years dramatically higher prices for sheep and better transportation have brought many of these marginal groups into contact with cash markets. It would be interesting to know if the Basseri have made changes similar to those of the Lurs or Arabs in response to this development. The transformation of pastoralism in Qataghan shows just how great an impact this change to a form of commercial ranching has had on all aspects of economic and social organization. Although the sheep and the people are the same, the underlying dynamics of each system are different.

Beyond the dynamics of these models, the Arabs are linked into the regional economy, state enterprises, and national government. Throughout their history, although they have been seemingly isolated, the Arabs have been affected by the outside world. Their nomadic pastoralism has been affected by political changes, international treaties, and changes in market demands. They do more than move sheep: nomadic pastoralists in Qataghan are intrinsically linked to the regional economy, and in comparison to wheat farmers they are more closely tied to urban markets. Policies that encourage sedentarization of "backward nomads" are, at least in northeastern Afghanistan, based more on misconceptions about what nomads are supposed to be like than on any real knowledge of what a nomadic pastoralist actually does for a living.

Bibliography

Akhramovich, R. T.
1966   *Outline History of Afghanistan after the Second World War.*
        Moscow: Nauka Publishing House.
Bacon, Elizabeth
1954   "Types of Pastoral Nomadism in Central and Southwest Asia."
        Southwestern Journal of Anthropology 10: 44–68.
Baily, Frederick G.
1969   *Stratagems and Spoils.* New York: Schocken Books.
Barfield, Thomas
1978   "The Impact of Pashtun Immigration on Pastoralism in
        Northeastern Afghanistan." In *Ethnic Processes and Intergroup
        Relations in Contemporary Afghanistan.* Edited by John
        Anderson and Richard Strand. *Occasional Paper of the
        Afghanistan Council of the Asia Society,* no. 15.
Barth, Fredrik
1961   *Nomads of South Persia: The Basseri Tribe of the Khamseh Con-
        federacy.* Boston: Little, Brown.
1969   Introduction. In *Ethnic Groups and Boundaries.* Edited by Fredrik
        Barth. Boston: Little, Brown.
Barthold, V. V.
1929   *Turkistan Down to the Mongol Invasion.* London: Gibb
        Memorial Series, n.s. no. 5.
Becker, Seymour
1968   *Russia's Protectorates in Central Asia: Bukhara and Khiva,
        1865–1924.* Cambridge: Harvard University Press.
Beveridge, A. A.
1921   *Baburnama in English.* London: Luzac.
Black, Jacob (Black-Michaud)
1972   "Tyranny as a Strategy for Survival in an 'Egalitarian Society':
        Luri Facts Versus an Anthropological Mystique." *Man* 7:
        614–634.
1976   *"The Economics of Oppression: Ecology and Stratification in an
        Iranian Tribal Society."* Ph.D. dissertation, London University.

Burnes, Alexander, Lieutenant Leech, Doctor Lord, and Lieutenant Wood
1839   *Reports on Missions in Scinde, Affghanisthan and Adjacent Countries, 1835–1837.* Calcutta: Bengal Military Orphan Press.

Canfield, Robert
1973   "Hazara Integration into the Afghan Nation: Some Changing Relations between Hazaras and Afghan Officials." *Occasional Paper of the Afghanistan Council of the Asia Society,* no. 3.

Clavijo, R. G.
1928   *Clavijo's Embassy to Tamerlane.* Translated by Guy Le Strange. London: G. Routledge & Sons.

Elphinstone, Mountstuart
1815   *An Account of the Kingdom of Caubul.* London: John Murray.

Etienne, G.
1972   *L'Afghanistan ou les aleas de la cooperation.* Paris: Presses Universitaires de France.

Farhadi, Ravan
1969   "Die Sprachen von Afghanistan." *Zentralasiatishe Studien* 3: 414–416.

Ferdinand, K.
1962   "Nomad Expansion and Commerce in Central Afghanistan." *Folk* 4: 123–159.
1969   "Nomadism in Afghanistan." In *Viehwirtschaft und Hirtenkultur.* Edited by L. Foldes. Budapest: Akademai Kiado.

Ferrier, J. P.
1976 (1857)   *Caravan Journeys and Wanderings in Persia, Afghanistan, Turkistan, and Beloochistan.* Lahore: Oxford in Asia.

Franck, P. G.
1955   "Technical Assistance through the United Nations—The U.N. Mission in Afghanistan." In *Hands across Frontiers.* Edited by Howard Teaf and Peter Franck. Ithaca, N.Y.: Cornell University Press.

Fry, M. J.
1974   *The Afghan Economy.* Leiden: E. J. Brill.

G.A.B. (Gazetteer of Afghanistan, Badakhshan)
1972 (1914)   *Historical and Political Gazetteer of Afghanistan, Badakhshan.* Edited by Ludwig Adamec. Gratz: Akademische Druck-u. Verlagsanstalt.

G.A.T. (Gazetteer of Afghanistan, Turkestan)
1979   *Historical and Political Gazetteer of Afghanistan, Mazar-i-sharif and Northcentral Afghanistan.* Edited by Ludwig Adamec. Gratz: Akademische Druck-u. Verlagsanstalt.

Geertz, C.
1963   *Agricultural Involution.* Berkeley: University of California Press.

Ghani, Abdul
1921   *Review of the Political Situation in Afghanistan.* Lahore: Khosla Bros.

Grötzbach, E.

1972 *Kulturgeographischer Wandel in Nordost-Afghanistan seit dem 19. Jahrhundert.* Meisenheim am Glan: Verlag Anton Hain.

Irons, W.

1974 "Nomadism as a Political Adaptation: The Case of the Yomut Turkmen." *American Ethnologist* 1: 635–658.

Jarring, Gunnar

1937 "The New Afghanistan." *Svenska Orientsalisk Årsbok.* 1937: 131–145.

Jenkinson, Anthony

1886 "The voyage of Master Anthony Jenkinson, made from the citie of Mosco in Russia, to the citie of Boghar in Bactria, in the yeere 1558: written by himselfe to the Merchants of London of the Muscovie companie." In *Early Voyages and Travels to Russia and Persia.* Edited by E. D. Morgan. London: Hakluyt Society.

Jenkyns, William

1879 *Reports on the Districts of Jelalabad, Chiefly in Regard to Revenue.* Calcutta: Government of India Publications.

Kakar, Hasan K.

1971 *Afghanistan: A Study in Internal Political Development, 1880–1896.* Lahore: Educational Press.

1979 *Government and Society in Afghanistan: The Reign of Amir Abd al-Rahman Khan.* Austin: University of Texas Press.

Karmysheva, B. Kh.

1964 "The Arabs and Jews of Central Asia." *Central Asian Review* 8: 271–274.

Khanykov, N.

1845 *Bokhara: Its Amir and People.* Translated by C. de Bode. London: J. Madden.

Krader, Lawrence

1955 "Ecology of Central Asian Pastoralism." *Southwestern Journal of Anthropology* 11: 301–326.

1956 *Handbook of Soviet Central Asia.* 3 Vols. New Haven, Conn.: HRAF Press.

1963 *Social Organization of the Mongol-Turkic Pastoral Nomads.* The Hague: Mouton.

1971 *Peoples of Central Asia.* Bloomington: Indiana University Press.

Kushkaki, Burhan-al-Din

1923 *Rahnuma-i-Qataghan wa Badakhshan.* Kabul: Afghan Ministry of Defense Press.

Lattimore, Owen

1940 *Inner Asian Frontiers of China.* New York: American Geographical Society.

Lewis, B.

1966 *The Arabs in History.* New York: Harper and Row.

Meyendorf, Georges

1826 *Voyage D'Orenbourg à Boukhara.* Paris: Dondey-Dupré.

Ministry of Planning
1355 A.H. (1976–1977) *Seven Year Plan.* Kabul: Ministry of Planning.

Napier, G. C.
1876 "Memorandum on the Condition and External Relations of the Turkoman Tribes of Merv." In *Collection of Journals and Reports from G. C. Napier on Special Duty in Persia 1874.* London: Her Majesty's Stationery Office.

Olufsen, O.
1911 *The Amir of Bokhara and His Country.* London and Copenhagen: William Heinemann.

Oshanin, L. V.
1964 *Anthropological Composition of the Population of Central Asia and the Ethnogenesis of Its People* vol. II, no. 2. Translated by V. M. Maurin. Edited by Henry Field. Cambridge, Mass.: Peabody Museum Russian Translation Series.

Radloff, Wilhelm
1893 *Aus Sibirien.* 2 vols. Leipzig: Weigel Nachfolger.

Sahlins, M.
1972 *Stone Age Economics.* Chicago: University of Chicago Press.

Schurmann, H. F.
1962 *The Mongols of Afghanistan: An Ethnography of the Mongols and Related People in Afghanistan.* The Hague: Mouton.

Schuyler, E.
1876 *Turkistan: Notes of a Journey in Russian Turkistan, Khokand, Bukhara, and Kuldja.* 2 Vols. New York: Scribner, Armstrong.

Stoddard, Laurence, and Arthur Smith
1943 *Range Management.* New York and London: McGraw-Hill.

Sultan Mahomed Khan
1900 *The Life of Abdur Rahman Khan.* London: John Murray.

Tapper, Nancy
1973 "The Advent of Pashtun Maldars in North Western Afghanistan. *Bulletin of the School of Oriental and African Studies* 36: 55–79.

Terentiev, M.
1876 *Russia and England in Central Asia.* 2 Vols. Calcutta: Foreign Department Press.

Trotter, J. M.
1873 *Central Asia, Part VI: Khanate of Bokhara.* Calcutta: Government of India Publication.

Tsereteli, George V.
1970 "The Influence of the Tajik Language on the Vocalism of Central Asian Arabic Dialects." *Bulletin of the School of Oriental and African Studies* 33: 167–170.

U.N. (United Nations)
1971 "Afghanistan." *Economic Bulletin for Asia and the Far East* 22: 24–53.

1973 *Afghanistan Development Assistance 1973 Report.* Kabul: United Nations Development Program.

1978   "Afghanistan." *Economic Bulletin for Asia and the Far East* 29: 10–27.

Vambery, Arminius
1864   *Travels in Central Asia.* London: John Murray.

Vavilov, N. I., and D. D. Bukinich
1929   *Agricultural Afghanistan. Bulletin of Applied Botany, Genetics, and Plant-Breeding.* Supplement 33. Leningrad.

Vinnikov, I. N.
1940   "Araby v SSSR." *Sovetskaya Etnografiya* 4: 1–22.

Watson, Burton
1961   *Records of the Grand Historian of China.* 2 vols. New York: Columbia University Press.

Wilber, D.
1962   *Afghanistan.* New Haven, Conn.: HRAF Press.

Wood, John
1872   *Journey to the Source of the River Oxus.* London: John Murray.

Yate, C. E.
1888   *Northern Afghanistan, or Letters from the Afghan Boundary Commission.* London and Edinburgh: Blackwood and Sons.

Yü, Y.
1967   *Trade and Expansion in Han China.* Berkeley: University of California Press.

Index

Abdur Rahman, Amir, 19, 23, 42, 160
Afghan Boundary Commission, 19–20
Afghanistan, Republic of: organization of, 160–161; transfer of officials by, 151; Seven Year Plan of, 115. *See also* Afghanistan government policies; Provincial administration
Afghanistan government policies: of conscription, 156; toward cotton, 83; toward imports, 89; of maintaining order, 46, 157; of nationalization, 112, 139–140; toward nomads, 62, 80–81; toward Pashtuns, 161–162; price fixing of, 93, 145–146; toward provincial areas, 19–20, 23, 163–164; of resettlement, 19–20, 22, 30–31, 46; of road building, 114; of state industries, 146–147; of state pasture, 42–43; toward wheat, 96–97. *See also* Afghanistan, Republic of; Provincial administration
Afghan Turkestan: Arabs in, 3, 17, 19–20; organization of, 17–19; raids against, 11, 17–20
Agriculture: among Arabs, 47–48, 72–76; in Badakhshan, 27–28, 104; in Bukhara, 9–10; comparison of highland versus lowland, 82; in Imam Saheb, 26, 95, 104, 158; impact of, on nomads, 69, 102; in Khanabad, 29; in Qataghan, 83–84, 90, 111–112; and sharecropping, 76. *See also* Cotton; Trade
Amanullah, Amir: land grants by, 46; reorganization of Qataghan by, 23; taxation policy of, 162–163

Amu Darya (Amu River), 19, 21, 25, 114
Amu Darya Valley: description of, 22, 25, 26; as pasture, 46–47, 50; settlement of Pashtuns in, 43; Turkmen in, 11
Andkhoi, 17
Anglo-Russian rivalry, 19, 41
Arabic, 4
Arabs, Bedouin, 4, 5
Arabs, Central Asian: in Afghan Turkestan, 6, 19–20; attitude of, toward state, 67–68; in Bukhara, 7–8, 11–14, 16; emigration of, from Bukhara, 6, 14–17; as ethnic group, 5; in Imam Saheb, 25–27; in Jalalabad, 6; language of, 4–5; origin of, 3–4; population of, 6, 16–17; in Qataghan, 23–24, 80–81; relation of, to *sayyids*, 5–6. *See also* Ethnic groups; Pastoral nomadism; Pasture; Political organization; Social organization
Arbob, 63, 151–152. *See also Bai*
Artisans, 90
Aw foroush clan: economic strategy of, 157–158; landownership by, 69–70; lineages of, 71; village structure of, 71–72

Babur, 4
Badakhshan: conquest of, 21; definition of, 25; description of, 27–29; migration to, 101–102, 134; mountains of, 17; nomads in, 103–107; pasture of, 29, 41–42; roads to, 115; salt trade

in, 50–51. *See also* Darwaz; Faizabad; Pasture; Rogh; Rustaq; Tajiks
Baghlan, 17
Bai, 62–68, 78, 151–152
Balkh, 4, 5, 17
Barth, F., 166–170
Basseri, 165–170
Bazaars: days of, 86; in Faizabad, 108–
109; in Imam Saheb, 85–100; in Kunduz, 89; relationship of, with state industries, 142–147; in Rustaq, 28;
temporary, 103. *See also* Trade
Black, J., 166–170
Brideprice, 77–80
Bukhara, Khanate of: Arab emigration
from, 14–17, 68; Arabs in, 3–4, 6;
conquest of, 14–15; description of, 4,
7–14; relation of, to Afghan Turkestan, 19; social and economic organization of, 8–14; trade in, 7, 17, 28,
100, 112
Burnes, A., 89

Camels: for sale, 94; as transportation,
39; wool of, 89, 102–103
Capital, access to, 54, 117–118,
125–127
Caravanserais: in Imam Saheb, 86–88;
ownership of, 74. *See also* Bazaars
Central Asia, 4. *See also* Afghan Turkestan; Arabs, Central Asian; Bukhara, Khanate of; Russia; Tajiks;
Turkmen; Uzbeks
Ceremonies, 72, 76–77
Chimkent, 11
China, 89–90
Cisterns, 27–28, 49
Commercial families, 135–137
Contracts, herding: of Basseri, 168; of
Lurs, 168–169; for shepherds, 53–54,
117–118, 126–127. *See also* Herd
management; Shepherds
Cotton: in Bukhara, 7, 15; by-products
of, 128–129, 141–147; as cash crop,
130, 140–141; fields as pasture, 46;
in Imam Saheb, 26, 73–74; in Kunduz, 30; price ratio of, 96; in Qataghan, 83–84, 112. *See also* Agri-
culture; Fodder; Spinzar Cotton
Company

Damascus, 4
Dari (language), 4
Darwaz: agriculture in, 29, 104; and
Bukhara, 13, 25; division of, 41; emi-
gration from, 41–42; pasture in, 29,
41–45, 51, 102–103, 113, 136–137.
See also Badakhshan; Dasht-i-Ish;
Pasture; Tajiks
Darya Panj, 25, 41
Dasht-i-Abdali, 27
Dasht-i-Archi: pasture of, 29, 42–43;
town on, 31
Dasht-i-Ish: air travel to, 122; pasture
in, 29, 42–43; troops in, 46
Dasht-i-Shirmahi, 27
Dasht-i-Shiwa, 29, 46. *See also* Shiwa,
Lake
Daud Khan, President, 140, 155, 160
Dispute settlement, 64–68. *See also*
Political organization; Provincial ad-
ministration
Dogs, 40, 53
Donkeys: sale of, 94, 106–107; as
transportation, 39, 50
Dost Muhammad, Amir, 19

Economic development: in Afghanistan, 113–114, 163–164; in Qataghan, 29–31, 111–112
Ethnic groups: in Afghan Turkestan,
16; in Badakhshan, 28; in Bukhara, 9;
cloth preferences of, 89; and conflict
between nomads and farmers, 102;
definition of, 5; encapsulation of,
162; in Imam Saheb, 26; political solidarity of, 70, 150; in Qataghan,
30–31; relationship of Pashtuns and
Arabs, 44–46, 64–66; relationship of
Tajiks and Arabs, 103–108, 124; in
Rustaq, 27; wage differentials among,
133. *See also* Afghanistan government policies; Arabs, Central Asian;
Pashtuns; Provincial administration;
Tajiks; Uzbeks
Europe, 89

Faizabad: air travel to, 114, 122; bazaar
in, 105, 108–109; competition of,
with Rustaq, 28; salt market of, 50
Farsi (language), 4

Fodder: from cotton by-products, 84–85, 141–142; difficulties in obtaining, 142–147; from hay, 49; on migration, 102; use of, 128, 134. *See also* Spinzar Cotton Company
Foreign aid, 112, 114–116
France, 90
Frontiers: with Darwaz, 41–42; within Qataghan, 30–31; with the Soviet Union, 25, 45–46

Goats, 39, 92, 106–107

Hazara, 23
Hazarajat, 42, 163
Herat, 114
Herd management: and fodder, 85; knowledge of, 57–58; labor needed for, 51–54; of size and growth, 52–53, 74; for urban investors, 130–132; and use of shepherds, 119–120, 122. *See also* Herdowners; Labor; Shepherds
Herdowners: and access to animals, 125–126; of Basseri, 166, 168–169; by inheritance, 51; of Lurs, 166–169; marks of, 57; of urban origin, 129–130. *See also* Herd management; Shepherds
Hilmand Valley, 112, 140
Hindu Kush Mountains, 17, 30, 112, 114
Horses, 39, 50, 94–95, 106–107

Imam Saheb: agriculture in, 83, 95, 104; Arabs in, 60, 63, 80, 121–122; bazaar in, 85–100; description of, 21, 24–26; irrigation system of, 25–26; labor in, 133; nomads from, 102; pasture in, 26, 131; provincial administration of, 150–159; relationship of, with Rustaq, 28; road to, 114; Spinzar Cotton Company in, 147
Inheritance, 51, 76
Involution, pastoral, 134–135
Iran, 12, 116, 133; nomadic pastoralists in, 165–170
Islam: Arab attitude toward, 76–77; introduction of, 3–4; marriage rules of, 80; and mosque congregations, 71

Jalalabad, 6, 31

Kabul: Arabs in, 6; officials from, 161, 164; prices in, 111, 115
Kandaharis. *See* Pashtuns
Karakul Basin, 9
Karategin, 10, 41
Kata poi clan: disputes of, 66, 69–71; land of, 158–159; sedentarization of, 122
Katta Kurgan, 4
Kazakh, 10–11, 63
Khanabad, 28; agriculture in, 24, 29–31, 83
Khanabad River, 21, 25
Khanykov, N., 4, 8
Khawan, 122
Khorasan, 6, 13, 18
Khulm. *See* Tashqurghan
Khwajaghar, 25, 27
Kinship: clan structure of, 59; in lineages, 71; and marriage patterns, 78; solidarity of, 52, 75–76; in villages, 68–70; and visiting patterns, 72. *See also* Political organization; Social organization
Kirghiz, 10–11
Kishem, 114
Kokand, Khanate of, 11
Kokcha River, 25, 27
Kolab, 10, 13, 41
Kunduz: Arabs in, 6, 24; bazaar in, 89, 92; cotton in, 29–31; government of, 150, 154, 158; khanate of, 18–19, 21; Spinzar Cotton Company in, 140–141, 149–150. *See also* Qataghan
Kunduz River, 21, 25
Kuwait, 115

Labor: in agriculture, 68, 76, 84; contracts for, 68, 132–134; in pastoralism, 51–56; by shepherds, 121–122, 133–134; by Tajiks, 108; for wages, 117–120; by women, 55–56, 123–124
Landownership: by nomads, 47–48, 68–76, 157–159; reform of, 159; taxes on, 23, 87, 163; of urban property, 87
Larkhabi, 5, 77

Livestock: in Bukhara, 8–11; sale of, 91–94; of Tajiks, 104, 106–107, 122; taxes on, 23, 163; theft of, 44, 64–65, 152–154; types of, 33–40
Lord, P. B., 21, 61–62
Lurs, 166–170

Maimana, 114; Arabs in, 6, 17, 20
Malaria, 21, 22, 30
Manzel Dasht, 103
Marriage, 77–80
Mazar-i-Sharif, 18–19, 92
Merv, 9, 11, 19
Meyendorf, G., 7
Migration: by airplane, 122–123; attitude toward, 121–123; to Badakhshan, 27–29, 102–103; end of, 121–124; nineteenth-century pattern of, 24–25; organization of, 52, 123–124; by Pashtuns, 134–135; by Uzbeks, 23. See also Ethnic groups; Pasture
Milk products: and commercial families, 136–137; decline in, 119, 123–124, 131; marketing of, 99–100; types of, 55–56
Mills, 96, 105
Mominabad, 21
Murad Beg, 18, 21, 22, 66
Music, 77

Nadir Khan (Shah), King, 23, 29, 42–43
Nesay, 122

Olufsen, O., 16
Oxus River. See Amu Darya

Paghman Mountains, 6
Pakistan, 115, 116, 162
Panj, Darya, 25, 41
Panjdeh, 20
Pashtunistan, 162
Pashtuns: autonomy of, 160; in government, 151; livestock of, 94; marriage of, 78–79; migration of, 102, 134–135; pastoralism of, 100, 112; pasture of, 43; in Qataghan, 19, 22–23, 30–31, 43; wages of, 133. See also Ethnic groups
Pastoral nomadism: of Basseri, 165–168; in Bukhara, 10–12; commercialization of, 117–122; and conflicts with farmers, 102; of Lurs, 166–169; for markets, 91–95, 97–100; and merchants, 88–90, 96; in Qataghan, 22–24; and the state, 12–14, 61–62, 80–81, 157. See also Migration; Pasture; Political organization; Sheep
Pasture: competition for, 43–46; on migration, 102; ownership of, 40–42; rental of, 45–46, 131–132, 136–137; sale of, 44; in spring, 26–27, 43–46; in summer, 45–46, 103–104; theft of, 44–45; for urban investors, 130–132; in winter, 46–49, 84. See also Badakhshan; Darwaz; Fodder; Rogh
Persian (language), 4–6
Political organization: of clan, 68–71; and disputes, 64–68; encapsulation of, 160; and integration with state, 61–62, 80–81; and middlemen, 142–144, 148–150, 158–159; structural problems of, 150, 158–159; of Uzbeks, 62. See also Arbob; Bai
Population: of Afghan Turkestan, 16–17; of Arabs, 6; of Qataghan, 30
Provincial administration: attitude of officials of, 151, 161; bribery of, 47, 154–155, 158–159; and criminal justice, 152–154, 163; evolution of, 162–163; isolation of, 155–156; in local affairs, 163–164; maladministration by, 47, 148–150, 155–156; reorganization of, 42; taxes of, 157. See also Afghanistan government policies
Pul-i-Khumri, 30–31

Qataghan: agriculture in, 82–84, 90; definition of, 25; development of, 29–32, 69, 140, 159; ecology of, 21–26; economy of, 108, 110–116; government of, 63, 71, 157, 160, 163; nomadic pastoralism in, 37, 97, 100, 102, 103, 117, 119, 127, 129, 134–135, 170; settlement of, 46, 162; Spinzar Cotton Company in, 140–142. See also Cotton; Imam Saheb; Kunduz
Qizil Qala. See Shir Khan Bander

Raids: by Turkmen, 11, 18; by Uzbeks, 18–19
Reza Shah, 166
Rogh: air travel to, 122; description of, 27–28; pasture in, 41, 44–45, 51, 136; wheat supply of, 104
Roshan, 13, 25, 41
Russia, 7, 14–15, 19. *See also* Soviet Union
Rustaq: bazaar in, 90, 105, 108; description of, 27–28; Uzbeks of, 27, 80

Salang Pass, 111, 114, 116
Salt, 50–51, 108–109
Samarkand, 9, 14, 15
Sarts, 9
Sayyids, 5–6
Schuyler, E., 4
Sedentarization: Afghan government policy of, 46; impact of, on women, 123–125; in Iran, 166; and polygyny, 80; by wealth and wage labor, 121–122
Settlement patterns: of Arab villages, 71, 76; in Badakhshan, 28–29; in Bukhara, 8–14; in Imam Saheb, 26
Shahrawan Canal, 25–26
Shahr-i-bozorg, 28, 103
Sheep: in Bukhara, 8, 11; care of, 49, 127–129; as investment, 72, 97–98, 127, 129–132; marketing of, 12, 35, 91–95, 98–100; in national economy, 116; ownership marks of, 57; prices of, 91–93, 98–99, 112–113, 116, 120; Qarakul, 8, 11, 100; slaughtering of, 57–58; smuggling of, 116; for subsistence, 112, 167–169; of Tajiks, 106–107; type and herd composition of, 34–38; wool of, 54–55, 99, 112, 119, 131, 137. *See also* Herd management; Milk products; Trade
Shepherds: contracts for, 68, 117–118, 132–134; increase in number of, 119–120, 129; owner's conflicts with, 57–58; trade with, 107; women's labor replaced by, 123. *See also* Contracts, herding
Shibar Pass, 30, 122
Shir Khan, 29, 140, 159
Shir Khan Bander, 30, 47, 114

Shiwa, Lake, 102, 122. *See also* Dasht-i-Shiwa
Shughnan, 13, 25, 41, 122
Sinjanis, 5, 77
Sinkiang, 11
Slavery, 7, 11
Social organization, 59–75, 80–81; of camp groups, 51, 70; impact of private property on, 69–71; of labor, 51–52, 55–56; stratification of, 74–75, 125–127; of villages, 68–77. *See also* Kinship; Marriage; Political organization
Sorkh Ab River, 25
Soviet Union: Arab population in, 4, 6; border with, 46–47, 112; foreign aid from, 114; goods from, 89, 90, 112; weapons from, 160. *See also* Russia
Spinzar Cotton Company: administration of, 140–141, 148–150; in Imam Saheb, 84–85; nationalization of, 112; permission to buy from, 142–147; in Qataghan, 30, 138–139, 163; relationship of, with bazaar, 142–147. *See also* Cotton; Fodder

Tajiki (language), 4
Tajiks: and Arabs, 5, 77–79, 103–108, 124; in Badakhshan, 23, 27–29, 50, 104–109; in Bukhara, 8–10; in Darwaz, 41; in government, 151; in Kunduz, 21–22; and nomads, 102. *See also* Badakhshan; Darwaz; Ethnic groups; Rogh
Taloqan, 24, 31, 50, 109
Tamerlane, 4
Tashkent, 11
Tashqurghan, 17, 22, 28
Taxation: amount of, 157, 162–163; and *arbob*, 151; as bribes, 47, 155; in Qataghan, 23; in Zarafshan, 15–16
Tents, 47
Trade: in Badakhshan, 28, 104–109; in Bukhara, 7, 9–12; of grain, 91, 95–99, 104–105; in Imam Saheb, 85–100; international, 30, 89–90, 112, 114–116; of manufactured goods, 88–90, 102–103, 105, 109; on migration, 102–107; in Qataghan, 24. *See also* Bazaars; Cotton; Economic

development; Sheep; Transportation
Transportation: by air, 122–123; by animals, 39, 94; in Badakhshan, 104; of fodder, 85, 128; of grain, 95; in Qataghan, 28–30; by road, 112–115. *See also* Migration
Turkmen: in Afghan Turkestan, 18–20; brideprice of, 78–79; in Bukhara, 11, 13; in government, 151; livestock of, 34, 94, 152–153; solidarity of, 150

United States, 89, 114
Upper Oxus River. *See* Darya Panj
Utarbuloqi, 5
Uzbeki (language), 4–5
Uzbekistan, 6
Uzbeks: and Arabs, 77–80; bazaar days of, 86; in Bukhara, 8–10; in government, 151; in Imam Saheb, 26; in northern Afghanistan, 17–20; political organization of, 61–62; in Qataghan, 22–23, 30–31; in Rustaq, 27; wages of, 133. *See also* Kunduz

Vambery, A., 18

Wood, J., 21

Yangi Qala, 47
Yurts, 47, 70–71

Zarafshan Valley, 9, 15–16, 80
Zerendaw Valley, 41–45, 136